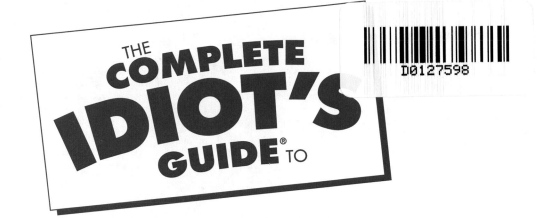

THE **COMPLETE** **IDIOT'S** **GUIDE** TO

Digital Photography

Third Edition

by Steven Greenberg

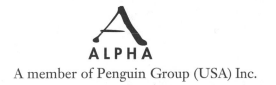

ALPHA

A member of Penguin Group (USA) Inc.

International Standard Book Number: 0-02-864453-0
Library of Congress Catalog Card Number: 2002113274

05   04   03   8   7   6   5   4   3   2

Interpretation of the printing code: The rightmost number of the first series of numbers is the year of the book's printing; the rightmost number of the second series of numbers is the number of the book's printing. For example, a printing code of 02-1 shows that the first printing occurred in 2002.

Printed in the United States of America

Note: This publication contains the opinions and ideas of its author. It is intended to provide helpful and informative material on the subject matter covered. It is sold with the understanding that the author and publisher are not engaged in rendering professional services in the book. If the reader requires personal assistance or advice, a competent professional should be consulted.

The author and publisher specifically disclaim any responsibility for any liability, loss, or risk, personal or otherwise, which is incurred as a consequence, directly or indirectly, of the use and application of any of the contents of this book.

Publisher: *Marie Butler-Knight*
Product Manager: *Phil Kitchel*
Managing Editor: *Jennifer Chisholm*
Acquisitions Editor: *Eric Heagy*
Development Editor: *Tom Stevens*
Copy Editor: *Cari Luna*
Illustrator: *Chris Eliopoulos*
Cover/Book Designer: *Trina Wurst*
Indexer: *Tonya Heard*
Layout/Proofreading: *Megan Douglass, Becky Harmon*

I want to dedicate this book with all my love and heart to my boys, Asher and Ari, who haven't seen much of me over the last few months. I would like to thank them for all the many deliveries of Coke and coffee. Guys, get those boots on—Dad is back, and we have a few new mountains to climb this summer! I especially want to dedicate this book to my wonderful wife, Tova, without whose patience, love, and support I would have never been able to write this book.

Also, this book is dedicated to my parents, who taught me to work hard and strive for excellence; to my friends and family, who supported me and cheered me on; and to the goddess of caffeine.

In Memory: Dad, thanks for all of life's lessons. I'll miss you.

Contents at a Glance

Contents

Introduction

We are in the age of information. With a few pecks at our keyboards and a glance at our monitors, we can find out almost anything. The massive amounts of information we can access, store, and manipulate are all due to the digital age.

When I was younger, everything you needed to know could be looked up in the encyclopedia set on the bookshelf or in the books in the library. Encyclopedias in my day were heavy, expensive, bound tomes of information printed on ever-so-thin paper. Today, my sons load their encyclopedia CD, which came bundled free with their computer, or with only a few clicks, race down the information superhighway to a website to learn what they need to know.

Our ability to rapidly acquire and process information coupled with the exponential growth of technology has led to the development of wonderful tools, including digital cameras. Image-enhancing software, cheap and transportable storage devices, and ever-increasing computing power have made it possible to photograph without film.

Computer stores are everywhere. You might be in a computer store at this very moment, reading this book (please buy it, it's great). Look down the aisles and you'll see cartons of computers, miles of monitors, and plenty of peripherals. But now, more and more shelf space is being given to digital cameras. Yes, it's true, Toto—we're not in Kansas anymore; we've entered a wonderful and colorful world.

This book takes in a wide view of digital photography. We'll start with a quick history of photography and along the way learn the basics of exposure and composition. We'll also learn how to purchase a digital camera and how to use and get the most out of it. Enhancing and manipulating an image can be fun and exciting, and we'll look at those issues, too.

For a little additional help along the way, you'll find these extras throughout the book:

Behind the Shutter
Here, I share some inside stories, notes, and general wisdom that can broaden your understanding of digital photography.

Say Cheese

Find all your digital photography tips and tricks here.

Flash

Be sure not to miss these warnings about hang-ups you might encounter while becoming a digital image enthusiast!

In Plain Black & White

If you just get fed up with all the jargon and buzzwords that surround technology, fret no more. This is the place to get up to speed on the latest "digitese" and impress your technophile friends with your word power.

Acknowledgments

I would like to thank the many vendors who supplied cameras and equipment for me to review, specifically Tara Poole for Kodak, Kylie Ware and Elise Eisenlaue for Epson, Emily Malech for Fuji, Karen Thomas for Olympus, Carla M. Vallone for Sony, Nicole Mendez for Nikon, and Steve Alessandrin for Minolta.

Also, Don Passenger deserves a tip of the hat for his valuable contribution in the chapters covering Adobe Photoshop Elements and all the image editing wonders it can perform.

Special Thanks to the Technical Reviewers

The Complete Idiot's Guide to Digital Photography, Third Edition, was reviewed by experts who double-checked the accuracy of what you'll learn here, to help us ensure that this book gives you everything you need to know about digital photography. They also suggested this revision highlight Adobe's Photoshop Elements 2.0, the program that many of the examples are demonstrated with. Special thanks are extended to Don Passenger and Tyler Regas for doing this job.

Trademarks

All terms mentioned in this book that are known to be or are suspected of being trademarks or service marks have been appropriately capitalized. Alpha Books and Penguin Group (USA) Inc. cannot attest to the accuracy of this information. Use of a term in this book should not be regarded as affecting the validity of any trademark or service mark.

Part 1

Digital Capture:
The Future Is Now

When does the future become the present? When does futuristic technology become new technology? When will we all have tri-corders? Technology becomes real when it can be seen and when it can be used. As a professional photographer, I have been using digital cameras almost exclusively for 10 years. If you look in the advertising sections of the newspaper or in the dozen or so computer catalogs you get in the mail each week, you'll see digital cameras everywhere. All the photographs in this book were taken with a digital camera. The future is now—and it's affordable!

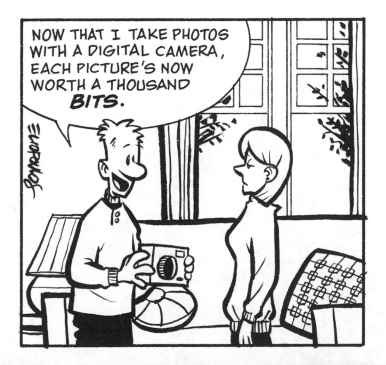

Chapter 1

Look, Ma, No Film: Why Digital Photography?

In This Chapter

◆ History of photography

◆ Advantages of digital photography

◆ Disadvantages of digital photography

Why digital photography? Because we are control freaks, that's why. We want to move, recolor, and manipulate our photos. We want to see them right away, and we want to show them to everybody. With digital photography, I can e-mail the most adorable picture of our dog to my parents, my in-laws, my wife's grandma, my sister, my wife's sisters, or anyone who has ever sent us a holiday card, or I can post it on our family website for all the world to admire. (Of course, the true power of digital photography is that I can make our dog, Wrinkles, look adorable in the first place.)

Painting with Light: A Brief History of Photography

The first cameras were not anything like what we use today. They were, however, used for the same reason: to capture light. The earliest cameras were, in reality, just darkened rooms. A small hole in a window shade or in the side of a wall let light in and a perfect (albeit upside down) image of what was outside the room would appear on a far wall or some other surface. This device was called the *camera obscura* (literally "dark room"). In 1558, Giovanni Battista della Porta's book *Natural Magic* was the first published account of the camera obscura being used as a tool to aid draftsmen and illustrators; the camera obscura also became a great source of entertainment for the general public.

Digital photos of Wrinkles have been the star of our family website many times.

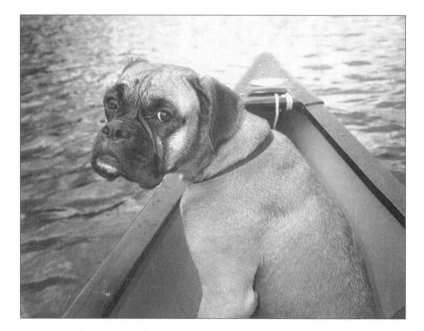

Behind the Shutter

Camera obscuras can still be found today. Unfortunately, many are in danger of being dismantled or are in poor repair—including the 50-year-old Giant Camera overlooking Seal Rock in San Francisco, which was slated to close at the end of 1999. After a campaign was waged by many friends of camera obscuras, the camera was added to the National Register of Historic Places on May 23, 2001. If you would like more info on camera obscuras, check out www.brightbytes.com/cosite/cohome.html. You can also find a great source of info by doing a web search.

Gradually, the camera obscura became smaller and smaller, becoming a box, usually made of wood, with a lens attached at one end. On the other end of the box, a mirror was placed at a 45-degree angle. Above this was placed a frosted or ground glass plate. An artist would place thin paper over the ground glass and trace the image that was projected there. Now, with just a little skill, anyone could draw or paint!

Behind the Shutter

When I was in college, some of my friends made a camera obscura of their dorm room. They blocked out all sources of light from a room, covered a window (which faced out onto a park) with opaque paper in which they cut a small hole, and fashioned a shutter out of tape. On the opposite wall, which was the focal point, they hung rolls of transparency slide film. After the tape was removed and the film was exposed, they rolled the film up, placed it in a light-tight box, and had it developed! To display the developed images, my friends built a huge backlit box with a frosted piece of Plexiglas. It was beautiful!

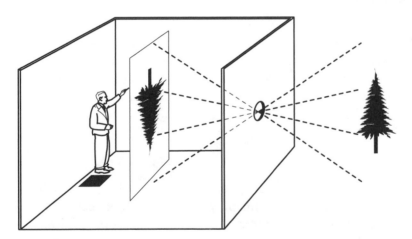

Some camera obscuras were as large as rooms. Others were small and portable and mounted on horse-drawn wagons.

In 1764, Count Francesco Algarotti devoted a chapter to the camera in his *Essay on Painting*. He said, "The best modern painters, among the Italians, have availed themselves greatly of this contrivance; nor is it possible they should have otherwise represented things so much to life." The camera had grown from an amusement center to a tool. This was also the beginning of painting by numbers.

As the camera obscura became much smaller, it began to be used in the field to help artists render life and nature.

Schulze's Silver Substance

In 1727, a German physicist named Johann Heinrich Schulze discovered that light could be used to alter substances. He put silver, chalk, and nitric acid together in a bottle, did the hokey pokey, and shook it all about. He then exposed the mixture to bright sunlight and found that the mixture darkened to black. To prove that this was a photosensitive reaction as opposed to a heat-induced reaction, he repeated the process but exposed the mixture to intense heat. Proving his theory, this experiment produced no change in the mixture.

Heliography

Joseph Niépce, a Frenchman, began to experiment with photosensitive materials around the early 1800s. Niépce found that bitumin, an asphaltlike substance, would harden when exposed to light. He coated metal plates with bitumin and exposed them to light inside a camera obscura. After a long exposure, the plate was washed to remove the "unexposed" bitumin, and was then dipped in acid, which etched the exposed metal. Finally, the plate was coated with ink and struck to paper. A print of the original image was produced. Niépce called this process heliography.

Daguerreotypes

Around 1825, another Frenchman, Louis Daguerre, was experimenting with the same process. Although Daguerre and Niépce did collaborate on the photographic process,

Daguerre took a slightly different direction. He chose to coat a copper plate with silver, and then expose the silver to iodine fumes, creating a silver-iodide salt. This made the plate photosensitive. The plate was then placed in the camera obscura and exposed to light for a long period of time. As demonstrated by Schulze, the silver-iodine would darken when exposed to light. The downside for Daguerre? Once exposed, the silver salts would continue to darken until, eventually, the entire image became black.

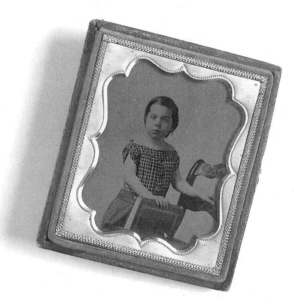

Daguerreotypes were originally rare and expensive; only the very rich could afford to have daguerreotypes taken of them. Later, after the Civil War, they became very common and affordable to the general public.

Daguerre solved this problem by accident: He left an exposed plate in a cabinet in which mercury was being stored. When he retrieved the plate, he noticed that the image had stopped developing; it did not continue to darken. The mercury fumes had developed the image. Because this was not the healthiest way to make a photograph or to remove the unused silver, Sir John Herschel, a British astronomer and scientist, suggested in 1819 that the plate be washed with a solution of *sodium hyposulfate*, which would chemically remove the unexposed silver. Daguerre called his photos *daguerreotypes*.

In Plain Black & White

Sodium hyposulfate, a.k.a. sodium thiosulfate ($Na_2S_2O_3$), is called fixer by those of us who still "do film." By the way, if hardener (potassium alum) is not mixed with fixer, it will not produce its famous odor.

Talbotypes

Working at the same time as Daguerre was Englishman William Henry Fox Talbot. Talbot used a similar process to Daguerre's, except that he used paper instead of metal for his "plate." The image he produced was a negative. (Remember, where light struck the silver, it turned black; where it didn't, the silver was unaffected or remained white. The daugerreotype was also a negative image, and had to be held at a proper angle for it to look "positive.") Talbot took the paper negative, waxed it to make it translucent, and re-photographed it to produce a "positive" image. Talbot could now reproduce his—you guessed it—*Talbotypes* over and over again.

Father of the Yellow Box

In 1888, George Eastman perfected the process of flexible, plastic-based films. Eastman's new company, Kodak, marketed a camera that contained a roll of film long enough for 100 exposures. The user would return the used camera to the Kodak Company, which would process the film, print the images, and return them to the owner with a freshly loaded camera.

Fast Forward: Digital Cameras

As with many of our modern inventions, digital photography owes much of its advancement to the military and to space exploration. The need to take sharper images and to view them as quickly as possible lent much to the development of digital cameras and imaging technology. Using digital technology, images could be beamed from miles above the earth to reveal hidden missiles or help predict crop growth. Unmanned spacecraft beamed back our first look at the dark side of the moon and the heavens above.

In 1981, the Sony Corporation produced the first consumer electronic camera, called the *Mavica*. Short for *magnetic video camera*, the camera produced still video images (the Mavica wasn't *truly* a digital camera, because its images were actually analog recordings). The race to produce "filmless" cameras was on.

The first truly digital camera, the QuickTake, was developed by Apple Computers in cooperation with Kodak. (How very forward thinking of both companies!) The hand-held camera had a fixed focus lens and could take anywhere from 8 to 32 images depending on the resolution of the images. Images were stored internally and could be downloaded to a Mac or PC via a serial port. It sold for about $700.

Behind the Shutter

There are many rumors about how George Eastman coined the word *Kodak*. Some thought it was in reference to the sound the shutter on his cameras made, but as he explained: "I devised the name myself. The letter K had been a favorite with me—it seems a strong, incisive sort of letter. It became a question of trying out a great number of combinations of letters that made words starting and ending with *K*. The word *Kodak* is the result."

Kodak also produced one of the first "professional" digital cameras, called the DCS 2. It produced, in a single shot, a 4MB color image. The camera was built on a 35mm Nikon SLR platform, but a digital chip was fixed in the camera's back.

If you ask companies like Kodak, Fuji, Agfa, or Polaroid why they produce cameras, you'll get an interesting answer: to sell film. Film is where they make the most profit. Why, then, would they become involved in the digital-camera market? My guess: They see the writing on the wall. It is very clear from these manufacturers' actions that film-based consumer-level photography is expected to become a thing of the past.

These days, everyone's in on the digital camera action. Of course, most of the major camera manufacturers are producing digital cameras; some, such as Ricoh, have stopped marketing film-based cameras in the United States altogether. In addition, companies that never produced film-based cameras, such as Dicomed and PhaseOne, are selling good-quality professional cameras. Even more interestingly, companies such as Leaf/Scitex and Agfa, which produce prepress scanning equipment, are now also producing digital cameras. These companies are evolving their scanning technologies into digital camera equipment. Many digital cameras are really "camera-mounted scanners."

Behind the Shutter

The DCS 2 was the first digital camera I owned. My introduction to digital photography cost me $35,000, not including the necessary computer, software, training, and aspirin. Don't worry—it won't cost you that much these days!

First, the Good News: The Advantages of Digital Photography

Digital cameras are everywhere. Store shelves are lined with them, and Sunday newspaper circulars are filled with advertisements for them. But why buy one?

If you are perfectly and completely happy taking pictures with your film camera, then don't buy a digital camera. But remember, you have to finish the whole roll, bring the film to the processor, and wait for the prints to come back, just to find out everyone in the "once-in-a-lifetime picture" had their eyes closed. Let's also not forget that you have to pay for the processing and buy film. Oh, by the way, you had better buy a few extra rolls, some for indoors and some for outdoors.

So what are the advantages of digital?

- **No more film!** That's right, ladies and gentlemen, children of all ages, you'll never need to buy film again. Using a digital camera means that you can take pictures without paying for film or wondering which type of film to buy.

- **No running out of film.** If you are careful with your storage, you will also never run out of film. The PCMCIA storage cards, which slip into the side of your camera, can hold up to 80 images. Many cameras now will accept mini-hard drives which have the storage capacity of up to a "gig." With a few of these in your camera bag, you can go on taking pictures for days. (There's nothing like that special feeling you get when you run out of film while on vacation. Not to worry; if you give the guy in the photo booth all your travelers' checks and promise him your first born, he'll gladly sell you a fresh roll with 12 exposures on it.)

- **No more processing costs.** No matter how you get your film processed, it gets to be expensive. You can't get around paying for processing unless you are taking digital photos—and you'll never have to decide about matte or glossy prints again.

- **"I wanna see them now!"** Digital photography enables you to see your photos instantly; no more waiting for your film to return from the lab. Many cameras have LCD preview screens, so you can see the image instantly, or you can download your images to your computer as soon as you take them.

- **Reshoot!** If somebody walked into your carefully composed shot or if the baby's eyes were closed when the shutter snapped, you'll know it immediately. You can simply retake the image. (On the flip side, you can also preview all the poses you just took of your dog and delete the ones you don't like.)

Behind the Shutter

As a professional photographer, digital photography has become an indispensable tool. My clients can use my computer monitor to view the image I have just taken; they can approve it on the spot or we can make changes. When the image is finished, I can then move on to the next setup or job. I don't have to wait for my film to come back from the lab or worry that I missed something in the Polaroids.

- **Control.** If you couldn't get close enough to your subject or the camera wasn't level when you took the picture, have no fear! You can fix it. You can easily crop or rotate your picture; remove spots; fix color; and lighten, darken, blur, or sharpen your images. With a little skill, you can even add Uncle Harry into the family photo even though he arrived late. Try that with a drugstore print!

- **Get out of the dark.** For those of you who spent hours splashing about in your darkroom to produce only a few prints, you are free. You can set up your computer in the light of day and image edit all you want. Imagine! You can be social and manipulate images at the same time. You can see and be seen by your family and friends. If you have special talents, you can even work on your computer and watch the football game simultaneously!

- **Everyone can see it.** With the advent of e-mail and modems, you can easily send a photo of a newborn to distant relatives or post it on your website. You no longer need to take the time or spend the cash to make multiple copies of an image and distribute them.

- **It will last forever.** Negatives and prints fade. They are subject to ultraviolet light, humidity and grubby fingers. Digital images, however, will last forever if carefully stored! And if your printout of the image gets damaged or you want to make a duplicate, all you need to do is pull up the file and reprint it. Your only cost is a sheet of paper and the ink/toner.

- **Get green!** Digital photography is environmentally sound. There are no processing chemicals to wash down our sewers, and the massive amounts of water and electricity used to process film are no longer needed. Plus, you won't need to worry about recycling those little plastic film containers. (You do recycle them, don't you?)

- **It's fun!** Photography is fun, and digital photography is more fun! And because you don't have to worry about having enough film with you or whether the picture came out, you might even say it's liberating. So grab a camera, take a few shots, and go have fun!

Now for the Bad News ...

There are some downsides to digital photography. Digital photography is not yet perfect, and we are all still paying for the manufacturers' research and development costs. Although storage devices are getting less expensive every day, they still are not as cheap as a cardboard shoebox. Here are some of the cons:

- **Image quality.** The amount of information that is contained on a piece of film or that can be reproduced on a photographic print is easily tenfold that of a typical digital camera. A camera crammed with enough chips to produce a film-like quality photo would be wildly expensive (remember that $35,000 I spent?); a disposable plastic camera will capture more info than your $300 bells-and-whistles digital job.

- **Limited resolution.** If you are going to use the image in a company newsletter or on a website, you will probably have no problem using a digital camera. If you plan to enlarge the picture to poster size and frame it on the wall, you had better use film. If, for example, I were to spend hours to climb to the top of a mountain (and I do), I would not use a midrange digital camera to capture the skyline for a print on my wall or to sell as a stock image. I would have no problem, however, using a digital camera to grab a shot of my wife skipping over the rocks and streams (and she does).

- **This stuff is expensive.** With digital cameras costing from $300 for a "point and shoot" to more than $1,200 for some of those bells and whistles, these cameras are not cheap. In addition, you are limited to using only a few accessories, such as lenses, filters, and the like (not to mention that any accessories you have for your current camera will likely be useless for a digital camera). And that's just for the camera!

- **Equipment upgrade.** Assuming you already have a computer, you might need to buy more RAM (memory). If you don't already have a good color printer, you had better put one of those in your shopping cart, also (while you're at it, please buy a decent surge protector). If you are serious about this new hobby, a larger monitor screen will help keep eye fatigue down.

- Have I spent all of your money yet? Don't forget the aspirin!

- **It's dark in here.** Digital cameras are not as sensitive to light as their film-based cousins. Simply put, they require more light to make an exposure. That probably won't be problematic outdoors, but problems might occur inside. Even if you are using a flash, you'll either need to augment with additional lighting or just settle for darker images.

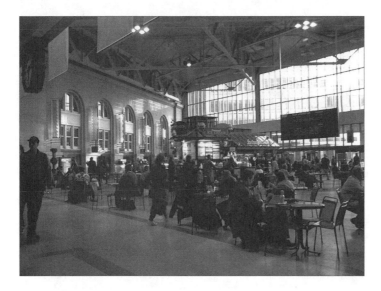

A dark interior, such as Boston's South Station, can wreak havoc with your camera. Bright areas, such as the windows, make automatic exposure even more difficult.

◆ **Noise.** If you were to look in the dark areas of an image, such as in a shadow or on a black surface, you might see *noise*. Hmm. Seeing noise. Now that's a funny thing! If you think of digital information as a television signal, noise would be just like the static you get when you try to tune in to a weak station. Noise generally appears as blue or red/blue static in the shadow areas.

◆ **Pixelation.** When you have enlarged an image too much, you'll see pixelation, or little squares in the image. These squares occur when the image file doesn't contain enough information to properly display the image at the size you've specified (another word for the information in a photograph is *resolution*). Sure, you can continue to make the image bigger, but that means your computer will only make up the information it needs to display the image, *interpolating* it.

In Plain Black & White

Interpolation is a technique that the computer and software use to estimate the tonal value for a missing pixel that should appear between two existing pixels. This is also known as an **intelligent guess**. It is much better to have the information there in the first place than to have your computer think it up for you.

◆ **Stair-stepping.** Another result of low resolution is *stair-stepping*, which usually occurs on diagonals in an image (you guessed it: they look like little stairs). The more information (resolution) your image has, the smaller those stairs become. You might also see stair-stepping on round objects or curved objects, such as balloons or wheels.

A very pixelated image due to a low resolution.

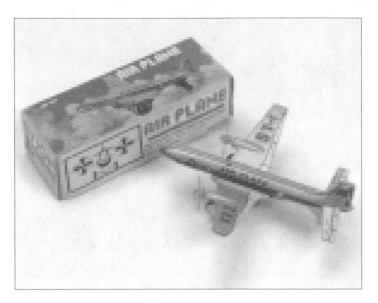

It is very difficult to avoid "stair-stepping," as seen on the diagonals of the scissors, unless there is adequate resolution.

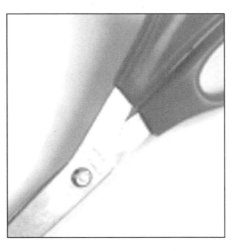

- ◆ **Color distortions.** A digital camera might just get the color wrong. No, you're not going to see blue grass or red skies (unless you're on Mars), but you might see orange when you expect to see yellow or purple when you expect blue. Color distortion is usually due to poor interpolation by the camera software. Most of the time, this can be easily corrected; I'll show you how in Chapter 14.

- ◆ **Wait, wait.** Most cameras, in order to save battery power, will automatically go into an energy-saving or *sleep* mode if not used for a few minutes. Depending on the camera and how "awake" it is, there can sometimes be a second or two delay between the time you press the shutter button and when the camera actually takes the picture. You might also have to wait a few moments after taking one picture before the camera is ready to take the next one (the camera might have to process the image and store it to memory).

◆ **The learning curve, again.** Taking a picture with a digital camera is not any more difficult than with a film-based one; it might be even easier for you. Getting the image out of the camera, processing it, and getting a great-looking print, however, are not going to be as easy as they were before (at least not at first). You are going to have to learn some new skills and invest some time in practicing them.

If you enjoy playing with your computer and learning new skills, digital photography can be a lot of fun. If not, you might not want to "do the digital."

Go for It!

Digital photography can be a load of fun and an inexpensive way to take pictures after you get yourself set up. It provides a spontaneous way to create images without having to worry about film, processing, and the costs involved, and it gives you the freedom to create images, to explore, and to be an artist. Digital photography also can be an invaluable business tool, providing a great way to communicate ideas and broadcast images.

So who needs a digital camera?

◆ Insurance agencies are using digital cameras to photograph for claim records. Agents can take a picture of a crumpled fender or broken window, attach it to the claim form, and instantly e-mail it to the central office. This can cut a day or two off the settlement time (oh, happy clients!). Also, the image can become a permanent (read: nonfading) part of the electronic record and can be accessed by anyone at the firm at any time.

◆ Realtors can use digital photographs to show off that beautiful house they are listing. The images can be shown to a prospective buyer, published into a listing sheet, or even posted on a website. With QTVR (Quick Time Virtual Photography), virtual tours of the inside of a home or office building can be produced to show to a client.

Behind the Shutter

With the advent of Quick Time Virtual Reality (QTVR) technology by Apple Software, photos can be taken of an object or a scene and then the images can be animated. To begin, the object is rotated in front of the camera, and a picture is taken each time the object moves 10° until it has completed a 360° revolution. To photograph a scene, the same process takes place—except that this time the *camera* rotates 360°, taking one picture every 10° for a total of 36 shots. You can post these QTVR images on a website or display them as part of a multimedia presentation. The viewers can see all 360° of the object, or take a virtual tour through a hotel lobby or museum. Recently, sports television has taken advantage of this technique by placing multiple cameras in fixed positions around the playing field or arena. They then can show the audience a replay and rotate the point of view as the play advances. Thank you, XFL!

While still in their offices, realtors can take pictures of homes for prospective buyers.

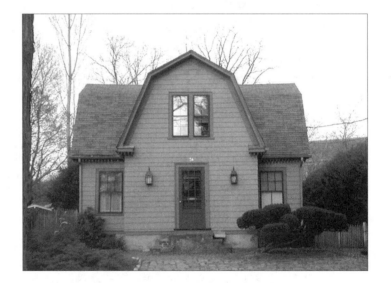

- Small business owners and professionals can use digital photography to help skip the traditional prepress scanning process. They can save time—and we all know time is money! A word to the frugal here: Be sure you know what you're doing before you try to "go it alone." It is very costly to have a press house fix your mistakes. A missed deadline can also be very expensive!

- Databases can include photographs of all those various gizmos you sell, which means your customers don't have to use their imaginations to see all the large and the small gizmos in red, green, blue, or whatever variation is available. Imagine the competitive edge you'll have! Again, using QTVR photography, you could even animate your gizmo so that your customers can see the top and bottom or all four sides.

◆ Digital pictures are perfect for the web. (Note: The smaller the image is, the faster the image can be delivered to your screen from a website.)

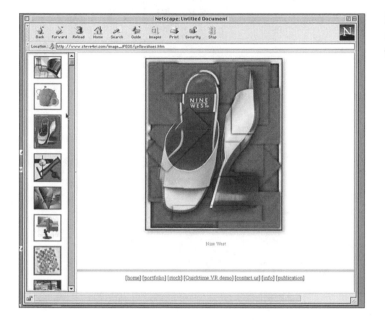

Digital cameras have more than enough resolution for website photos.

◆ Digital photography is great for use in small offices. You can produce newsletters or take reference photos of products for your sales force. You can use a digital camera to photograph a new client so all your staff and sales team will be able to greet your new client on sight and by name. Interoffice mail can be made more personal and websites more informative.

◆ Doctors, dentists, and surgeons can use digital cameras to take reference photos of patients. You can show your patients before and after images; you can use images for your medical records, or attach them to an insurance claim. But before you spring for a digital camera, spring for a few new magazines in your waiting room!

◆ Newspaper and other journalistic photographers are using digital cameras on an increasing basis. The resolution from a mid- to high-end camera contains plenty of information for the typical newspaper or magazine. In fact, many of these digital images are being delivered via satellite. Photographers are carrying small up-link satellite dishes to beam their images directly to their editor's desk.

◆ At home, you can take pictures of all your valuables—not to show to your friends, but to be kept as a record for insurance purposes. (It might be a good idea to keep a copy of the files in a safe place outside of your home.)

I use a newsletter to inform my clients about recent events at my studio. Digital photography is a great way to facilitate the newsletter and improve its visual appeal.

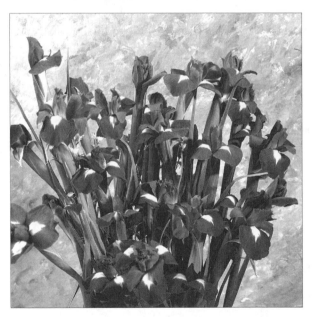

Digital photography can be used to enhance reality. Can you tell which flowers are original, and which were cloned?

◆ Take family pictures. You can take these cameras anywhere. You can take tons of shots and edit out the ones you don't want later. You'll be surprised at what pictures you'll take when you are not worried about wasting film.

♦ You can make art! You can have loads of fun being creative and manipulating images. You can take many views or variations of a picture; you can take pictures at different times and places and collage them together. This can be a very liberating experience.

The Least You Need to Know

♦ Photography as we know it began with the invention of the camera obscura.

♦ There are many pros to using a digital camera, but there are some cons as well.

♦ You can use digital photography for many purposes.

♦ Digital cameras are great and convenient, however, their image quality, though good, cannot surpass that of a film camera.

2

Pixel, Pixel, Little Star, How I Wonder What You Are!

In This Chapter

- ◆ What's a pixel?
- ◆ All about light
- ◆ How digital cameras work

So what is a pixel? Are they small and do they have rapidly beating wings? What is light? How does the camera work, and how do you change those light rays into electronic data? Read on!

It's a Three-Color World (RGB)

When white light is passed through a prism, a whole spectrum of color is visible. You could reverse this process, stuffing the entire spectrum of color back through the prism to get back to white light, but you don't need to—all you really need are red, green, and blue. If you don't believe me, go and try it yourself. If you do believe me, go and do it anyway; it's an impressive demonstration.

We call this color world the *RGB color world* (where *RGB* stands for *red, green, blue*). And because we *added* the three colors together to get to white light, the process is called *additive color*. While we're at it, we might as well call those three colors—red, green, and blue—*primary colors*.

Behind the Shutter

If you're a nonbeliever, conduct the following experiment: Get three strong flashlights, and cover one with a red gel, one with a blue gel, and one with a green gel. Then tack a piece of white paper on your wall. Darken the room, and shine the lights on the paper. You should get white light. (If you feel foolish doing this, get your kids to do it as a science fair project.)

Some of you might be jumping out of your seats and yelling, "But green isn't a primary color!" Well, you're right and wrong. The primary colors of the *light* spectrum are red, green, and blue. For any coloring matter such as dyes, pigments, or paint, the primary colors are red, *yellow*, and blue. If you don't believe me, check out a few books on color theory from your public library and look it up for yourself. If you are curious, it makes for a mind-boggling, but fascinating read.

The classic double triangle.

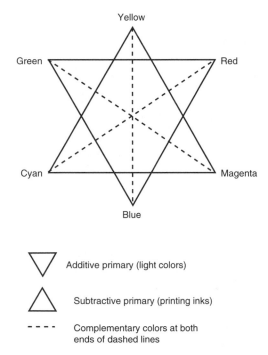

Okay, this part gets tricky, but hang in there. It will all make sense in the end. Take a deep breath; I promise there will be no test. Let's say the green light that you're stuffing back through the prism was blocked. The resulting color would be magenta, a *secondary color* that is opposite green in the classic double-triangle illustration shown previously, and a combination of two remaining primary colors, red and blue. The other secondary colors are yellow, which is the opposite of blue, and cyan, which is the opposite of red.

To make this discussion more relevant to photography, suppose you were to reduce the amount of green in a photograph. Yes, you guessed it, the picture would appear to be more magenta.

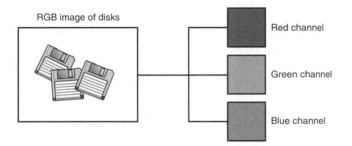

A photo broken up into three channels.

Eye to Eye: How the Camera Mimics Your Eye

The color our eyes see is a result of light reflecting off an object. An apple appears to our eyes as red because the apple's skin absorbs both blue and green light and reflects back only the red. (Unless, of course, you are looking at a Granny Smith apple.)

Our eyes are made of three basic parts:

◆ A *lens* focuses the light on the back of the eye.

◆ The *iris* helps form the *pupil*, the little black hole, which regulates how much light enters the eye.

◆ In the back of the eye is the *retina*. On the retina are the nerves that send the light pulses to the brain. Some of the nerves on the retina see red, some see green, and some see blue. Your brain processes all the information and voilà, you see color! (See what I mean about RGB being primary colors?)

It's no wonder that the camera mimics the eye almost exactly. Both incorporate the same two fundamental laws of light:

♦ Light travels in a straight line unless it is interrupted. This helps explain why an image is inverted when it travels through a lens. As the light travels from the top of your subject, it continues through a hole in your camera (the lens) and to the bottom of the back of your camera. As light travels from the base of your subject, it again passes through the lens and continues to the top of your camera back. Voilà, your image is inverted. This theory works for eyeballs, pin holes, lenses, and camera obscuras.

♦ When light enters a denser medium, it bends. To get a little more complicated, when entering a thicker medium, light bends toward the denser part of the medium. This is how a lens works.

Just as early inventors of flying machines mimicked birds, camera designers mimic the eye.

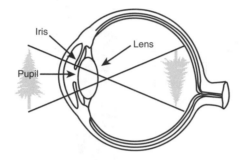

The eye is a good model to copy for our camera. It has all the necessary parts we need. First, we'll use a few lenses to focus the light. Next, we'll use a mechanical diaphragm to replace the iris and regulate how much light enters our camera body. And finally, we'll use film as our retina.

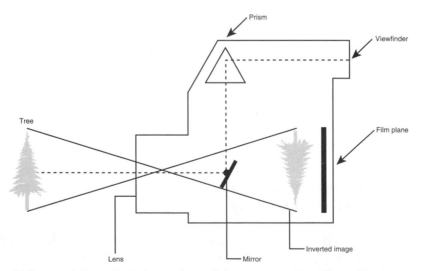

Light travels through the lens, reflects off the mirror, and is redirected by the prism to your eye. When the mirror is in an up position, the light continues to the back of the camera and strikes the film.

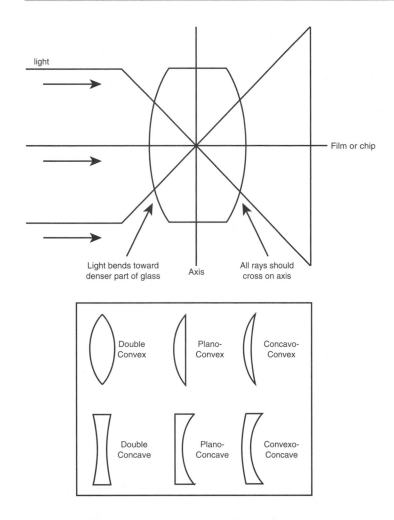

Notice how similar the lens is to the eye!

In the Beginning ... There Was Film

Let's start by discussing how black-and-white film works:

1. Silver nitrate crystals are suspended in an emulsion. Think of emulsion as gelatin (Jell-O) with pieces of fruit (silver nitrate crystals) floating in it. The emulsion is bound onto a clear substrate. (We call this substrate *film*.)

2. The silver is exposed to light (a picture is taken).

3. The film is developed. If the silver on the film has been fully exposed, it turns black. If the silver has been partially exposed, it turns a shade of black (a.k.a. gray).

4. The development is stopped (stop bath) and the unexposed silver is removed (fixer).

5. The film is dried. We now have a negative!

6. Light is sent through the negative onto another film (or paper) to make a positive. (Remember, two negatives make a positive.)

So just how does color film work, exactly? To put it simply, color film is broken down into three basic layers. (Actually, there are many more layers, but I'm trying to keep things simple.)

◆ The red layer turns red when red light strikes it.

◆ The blue layer turns blue when blue light strikes it.

◆ You guessed it: The green layer turns green when green light strikes it.

The photochemical process.

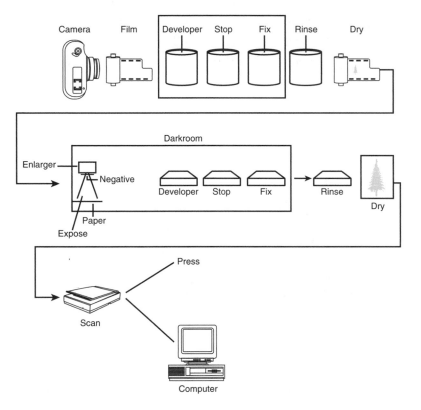

Sound familiar? When light is passed through the film and all the layers of color, we see a colored picture.

Pixel Schtick: How Digital Cameras Work

Instead of film, digital cameras contain *imaging arrays* onto which the lens focuses light. (Many people call arrays *chips*, which is perfectly legal; no points will be deducted from your score.) On these chips are CCDs (*charged coupled devices*).

Behind the Shutter

In case you're curious, here's how this all works: When light strikes its corresponding layer, it excites the silver residing on that layer. The layers are filtered so that only red light affects the red layer, only blue light affects the blue layer, and so on.

But wait! Doesn't silver turn black or shades of black? How can silver turn into a color? Here's how: The silver, in its excited stage, activates a *color coupler* (the color coupler is mixed with the silver in the emulsion).

When the film is being processed, it is dunked into a solution called *developer*, which contains color dyes. Those excited color couplers grab these semitransparent color dyes out of the developer solution and lock them onto the film base in layers.

After the chemical developer is stopped, a bleaching bath is used to strip away the silver, leaving only the color dyes. There is no silver in a color negative or in a color print—it's all left in the bleach.

When the CCDs are struck by light, they emit an electrical charge that is turned into binary information by the camera's processor. This digital information, the ones and zeros (or offs and ons), are the heart of how computers work. In fact, the capability of the processor to change color and brightness information into machine code is the reason we are able to manipulate a photograph in the first place. In a color camera, the CCDs are filtered, or *tuned*, to accept only certain colors—you guessed it: red, green, and blue.

Digital cameras capture information in many ways:

◆ CMOSes (*Complementary Metal-Oxide Semiconductors*) work like CCDs to produce electrical charges when struck by light. CMOS chips tend to be a bit noisy and less sensitive to light, but they are less expensive to produce and use less power than their cousins, CCDs. CMOS chips can be found in certain modestly priced digital cameras and web cams.

◆ The simplest type of array aligns the CCDs in a line. This is called a *linear array*. A linear array can capture only one color at a time; the array is moved across the long direction of the image plane three times to capture color (once for red, once for green, and once for blue). The major drawback of a linear array is that the subject cannot move, and the lighting must be constant during the exposure. Many photographers will use photo-floods or filmmaking equipment to light their sets. There can also be color registration problems if the camera moves because the chip must return to the exact same starting place at the beginning of each scan.

The CCDs on a linear array digital back travel across the back of a camera three times to make an RGB exposure.

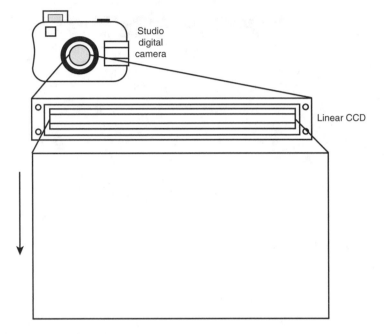

In Plain Black & White

So what is a pixel? I've been throwing the word around a lot so far. A **pixel,** which is short for **picture element,** isn't a thing, exactly; it is more of a description of a thing. If you were to enlarge a digital photograph, eventually you would see little squares of color. These are pixels, which are created by the CCDs.

You might say you are seeing the CCDs themselves, but you would be wrong, so don't say that. CCDs only tell the imaging software to draw or create a little square to represent how much light struck it and what color the light was.

The more pixels there are in a given area, the more resolution the area is said to have.

Behind the Shutter

CMOS chips are being used by only two or three camera manufacturers at this time. After more research and development, however, CMOS chips might make their way further into the marketplace. The CMOS cameras currently on the market are being used by professional photographers to capture images where high resolution is not needed, such as for Internet and small catalog shots. These cameras are not as expensive as high-resolution digital cameras, and are a good alternative.

♦ The next step up the evolutionary chain is the *tri-linear array*. This array has three rows of CCDs on it; each row is filtered for one of the primary colors. The array *scans* the image plane only once, which greatly reduces the time it takes to make an exposure. Color registration is also greatly increased. Because there is little to no interpolation, these arrays are very accurate when it comes to color. If these arrays are long enough and allowed to travel over a large distance, they can produce very large files—100MB or more. These arrays are commonly used in professional still-life photo studios, but again, the array must be moved down the image plane, the subject cannot move, and the scene must be constantly lit.

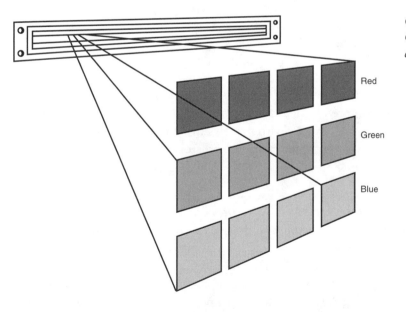

On a tri-linear array, the CCDs need travel across the camera back only once.

Red

Green

Blue

♦ If you take the chip and line the CCDs up in rows and columns, you can create a great black-and-white (B&W) chip. With this type of chip, you can use a flash instead of a constant source, and can photograph live action. To produce a color photograph, the camera must make three exposures, or passes. To do this, a rotating color filter is placed in front of the lens. First, a red filter rotates in place and an exposure is made, then green, and then blue. The color in the image will be very accurate. Also, the exposure times are greatly shortened because a flash can be used during each pass. The subject, however, still cannot move.

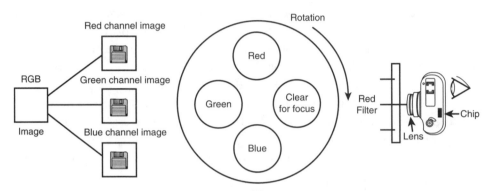

Light passes through each of the color filters to strike a black-and-white chip set. When the colors are combined by the camera software, a full-color RGB image is produced.

♦ Some manufacturers are placing a glass filter called a *liquid tunable filter* in front of the lens or inside the camera on the surface of the chip. The filter rapidly changes from red to green to blue within the time duration of a flash, which has the effect of making three passes with one flash! With this technology, you can get the best of both worlds: accurate color and stop-action photography. The technology is still young and there are still a few bugs to work out, but it is promising.

♦ Single-shot color can be produced by a *stripped array*. This will be the most common type of chip set you will find in today's cameras. The CCDs are again arranged in rows and columns, but tiny (one might say itty, bitty) colored filters are arranged over the individual CCD. The filters can be arranged in a repeating simple pattern (RGBRGB) or in a more complex pattern (RRGBRRGB). The patterns differ depending on the chip and camera manufacturers; color resolution depends on what type of chip is being used and what type of interpolation is being done.

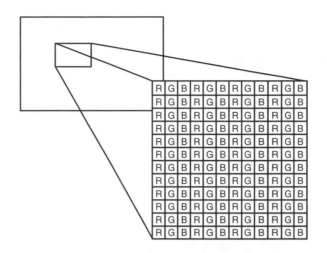

The stripped array arranges tiny filters over the CCD devices, enabling one-shot color photographs.

Behind the Shutter

On color film, the red, green, and blue layers are stacked over each other. As the light passes through these layers, true (accurate) color occurs. Because the CCDs are not layered over each other but rather sit side by side, you can run into some problems with the color. If a beam of red light strikes the red-filtered CCD, everything is fine; life will be beautiful. But if the red light strikes a differently filtered CCD or a different color strikes the red CCD, you have problems.

But not to worry. Interpolation algorithms look at the information as it comes off each CCD and decide whether the information is correct or not. The algorithms look at the information and say, "Yup, that looks like red light. Pass it on," or "Nope, that's not red, but it looks like blue." (Go ahead, put your ear up to the back of a camera!)

The Least You Need to Know

- The visible spectrum can be broken down into red, green, and blue primary colors.

- Cameras and lenses mimic the human eye.

- CCDs are activated by light and send electrical impulses, which are changed into digital signals.

- There are many variations of digital cameras. These include scanning backs and one-shot action backs. These produce black-and-white (B&W) and color (RGB) images.

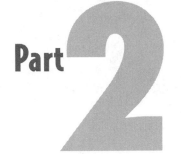

Part 2

Cameras, Computer Hardware, and Software for Digital Capture

The blazing speed of computers has spawned a revolution in software development. Software has, and probably always will, lag behind CPU development. Nevertheless, today's software programs allow us to manipulate images in ways we've never dreamed of before. Once upon a time, we were happy if we could rotate a black-and-white image. Today, we can correct the color of an image, triple its size, and sharpen it while we sit in front of our monitors.

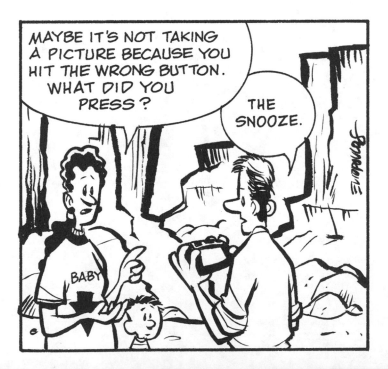

So Many Choices: Camera Models That Show Off Their Style

In This Chapter

◆ What's the best camera for you?

◆ Camera types

◆ The inside scoop on pixels

Digital cameras are being produced with so many variations in size, design, and features that it's hard to choose the best one. It seems as if almost every day a new camera is coming out with a new or better feature list than the last. Although we will be looking at specific cameras and their features, reviewing specific camera models would be fruitless because the industry is moving at such a quick pace. By the time you read this book, some of the camera models on the shelves today will no doubt have been replaced by newer and fancier siblings.

The most enjoyable part of writing this edition was to see the advances in camera technology, specifically the chip technology. The chip sizes have increased in size from 1 megapixels to 4 or more megapixels. (Don't worry—read on to find out what a megapixel is.) Not only is that a huge size increase, but the most amazing thing is that the price has stayed the same! There are many new bells and whistles but on-board storage technologies have really advanced. It's now an easy thing to take tons of photos without having to fill your pockets with storage chips.

Research, Research, Research

The best way to get the down and dirty about a specific camera is to do a bit of research. Most of the popular photography and computer magazines review digital cameras regularly—it seems as if a new review about a specific camera comes out each month. Also, you will find overall "compare and contrast" reviews about cameras grouped by price range, resolution, or ease of use. Many of these reviews rate the cameras, such as on a scale of 1 to 10, or with stars, shutters, or other weird icons. You might even see a "best buy" or "editor's choice." You can also find great information on the web or in a consumer's guide magazine such as *Consumer Reports*.

Another good way to learn about what's new and hot is to look at the manufacturers' advertisements. See what they are hawking and why, and what gizmo or feature they have that is different or new. Watch out for confusing terminology, however; one manufacturer's "supersonic zoom system" might be identical to another's "wonder wizard system."

Say Cheese

It's important to set up a budget before you go out to buy a camera. A budget helps you decide which camera, printer, or accessories to buy. Plan for the future. Will this be the last camera you ever plan to buy? (I hope not.) Is your purchase planned to get you started or will you upgrade your equipment in a few years? Do you want to invest in a system that can be upgraded, or will you just go out and buy new stuff in a few years? Do you want to get cutting-edge equipment, or will last month's "wonder" technology do? Some of these decisions might be influenced by your economic advisor (in my case, my wife); other times, you just gotta have the best camera on the block!

Narrowing It Down: Camera Types

First, let's figure out what type of camera you need. Basically, four major groups of camera designs are available, each with advantages and disadvantages:

◆ **Range finders.** Range finders are simple (not to be confused with *inexpensive*) cameras. You will find both traditional and digital cameras in a range finder configuration. With a range finder, you view the subject through a viewing-only lens (called a *viewfinder*) that is separate from the lens through which light exposes your film (I'll refer to that lens as the *photographic lens*). On a less-expensive model, the viewfinder might be a simple hole in the camera body, covered by clear plastic. On a more expensive model, a range finding (read: distance measuring) system allows the viewfinder lens to be focused and otherwise manipulated. The photographic lens is separate from the viewfinder.

The good thing about range finders is that they are usually smaller and weigh less than the other types. The downside is that you experience *parallax* because the viewfinder and photographic lens are not one and the same; the image you see is not identical to the image that is captured on film (see the following figure).

In Plain Black & White

The best way to demonstrate the effects of **parallax** is to look at an object first with one eye closed, and then the other. The object you are looking at appears to shift! Which view is correct? Try this again with your finger held in front of your face; the effect intensifies when the object is closer.

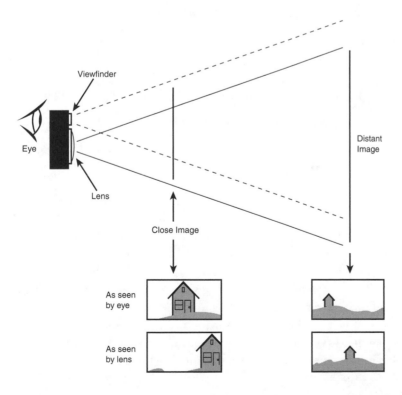

The problem of parallax.

♦ **Single Lens Reflex (SLR) cameras.** The single lens reflex (SLR) camera corrects the parallax problem because, through the use of a prism and mirrors (not to be confused with smoke and mirrors), you look directly through the photographic lens to view your subject. The Olympus 620 DL is a fine example of a digital SLR.

The trusty workhorse …
I haven't used mine in
years!

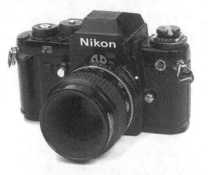

Boston's Federal Reserve
Bank; a classic example of
keystoning.

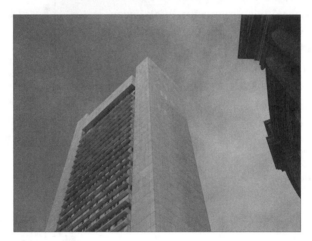

Types of Digital Cameras

One of the most important features of a digital camera is the size of the CCD array. After the chip size is taken into account, there are many other bells and whistles that have found their way into the mix. There are simple and advanced metering systems, focusing systems, color-management systems, and so on. Please don't be alarmed or overwhelmed by all the options. Even the simplest of digital cameras will take a good picture. Read through the description of camera types and options, a few times if necessary, before you decide which camera to buy. Decide how you will use the camera and how much control you want to have over your picture taking. Don't buy more camera than you can handle. It will be a waste of money and might frustrate and hinder your photographic experience. The most important thing is to feel comfortable with your camera.

One Megapixel Cameras

Most commonly, you will find cameras that have chip arrays measuring 1,280 × 960 CCDs on the chip (see Chapter 2 if you need more information on CCD arrays). These are called *1 megapixel* (1Mp) cameras, and will give you great snapshots. If you are planning to only use your camera to post your photos on a website this type will provide you with everything you'll need.

Flash

Some cameras depend on interpolation to increase image size. Be careful of these and try not to get confused by the actual array size versus the size of a finished image. Interpolation is an increasing in size of an image by the camera. The new information (data), which is created during the interpolation to increase the image size, is a result of a "best guess" by the camera's brain. It is not as good as the original data. Typically, poorly or overly interpolated images will have poor color quality and will be soft (lack focus and sharpness). Unless you are working on a tight budget, stay away from cameras that depend on a lot of interpolation. These cameras won't provide an image with a lot of detail.

These types of cameras come in a variety of shapes and sizes, ranging from *P and S* (point and shoot) range finders to SLRs (and with a price range from $300 to $1,000—the SLR cameras tend to be the more expensive). The cameras also range in complexity, from the simple P.H.I. (Push Here Idiot) to some that have so many bells and whistles you should expect to keep the instruction manual always at the ready. Using a 1Mp camera, you can expect to make good-quality prints from a 4×5-inch to a 5×7-inch, depending on image quality.

Flash

The "depending on image quality" caveat is not meant to be a dodge. If your image has a lot of diagonals or detail, such as texture, the image quality is going to suffer if you make too big of a print. You can still make a big print—just stand back from it a bit! If, however, your image doesn't have a lot of detail (it's a nice big blue sky, for example), you can make bigger prints.

Fuji's Finepix 2600 camera offers compact size, 2.0 megapixel chip size and USB file transfer.

(Courtesy of FujiFilm)

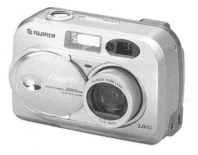

Behind the Shutter

One camera I reviewed while doing research was the Barbie camera, a great point-and-shoot camera for girls or boys. It comes with software that enables children to take images and manipulate them. In addition, the software allows the young photographer to make animations with his or her images. I think it is a wonderful way to get children excited about photography; I'm sure the GI Joe camera will follow soon!

Every kid has to have one!

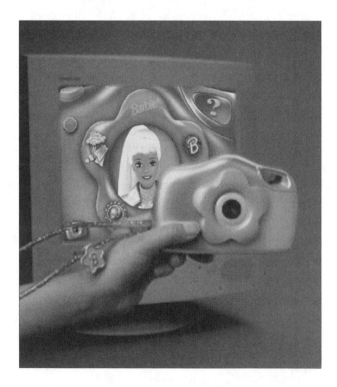

2 and 3Mp Cameras

Although 1 megapixel cameras are still available on the market, for "short money," 2 and 3 megapixel cameras are very common and very plentiful.

Let's take a moment to do some math and see just what all those megapixels are adding up to. A 2 megapixel camera has a CCD chip size of about 1,200×1,800 pixels, give or take a few. A 3 megapixel camera has a chip size of about 1,536×2,048 pixels. Let's look at this in another way that may be more familiar to you. A 2Mp camera will produce a 6 megabyte file. At 150 dpi, this would yield a 8×10-inch print. A 3Mp camera will produce a 9 meg file (that's 50 percent bigger) which in turn will print up at almost 10×14 inches. Better yet, you could increase the dpi and produce a 8×10-inch print at 200 dpi or better. Not bad!

So which one to buy? This is not an easy question to answer. There are two ways you can go. One, you can get the highest megapixel camera with a small set of features. Two, you can get a low megapixel camera with a large feature set. Another thing you can try is to buy some digital media and take it with you when you go to test cameras. If you have a Pocket PC PDA or recent Palm (m500 or m125) that's all the better, as most PDAs can handle the same storage CompactFlash and Secure Digital media as digital cameras. If you don't have a PDA, you can get a USB or Serial card reader for $30 and up at your local computer retailer. You should consider buying one anyway, if you're that serious about a nice digital camera. Take a few shots, jot down notes about the order that you tested cameras in, and take them home to view and print.

If you can look at the images on a computer monitor, take a look at the shadow areas. See if you can see "noise" or grainy color variations in the deep shadows and/or blacks. This is a really good test of how well a chip handles low light and reproduces color. If you see a lot of noise, gently put the camera down, smile nicely at the salesperson and try another one.

As I mentioned before, digital cameras are getting better all the time. Right now some engineers in a lab are tinkering with the next generation chip. These advances, and the advances that are soon to come, are going to greatly increase the quality of digital images, bringing digital cameras into the mainstream and ultimately replacing film cameras in sales.

Say Cheese

When you take a storage card and insert it into a camera, the camera creates a folder on the card. The folder is typically named after the model of the camera, so it's easier to tell where each picture sample came from. You can see these folders on a PDA or desktop computer using file browsing software that came with the PDA or the card reader.

Midrange/Semipro Cameras

Midrange, or semipro, cameras have chipsets that deliver images between 8MB and 16MB. Not surprisingly, these babies are on an average pricey—from $1,000 to $5,000—but remember that for this type of money you are going to get a lot of camera (usually an SLR) with a lot of bells and whistles. Most important, you can be sure that the image quality of photos taken with these types of cameras is going to be a lot better than with the 1Mp or 2Mp cameras. (For that money, I certainly hope so, Ollie!) You should expect to be able to easily make a 5×7-inch to just under 8×10-inch print and still hold good detail.

There are, however, still deals to be had in the 4MP+ range. Both the Minolta Dimage F100 4MP and Olympus C-4000 4.1MP cameras retail for around $500, which is a great deal if you need a high resolution camera now. If you don't need one right away, trends indicate that prices should drop dramatically on 4MP cameras over the next six to nine months.

Be ready for life's big moments!

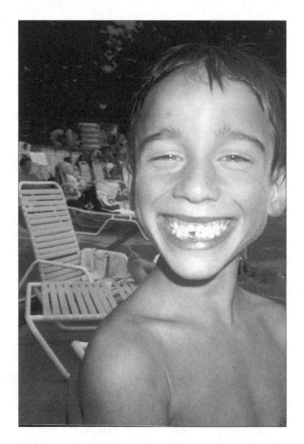

Professional Cameras

Professional-level digital cameras start at about $17,000, and range up to just short of the cost of some lakefront property! You can expect image sizes of 18MB to 36MB with one-shot professional cameras.

Models such as the Nikon D1 have chipsets built into the camera at the film plane, making them extremely thin and lightweight (see the following figure); these cameras have been adopted by many news and sports photographers.

Other companies, such as MegaVision and Phase One, manufacture detachable film backs, which slip onto the camera. These typically are mounted on a Hasselblad or Fuji 680.

> ### Behind the Shutter
>
> Did you ever wonder how the daily newspaper was able to run a photo of an "Olympic Moment" within hours of it actually happening? Many news photographers now carry wireless and satellite equipment that allows them to send images directly from their current location to the photo editor's desk. As Jimmy Olsen would say, "Holy Cow!"

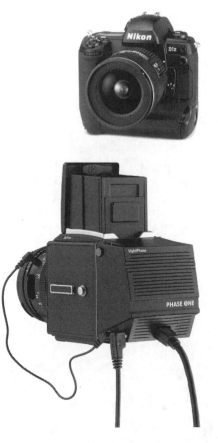

Nikon offers professional photographers the D1 series of camera that use traditional camera bodies and lenses married with digital chip sets on the film plane.

Phase One LightPhase, one-shot digital back.

Scanning-back cameras usually are designed to slip onto the back side of a 4×5-inch view camera. These babies put out 100 to 200MB files. You can do a whole lot with that much information! A good example is shown in the following figure.

Phase One PowerPhase FX
scanning back.

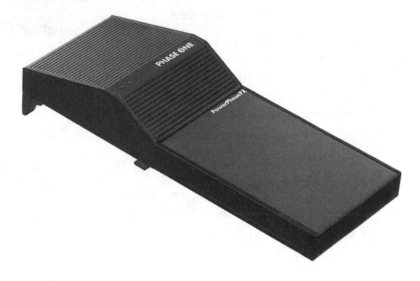

The Least You Need to Know

- With all the available options and choices, your best bet is to do your homework to find the best deal.

- Decide how involved you want to get when taking pictures. Don't buy more camera than you need, but leave yourself some room to grow.

- Don't become "camera poor." Be sure you have enough cash left over to buy a few batteries and any computer equipment you might need.

- The bigger chip size your camera has (megapixels) the better. If you're on a budget, don't buy more than you need.

Chapter 4

Attention to Details: Features You Need to Know to Get the Camera You Want

In This Chapter

◆ Useful camera features

◆ A lot depends on the lens

◆ Don't be fooled by flashy promises of flash

◆ How to spot a quality LCD screen or viewfinder

◆ Understanding image storage and downloading

When it comes to which features on a camera you want or need, the decision-making process can get very confusing. Again, I suggest you first decide how you will be using your camera. Will you use it mostly outdoors or will you need to make very detailed reference photos? Is a powerful flash needed or do you need an accurate metering system, or both? Do you want a camera that can slip into your pocket or are you comfortable lugging around a camera bag? The LCD screens, which are prevalent on most cameras, can be difficult to see well. Take the camera outside and look at the screen in bright light. Look closely at these types of details.

Take your time when you make these decisions. Don't fall in love at first sight. If you can test the camera out before you buy it, great. See whether your camera dealer will let you walk around with a demo model for a while.

Camera Design

Digital cameras are being manufactured in many new sizes and shapes; some no longer look like their traditional film-based cousins. The main reason for this is that they do not have to adhere to many of the mechanical restrictions that film-based cameras do, such as film transport systems. The only two parts of the camera that need to be aligned are the lens and chip field. After that, anything goes!

Split/Pivot Cameras

Many new digital cameras *split*, or *pivot*. This design is found mostly on cameras that have LCD view screens. Although the LCD screen stays with one half of the camera, the lens, flash, and optical viewer (if there is one) stay with the other. This design can enhance your ability to see the image on the LCD screen and, at the same time, make taking the picture easier. These cameras are great, especially if the LCD panel can be used as a real-time viewer (like a movie camera). For example, you can hold the camera over your head in a crowd, point the lens toward the subject, and follow the action on the LCD screen. Up periscope!

Nikon's 995 split-body camera takes a little getting used to, but after that, it's great!

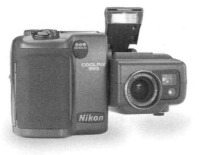

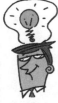

Say Cheese

Many times you'll see news photographers holding cameras over their heads in a crowd to get a shot. These guys, including me, have a pretty good idea what the camera is seeing. We also cheat a bit by putting on a wide-angle lens, ensuring coverage. It is a lot better than missing an important shot or photographing the back of the head of the photographer in front of you. Try it out. You've got nothing to lose—you're a digital photographer now!

One camera, the Minolta Mirage V, even has a *detachable* lens and chip assembly. The assembly is tethered to the camera body via cable; you detach the lens and place it in a spot that is awkward to get to or out of reach. I'm sure James Bond must have one of these!

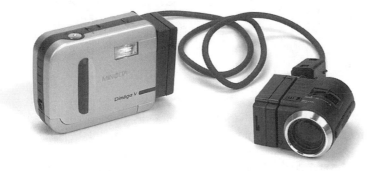

Now you can take pictures around the corner.

Other Design Considerations

Many of the SLR cameras are also breaking new design boundaries; specifically, their bodies are being designed to make holding them easier, or to incorporate larger flashes. Some of these look so aerodynamic you might think they could fly!

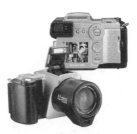

A very slick-looking Olympus DL 620.

No matter what the camera looks like, however, you should pick it up before you buy it (if you were to spend this much money on a new sports coat, you would try it on, wouldn't you?). You are going to be holding this thing for a long while, so you should see how it feels. Those of you who "hunt" with your cameras (you know who you are) will appreciate a comfortable camera. Ask yourself the following questions:

◆ Is it well balanced?

◆ Is there a good place to hold it?

◆ If you are a southpaw, does it work for you?

◆ If you hold the camera up to your eye, does your elbow end up in a place that would be uncomfortable after a while?

Of course, it isn't *that* important that the camera be able to twist, bend, or tie itself into a knot. Many of the basic camera shapes still function perfectly well. So before you purchase a camera, it is important to evaluate how you have been taking pictures or how you plan to take pictures in the future. It is also important to determine how the camera fits into your budget. You can save a lot of money if a simpler camera style will work for you. That way, you can spend the money you save on more important items, such as a better printer or an autographed Mark McGwire baseball card.

Battery Life

Simply put, no digital camera works with dead batteries, so you should check out how many batteries your camera needs, and what kind. Not only do batteries add to the weight of your camera, they also reduce the weight of your wallet. Are the batteries your camera requires readily available for purchase, or are you going to be chained to the local Radio Shack? Also, pay attention to the camera manufacturer's specifications. Many of these specs tell you how many pictures your camera will take on one set of batteries. Be sure the specifications include flash use, because you are going to be using one a lot!

Flash _____

Many rechargeable batteries, especially NiCad batteries, develop a memory. If they are not fully drained before you recharge them, they will either not fully charge again and/or not deliver their full capacity.

If you suspect your batteries are weak, or if your camera is acting a little slow, here's a great way to drain your batteries before recharging them: Place the batteries in a flashlight that can be left on. When the flashlight no longer works, you can be reasonably sure that the batteries are completely drained. Then go recharge them.

There are many types of batteries on the market today. Some batteries, which are usually rated for photography, deliver full output and then die, although others, usually cheap, general-use alkaline batteries, output less and less power until they're dead. Alkaline batteries are the most common and the cheapest, but it is not recommended that you recharge them. Lithium batteries, which are also nonrechargeable offer longer life, but are a little on the pricey side. NiCad (Nickel Cadmium) batteries are rechargeable and make good economic and ecological sense. NiCad batteries must be completely drained before they are recharged; otherwise, they develop a "memory." In other words, if your battery is recharged while it is two third full, it will always need to be recharged when two third full and will take only a two third charge. NMH (Nickel

Metal Hydride) batteries are also available for use in cameras; they provide even greater power and endurance than NiCads. NMH batteries also have the great advantage of not developing a memory, and can be "topped off," or recharged to full, at any time. These batteries are a little more pricey, but well worth the extra cash.

When you're buying a camera, you should consider whether it comes with a battery charger or whether you will have to buy one. If the camera does come with a charger, determine whether it is a quick charger or one that requires 8 to 12 hours.

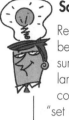

Say Cheese

Rechargeable batteries should be kept in sets to help you be sure all the batteries in a particular set are totally drained. Color code your batteries or write "set one," and so on, on them.

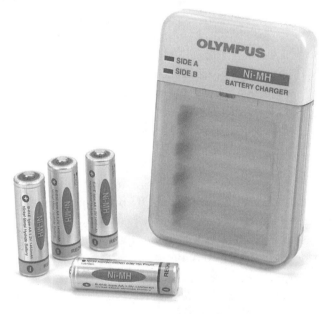

NMH batteries and charger are included with Olympus DL 620.

Many battery chargers allow you to "trickle-charge" the batteries. Trickle chargers supply a small charge to the battery, after it has been fully charged, without overcharging them. That way, you can keep your batteries in the charger, always at the ready. Nontrickle chargers can overcharge or ruin your batteries. Be careful where you charge your batteries. I have found that the charger and the batteries can get quite hot. Be sure there are no combustibles, such as paper, near the charger.

Some cameras come with an AC adapter, which allows you to plug your camera into the house current and charge your batteries while they are still in the camera. If you don't mind trailing an extension cord (or if you forgot to charge the batteries and have no choice), you can run the camera from the wall outlet.

The most frustrating problem with digital cameras and their "weakest link" (spoken in an English accent that befits the host on the popular American show that goes by the same name) is dead or dying batteries. As you're toting your camera around keep the following in mind:

◆ Keep your AC adapter handy. Try to use it when you are at home or transferring files to your computer.

◆ Turn off your flash, if you can, when you don't think you'll be using it. (See Chapter 10 for more flash hints.)

◆ Run the camera with the LCD screen in the off mode as much as possible. Especially if you just have the camera dangling around your neck, but still on.

◆ Let it sleep! When the camera is turned on you'll notice it whirs and spins for a few moments. Also you will notice that the zoom lens will come out and set itself. When the camera goes into it's power saver or sleep mode, it will turn off most of it's power use and wait for you to awaken it. Usually a simple tickle of the shutter button will do. If you would like to play Prince Charming you may try kissing the camera. Results will vary!

CAUTION

Flash _____

Be sure to check the batteries in your camera before you plan to take pictures. Keep an extra set charged always. If you plan to be taking a lot of pictures, take a few sets of batteries with you; you won't regret it.

You may find small auxiliary battery packs which contain four to six high-capacity batteries. These batteries can be plugged into the DC power port on the side of your camera, where the charger or external power source is normally plugged in. These power packs may last two to three times longer than the on-board batteries. Many professional photo or video stores will carry these.

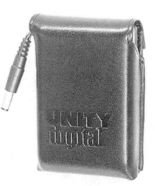

Battery packs like this one hold four to six high-capacity NMH and can be connected to the external power port on your camera.

Lenses

Unless you are going to be the first digital "pin-hole" photographer, you need a lens. With the exception of some upper-end SLRs, most digital cameras come with one lens—usually a wide-angle to telephoto lens combination (28mm to 150mm), commonly called a zoom lens—permanently attached. (You'll learn more about lenses in Chapter 8.)

If you want to know how much of a zoom lens to buy, consider the following:

- **Look through the lens.** Place a group of people 10 or 15 feet away, zoom all the way out to wide angle, and see how many people will be in the shot. If you think you need even a wider view, you can either go buy a wider zoom, or take a few steps backward! (Taking a step back can be the difference between a 23mm and 28mm lens, for example.) The same test can be applied to the telephoto end of a zoom. If your kid is playing center field, you need more of a telephoto lens than if he or she is pitching. With a camera that has a smaller chip array, or that depends on interpolation, filling the frame of the viewfinder is much more important. Remember, you want to get as much original image data into the camera as possible. This way, you will end up with a better-looking image if you need to crop or enlarge the image later. A longer focal length telephoto helps here.

- **How does the lens operate?** Can you zoom manually, or do you have to push a button and let a motor do it? (Remember your batteries!) How fast does the lens zoom if it is motor driven?

- **How crisp is the lens? How good does the image look? Is there good contrast in the picture?** Evaluate these criteria by viewing images photographed by the lens on your computer screen. (Be sure you use the same computer screen when you compare lenses! No fair looking at images taken with one lens at home and images taken with another at work.)

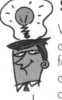

Say Cheese _____

When you are comparing cameras to buy, don't be fooled by a lens that might be a few millimeters better than another. If there is less than a 10 to 15 percent overall difference, it's not a consideration.

Flash _____

Many cameras depend on interpolation to increase the size of an image, or "zoom in." This is not a true telephoto. The problem this might cause is that the image might degrade due to the interpolation when enlarged. Be careful to check what is the true optical focal length of your lens.

- **How sharp is the image?** Many lenses use plastic optics. Plastic optics generally do a good job, but glass optics are better. However, and this is important, a camera that does not have a big chip array or is depending a lot on image interpolation does not need glass optics. The camera won't be able to reproduce the difference in detail that a glass lens offers over plastic optics.

- **Can you attach filters to your lens? Do you need to buy filters that will work only with this camera, or can you use them on other equipment? Can you use previously purchased filters?** Some cameras offer a built-in lens cap device that automatically covers the lens when it is not being used to protect it. But as a matter of precaution, it is a good idea to always have a UV (ultraviolet) filter over your lens if possible. The UV filters are clear and serve two useful purposes: They filter out UV light (haze) and protect the lens from dirt, fingerprints, and dog noses.

- **How fast is the lens?** The more light a lens can pass through to the chip or film, the faster it is said to be. Because digital cameras are not as sensitive to light as film cameras are, and perform poorly in dimly lit situations, the faster the lens, the better.

  Lens speed is calibrated in *f/stops*, which are numerical values that tell you how much light can pass through a lens. The lower the f/stop number, the faster the lens. For example, an f/stop of 2.8 lets in more light than an f/stop of 3.5. Why the goofy numbering system? Bookmark this page and go read Chapter 7; otherwise, just take my word for it for now!

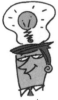

Say Cheese

Is an f/stop of 2.8 faster than an f/stop of 3.0? Yes, but not by much. If it came down to deciding whether to buy a camera with an f/2.8 lens versus one with an f/3.0 lens, all other things being equal, including the cost, I would buy the faster f/2.8 lens.

- **Does the camera have auto-focus?** Many cameras employ sophisticated methods of automatically focusing the lens. Some use sonar to determine distance, and others judge the contrast of an image to determine whether it is in focus. It really doesn't matter how a camera auto-focuses, as long as it does it well.

  My suggestion? Pick up the camera you are planning to buy, and see how long it takes to focus. If you are using a non-SLR camera, listen for the whirring (if there is any) to stop. See how well the camera focuses, and on what, when two objects are at different distances from you (an example of this would be if your image depicted a single person standing a few steps in front of a group of people).

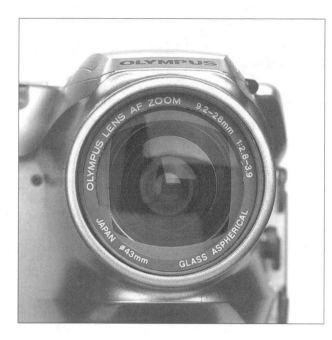

Check out the information on your lens to find out the maximum f/stop and focal length.

A fixed focus, for instance, is generally found on less-expensive cameras. Though it might well be your only option, it can serve you well. You are limited as to how close you can get to your subject, but all cameras focus to infinity (and beyond). If your camera really wants to focus on a group of leaves and not the flowers in front of them, an override capability comes in handy.

Flash

If the camera you are planning to buy does not have an onboard flash unit, don't buy it (unless it's a professional model). As I've said before, digital cameras need all the exposure help they can get!

Most camera manufacturers do not tell you how powerful their flashes are, but they should! A bigger-looking flash doesn't necessarily mean it is more powerful than a smaller one. The best way to tell how much *flash in the pan* you're going to get is by testing. Shoot the same subject, at the same distance from the camera, with two different cameras (be sure to test cameras with equal chip sensitivity/ISO ratings), and then see how bright the subject appears after you've downloaded each image to your computer and opened them in your image-editing

In Plain Black & White

Flash in the pan refers to old-time photographers who would put flash powder in a pan and ignite it to serve as a light source.

program. Also look behind the subject to see how much of the background is lit. The more the background is exposed, the better. Set the camera to wide angle, and repeat the test. Again, the more area that is exposed, the better.

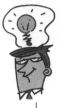

Say Cheese

Borrow a flash meter, to get a qualitative answer to flash output. Most photo stores that carry professional equipment should have a flash meter available for you to use.

You should also consider where the flash is located on the camera body. The flash should be as far away from the lens as possible (this might be a little tough to accomplish on a camera with a small body). This distance helps render better shadows and helps you avoid the "deer caught in the headlights" effect. Cameras with flash units right next to the lens greatly increase the odds of your subjects getting *red eye*.

Small but effective flash mounted on a Minolta body.

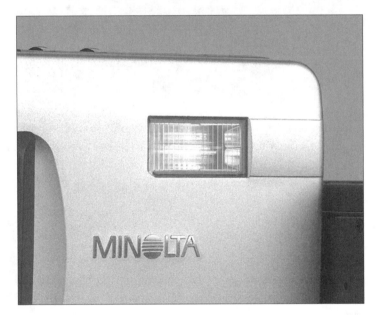

In Plain Black & White

Red eye occurs when the flash is too close to your lens. Because the flash is directing light straight into your subject's eye, you are actually photographing your subject's retina. This happens more frequently when your subject's iris is dilated (opened wider), such as in a darkened room. Some cameras employ "red eye reduction" gizmos—most work by strobing the flash a few times before the actual exposure is taken, to force the eye's iris to close. This technique works adequately, although it does rob the strobe of a lot of its firepower for the actual exposure. Also, if you notice, most of the people in the photo have annoyed or quizzical looks on their faces! Check out alternative lighting techniques in Chapter 10.

Recycle time, the time it takes the flash to recharge, is also important. There is nothing worse than waiting for your flash to charge. When the batteries in your camera are fresh, this should happen almost instantaneously. A good indication that your batteries are getting *tired* is when the flash starts taking too long to recharge. How long is too long? Without getting too philosophical, too long is when you have to wait for the strobe instead of taking pictures! Swap out the batteries for a fresh pair.

On cameras that split or twist, the flash should "travel" with the lens and remain pointed in the same direction as the lens. Although I have not seen this yet, another option would allow the flash to point in another direction to help facilitate bounce-flash techniques.

Viewfinders

Two types of viewfinders are available on point-and-shoot cameras:

♦ Most cameras incorporate an LCD (liquid crystal diode) screen on the camera body. These flat screens show you what the lens is seeing. (They might show you the image you have just photographed, or they might be *active*, and show you a real-time view of what the lens is pointed at.) These types of viewfinders can be a lot of fun; using an LCD screen, you can take a picture, and then pass the camera around for all to see. LCD screens can be difficult to see in bright light. I found myself shading the LCD with my hand in order to see the image more often than I liked. The Epson Photo PC 750 offers a nice little switch that allows the LCD to be "backlit." This made it much easier to view in bright light. You may find this feature on other cameras as well. I strongly advise you to check the camera you are considering purchasing in a brightly lit area or outdoors. If you have trouble seeing the LCD panel, don't buy it!

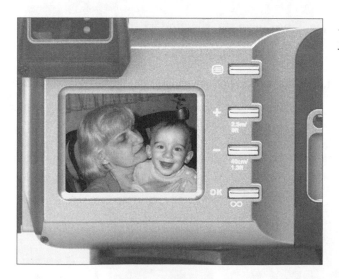

A bright LCD screen helps you preview your images.

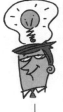

Say Cheese _____

Most LCD screens must be looked at straight on to work; you should see how well they work in subdued or bright lighting situations. Also, look to see what intelligence is offered on the screen. (Is frame count, compression rate, battery condition, time and date, or other information available?) Although it might not be a significant amount, be aware that an LCD screen is going to draw power from your batteries.

◆ A simple optical viewfinder might also be incorporated into your camera (if no LCD screen is available, this is your only way of seeing your subject). Depending on whether your camera has a metering system, you might see _intelligence_ (lights and dials) in the viewfinder; you might also see scribed markings indicating what your camera sees when it's in the telephoto or wide-angle mode. Ideally, your viewfinder will have an indicator to tell you that the strobe is recharged, as shown in the following figure. I like this feature; it lets me frame up a subject and fire the camera without taking my eye from the viewfinder.

If your camera relies on an optical viewfinder, think about the following:

◆ Can you see through the viewfinder?

◆ Is the viewfinder too small?

◆ Will your nose get in the way?

◆ If you wear ocular enhancers (eyeglasses), will they get in the way?

◆ If there is no protection on the eyepiece, will you scratch your eyewear or your forehead?

◆ What information, if any, is in the viewfinder? If a metering system is present, can you see it well?

If, on the other hand, your camera relies on an LCD viewfinder, consider these issues:

◆ Can you see it well?

◆ Does the LCD viewer work well in brightly lit situations?

◆ Can you see the LCD viewer in dimly lit situations?

◆ Is the LCD viewer big enough?

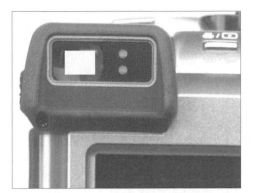

*Detail of optical viewfinder.
Note LED readouts.*

I like an LCD screen on the camera, but it might take a bit of getting used to—
especially if there is no optical finder. You have to hold the camera a few inches away
from your body to see the screen. If you have shaky hands, this might be a problem.
(I might suggest that you drink a little less coffee.)

Selected Delete

Although this might sound like a type of weapon from a *Terminator* movie, selected
deletion makes great use of the LCD screen. With the LCD screen, you can review—
on the camera—all the images you have taken that still remain in memory. You can
then delete the images you don't want, like the one where everyone has their eyes
closed. This is a great way to save space in the camera's onboard storage.

Onboard Storage

Unless you plan to have your camera permanently tethered to your computer, which
is no fun at all, it needs some kind of onboard storage. Many storage options are
available; if you are comparing cameras, trying to decide which type of memory to
buy is going to be the most difficult part. Here are some considerations:

♦ If a camera offers no removable memory (storage cards), it has built-in memory,
  usually RAM (Random Access Memory). Obviously, the more memory available,
  the fewer times you are going to have to download images from your camera to
  your computer. It can be frustrating to take only six or eight shots and then have
  to go running to your computer to download them.

◆ Some cameras, usually the higher-priced ones, have built-in RAM alongside removable memory. Cameras can access the built-in RAM memory more quickly than they can access memory on a removable card, which is why the built-in memory is usually used as a buffer. That is, the camera saves images in its buffer before sending them to the hard-card removable memory; this enables you to more quickly take your next picture. You might also have the option to save your image with different compression modes while the image is still stored in the camera's built-in RAM.

◆ Flash card memory (removable storage media), often called flash film, uses SRAM (static RAM technology which will hold its data without electric current applied), and is found in many sizes, shapes, and storage capacities. For example, the larger-bodied and/or more professional cameras use PCMCIA cards (also called PC cards), the size and shape of a thick business card. These cards are actually miniature hard drives as opposed to flash card memory, which relies on SRAM chips. A stack of five or six PCMCIA cards, which are made of metal and very durable, consume as much space as a box of film; each card holds 8-, 16-, or up to 32MB of memory. You can expect to pay about $4 per megabyte for flash card memory.

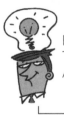

Say Cheese

PCMCIA cards, PC cards, Type 1 memory, ATA cards, and AT cards are all similar devices.

◆ Type III memory cards, which are actually mini hard drives, hold more memory than the SRAM cards—typically up to 240MB. They cost about $4 per megabyte.

◆ Compact flash cards are similar to PC cards, except they are about two-thirds the size. Each card can hold anywhere from 8MB to 45MB, and they cost about $4 or $5 per megabyte.

A compact flash card.

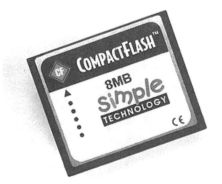

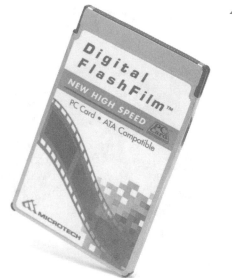

A PC card.

◆ SmartMedia cards, also called SSFDC media, are another form of removable storage. They are the size of a matchbook, are about ⅛ inch thick, can hold 2-, 4-, 8-, or 16MB of information, and cost about $4 per megabyte. Although they look sturdy, SmartMedia cards are a little more fragile than PC cards. However, this consideration is outweighed by the portability of smart media cards. For example, you can use a SmartMedia adapter—a small device into which you insert your SmartMedia card—to transfer images to your computer. In addition, many devices, such as printers, now feature slots to allow you to insert SmartMedia cards directly into them. Because of their size and portability, SmartMedia cards will likely become the standard removable device.

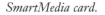

SmartMedia card.

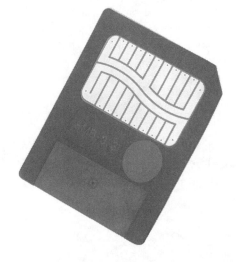

Check out how small the SmartMedia card is in comparison to the Minolta camera!

Many new storage devices are always in development. For example, IBM manufactures a mini hard drive, called the *Microdrive*, which has a capacity of 340MB and ranges from $340 to $500. In addition, Sony Corporation markets *memory sticks*, which will measure $0.85 \times 1.97 \times 0.11$ inches, hold 4-, 8-, 16-, and 32MB of information, and cost less than $4 per megabyte. These SRAM devices will be designed to interchange between cameras, printers, and CPUs.

Behind the Shutter

Some camera manufacturers design and manufacture their own memory cards as well, using unique sizes and shapes to fit only in equipment made by them. Compact flash cards are a good example of this. If you are going to be buying a few memory cards, and you will, be sure to buy cards that will fit other cameras. After all, you might buy another camera in the future, or hang out with a group of people who have cameras of their own and want to swap or loan cards. These cards are an investment, so plan to use them as long as possible.

Sony also markets a mini CD that fits into their Mavica CD camera line. This CD is actually burned onboard by the camera and can hold 156MB of data! The cost of the CD is about $5. For $10 you can get a CD-RW disc which can be read and burned over and over.

Downloading Options: Kodak DOCK

Cameras offer two ways of getting information from them to your computer (or vice versa):

- ◆ **Direct cable.** If you download by direct cable, it's best to leave the cable attached to the computer. That way, you'll avoid playing with cables instead of downloading.

- ◆ **Removable disk.** If you use a removable disk, you will need some sort of docking device or reader. These also can be left attached to the computer to avoid hookup confusion.

Consider the following options when deciding which way you want to download your images (you should also consider the additional cost of cables or readers):

- ◆ Most cameras, especially ones with no removable memory cards, allow you to download via a cable (usually through a serial cable that connects to the back of your computer).

- ◆ Universal Serial Bus (USB) cables are becoming more and more common; they also make it possible for manufacturers to produce equipment that can be made for either the Mac or the PC. USB cables and connections, which allow much faster data transfer, will soon replace the traditional serial cable and port as we know it. Some cameras are being manufactured with USB connections only. You should definitely purchase a camera, or any device, with a USB port before a regular old-style one.

Flash

Keep those memories:

- ◆ For those of you who must have something in their hand to play with (like me) may I suggest a smooth stone or small ball. Please don't bend, spindle or otherwise mutilate your memory cards. Treat them as fragile objects.

- ◆ These are not scratch lottery cards. Be careful not to scratch the contacts.

- ◆ Do not rub these on your sweater and try to stick them on the wall, please use balloons for that trick. Be very careful of static charges. If you've just walked across a carpet, don't grab your card, or your camera for that matter, or you may be very sorry.

- ◆ And while we're at it. Don't drop them. They will take a bit of a beating, but not much.

- ◆ Be careful to insert the card into your camera with the pins correctly orientated. You can do some pretty heavy damage to the card and your camera by shoving a card in the wrong way.

The business ends of a USB cable.

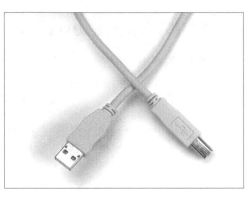

♦ FireWire connections are found mainly on high-end cameras (used primarily in conjunction with Macintosh G3 and new G4 computers), so don't look for these on any sub-$7,000 cameras. FireWire connections are very fast, and offer the wonderful option of being disconnected, and plugged into another computer, or simply put away while the original computer equipment is on. This is called "hot swapping."

CAUTION

Flash _____

You should never connect or disconnect any peripheral device to a computer while it is powered up (unless it is a FireWire or USB device). You risk seriously damaging the machine or at least the hard drive.

♦ PC cards and compact flash cards require some sort of reader to allow you to send image data to your machine. Most laptops come with PCMCIA slots built into them, and you can buy adapters for most PC card readers that enable you to use compact flash and SmartMedia cards. However, if you don't use a laptop, you'll probably have to buy a PC reader for your desktop machine.

PCMCIA card reader.

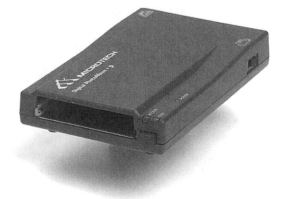

◆ Some camera systems, especially the Sony Mavica, actually use common 3½-inch disks. Imagine that! Then again, with the recent disappearance of floppy drives on iMacs, you should probably avoid this option; you might have to buy a separate floppy drive.

◆ SmartMedia cards can be put into adapters that fit into the floppy drive of your computer. This makes good sense, as most of us still have floppy drive slots. (If you own an iMac, you'll have to buy a drive, download your images via a network, or download directly via the USB port.)

◆ Kodak has developed a system dock, which allows a Kodak camera to be placed into a cradle to transfer files to the CPU or printer. The dock is attached to the computer via a USB cable. This is a very quick, no fuss way to transfer info. The dock can also be used as a battery charger and will power the camera while attached. Kodak calls this the core of their "Easy Share System." Of course, the cameras have to be part of the Easy Share System. Look for other camera manufacturers to pick up on this cool idea.

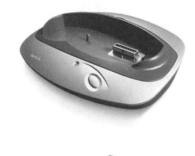

Kodak "Easy Share System" allows the user to place a camera onto the dock and transfer images.

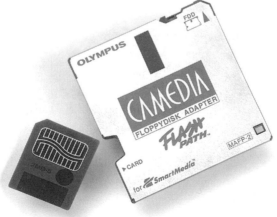

The SmartMedia transfer card fits in a 3½-inch floppy drive.

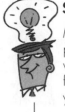

Say Cheese _____

Many cameras are equipped with NTSC video out plugs, which allow you direct output from your camera to a television set. You can preview your images on your set or, with included software, give a slideshow. This is a great way to show your family and friends the images you have taken without first downloading them to your computer. If you're visiting your computer-phobic grandmother, this can be a great option!

Burst Exposures

When you take pictures with a digital camera, there is usually a lag time between exposures, which is due to the camera processing or shuttling information between the RAM and the storage device. To counteract this, some higher-end cameras offer a *burst mode*, which allows you to take up to 10 exposures in a rapid sequence (the number of exposures and the lag time between differs by manufacturer). This is excellent for taking live action shots such as at a sports event or of a fast-crawling baby. As if that's not cool enough, some auto-exposure cameras use burst mode to quickly take four or five shots of the same image, varying the exposure, and then select which exposure is the best!

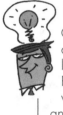

Say Cheese _____

One nice thing about using PC cards is that you can be downloading information from one PC card into your computer while shooting pictures with another PC card in your camera.

Metering

If you really want to have as much creative control over your photography as possible, you should buy a camera with an exposure meter built in (you'll usually find exposure meter readouts in the viewfinder). This will allow you to precisely control your exposure. This comes in handy in toughly lit scenes, such as with backlighting, which can fool an automatic meter. But even if you don't have an exposure meter, some cameras enable you to select either the shutter speed or the f/stop. This is called *shutter* or *aperture priority exposure*, and is a nice compromise over fully manual exposures.

We'll get into the topic of exposures a bit more in Chapter 7.

Resolution

A camera usually records your image in full resolution (using every CCD on the chip) as a TIFF file. To save space on your hard drive, however, your camera might offer you the ability to take images with lower resolutions. Each manufacturer handles this in different ways; one is to actually take a photograph, reduce the image in size, and then store it (some cameras compress the image even further after this process). Although this allows you to pack a lot of images in storage, it has the disadvantage of making your files low resolution.

You can also shoot a full-resolution image and then compress it using a compression rate that you select. Although the compression process degrades the images slightly, this is a better way to go. (Resolution and compression are covered in more detail in Chapter 12.)

Speed and Sensitivity

Some cameras allow you to vary the sensitivity, or ISO rating, of the chip, which has the same effect as using a higher- or lower-speed film. Not too long ago this system used to be called ASA. Specifying a faster ISO rating enables you to shoot in lower-light situations, and gives you some degree of control over the exposure. Realize, however, that using a faster ISO rating usually means that some sort of amplification is being done on the chip, which produces noise. Noise appears mostly in dark areas of your image as blue and red/blue "static."

A good way to compare cameras for sensitivity is to look at their slowest ISO rating. If you find one camera's specification with a minimum rating of, let's say, ISO 100, and another with a "spec" minimum rating of 200, opt for the ISO 200 camera (provided that the ratings are true and not already amplified).

Generally speaking, only cameras with bigger chips and/or cameras in the mid to professional range offer this option. However, it could be a good deciding factor when trying to choose between two otherwise similar cameras.

Extras

You should look for a few more bells and whistles on a camera when buying one:

◆ Your camera should have a threaded hole on its bottom to allow you to attach it to a tripod. If it doesn't, don't buy it. Be sure the tripod mount will not be in the way of the door for the memory cards. Otherwise, you will have to remove your camera from the tripod to change cards.

◆ Another good thing to have is a flash cord socket. This allows you to fire a flash, via a wire, that is mounted off the camera. You'll probably find this on a more expensive camera.

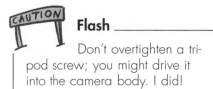

Flash _____

Don't overtighten a tripod screw; you might drive it into the camera body. I did!

◆ How are you ever going to be in your group shots if you don't have a self-timer on the camera? Most cameras do, but double-check!

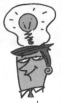

Say Cheese

If you don't have a cable release, try setting the camera on a tripod or a surface that is not moving, and set the self-timer. Your camera will go off with nary a shake!

◆ A cable release (a mechanical or electrical cord that you attach to your camera and use to fire the shutter) is a great thing to have if you are going to be taking pictures with a slow shutter speed or in low-light situations. Using a cable release prevents you from shaking the camera when you press the shutter button.

Bundled Software

Most cameras come with some sort of bundled software. Be aware that while many of these might be complete programs, some might be "lite" versions or timed versions that stop operating after a specific amount of time. Check this out before you think you're getting the deal of the century.

A Final Word ...

It is always hard to decide when to buy new equipment, but if you need the new equipment immediately, for whatever reason, find the best deal out there and go for it. On the other hand, if you're in no real rush, remember that there is always something better—some new gadget—on the horizon. Do your research to find out whether something big and new is about to come out, and decide whether you can live without it. If you can live with yesterday's technology (which worked great yesterday), you can get a good deal. (Remember when the new Intel Pentium III chipset machines came out? The P-II machine prices fell, big time.) If, however, you want the newest and best, get the new stuff—but be careful what you buy. The technology might still have a few bugs in it, or it might eventually be replaced (can you say *Betamax?*). But whatever you decide, don't miss any great shots by putting off your decision!

The Least You Need to Know

◆ Features can drive the cost of your camera up. Deciding which features you'll need and which you want will help your camera buying decision.

◆ Learn to preserve your batteries. Take extra batteries with you and don't forget to bring the charger along.

♦ Lens choice is a very important factor when deciding which camera to buy. Check out your image quality carefully be before you buy.

♦ Images are stored on removable media cards. Be sure to leave money in your budget for a few extra cards.

♦ Your images can be viewed through the lens or via an LCD screen on the back of the camera, The images can be seen in "real time" or as "on demand" review.

♦ You can download your images directly from the camera or by removing the media and "reading" it. Also, many printers can also read and print directly from the media cards.

Chapter 5

Mac Versus Windows: System Requirements for Digital Capture

In This Chapter

- ◆ Which computer will do, a Macintosh or a Windows platform?
- ◆ How much computer do you need?
- ◆ What is the best monitor for you?
- ◆ What peripheral devices do you need?
- ◆ How to buy a printer
- ◆ How to buy a scanner

There are so many automobiles on the market today! There are sports cars, family cars, and SUVs (we'll buy anything that is spelled with an acronym); some cars offer huge, powerful, gas-guzzling engines, some cars offer tons of cargo space.

No, I haven't suddenly switched to writing *The Complete Idiot's Guide to Buying a Car*; rather, I want to make a point. Almost any car can get you down the road. Likewise, you can use almost any computer to store and manipulate images you obtain with a digital camera. The issue is how well the computer you use can handle the task.

Windows or Mac?

The first question that might come to mind is do I need a Windows machine or a Mac? The answer is simple. They both work, and work well!

The Apple Macintosh was the first computer to offer any graphic software and photo manipulation, and in the beginning, most photo-manipulation software was developed solely for Macs. Macintosh computers also were the first to offer millions of onscreen colors, which is very important when working with onscreen photographic images.

Nonetheless, Windows OS (operating system)–based machines have come a long way since they first appeared. Windows offers a usable GUI that is an alternative to the Macintosh computers. Windows computers are powerful graphic machines. Windows-based systems are also capable of displaying millions of colors and tack-sharp resolution as long as the video card and monitor supports it.

Camera manufacturers design their equipment to work on either platform, mostly. Most also include software that will work on both systems. If you own a Windows platform and are comfortable with it, stay with it. If you own a Macintosh system, ditto! If you don't own a computer at all or are considering changing sides, go do your research. Macs are generally easier to learn than their Windows counterparts, but price can be a factor.

It is possible to purchase a complete Windows system for around $600 to $700 or an old iMac for as low as $500, but I'm not sure you'd really want it. Low-cost systems are so inexpensive because several corners must be cut to drop the cost of manufacturing them. These systems are also far more likely to be way out of step with current technology. You wouldn't skimp on buying tools or children's safety equipment, so why should you skimp on a computer? Expect to spend anywhere from $1,000 to $2,500 on a new computer.

Say Cheese

The prices listed were sampled at the time this book was written. It's very likely that they have gone down, even a little, by the time this book is published. Be sure to check on current prices before you get disturbed over newer systems not released when I wrote this. The good news is you'll typically find better deals then what I quote!

If you've never purchased a computer, consider a Mac first. The new Apple eMac is a powerful, low-cost winner that can be had for as low as $1,099 and has an integrated 17-inch monitor. The new LCD iMacs go for $1,399, and G4 desktop systems start at

$1,599, although you'll have to buy a monitor for a G4 Mac. On the PC side, the Dell Dimension 8200 is going for $1,069, and deals like that can be had from any PC retailer.

Before you buy a system or a camera, decide where you are going to get technical help. Will your dealer supply it? If you buy equipment from a superstore, can they supply help? If you live near one of the growing number of Apple retail stores, you can take your Mac in for service. Many equipment manufacturers offer websites for help; phone support might also be offered. Call up a manufacturer or visit its website, ask a question (make one up!), and see how long it takes to get an answer. Are you put on hold for an hour? When you get through (or find the right web page), do you get the right answer?

If you already own a system, you might find that the software packaged with the camera is out of date. You can typically find updates at the cameramaker's site. If not, call technical support fast as they owe you an explanation. Most of the software and equipment that is on the market now is designed to work with Windows 95/98/2000 or with a Macintosh. Ask your dealer/supplier questions. Will the software work on your system? Remember that you might need to upgrade software down the line; will the upgrades be backward-compatible to your system? If you can get a demo version of the software before you purchase the camera, install it and see how it performs. Does it choke your machine? Does it bother you to have to work a little slower? You might ultimately decide to start out with your current system and buy new equipment later.

> **Behind the Shutter**
>
> Macintosh machines are easier to plug and play, meaning that adding equipment and new software or upgrading is generally easier and less time-consuming.

> **CAUTION**
>
> **Flash** _____
>
> Right now, Apple is migrating toward their new Mac OS X operating system, so there are still things available for both Mac OS 8.x or 9.x and others just for Mac OS X. Apple has, however, announced that new Macs made in mid-2003 will no longer be able to start with Mac OS 9 or earlier. Make sure the software you're looking at supports the exact Mac OS you have before acquiring it.

General Requirements

It can be frustrating to use a computer if you don't have enough under the hood. Let's take a look at what you'll need.

Central Processing Unit (CPU)

The CPU of a computer is the part that does all of the thinking. It also plays the role of traffic cop for all of the other components in a computer. For Windows systems, these are from Intel and AMD. From Intel, the low-cost chips are called Celeron and the current cream of the crop is the Pentium 4. AMD offers the Duron and Athlon chips to compete. Apple, however, uses Motorola's G3 and G4 processors. The Apple systems may be marked slower than their PC counterparts, but don't think that this means they're slower. Apples are very capable machines and can match faster MHz Intel and AMD processors easily.

Random Access Memory (RAM)

RAM is where the CPU stores data it's working on. The CPU gets that data from the hard drive in your computer, and when it's done with that data, it puts it back on the hard drive. So why not just get it straight from the hard drive? RAM is a great deal faster than the hard drive. For Windows 98, 98SE, Me, or Windows 2000 Professional I strongly suggest 128MBs of RAM. Windows XP Home and Professional both require 256MBs of RAM. For Macs, the amount of RAM the system comes with is generally fine for most everything, but adding never hurts.

Because RAM is cheap, buy more. There's nothing wrong with having 1GB of RAM (if your computer can handle that much) and it makes a great brag when talking with your neighbors at the hedge.

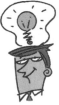 **Say Cheese**

If you want to purchase more RAM, shop around either on the web, in the back of computer magazines, or by making a few phone calls. You can find great prices, but beware! Not all RAM is created equal! Try to get RAM from reputable makers like Kingston and Crucial. Also, RAM is sold in many configurations; be sure the RAM you buy will work on your machine!

Although installing RAM is not difficult, you might want to have a qualified repair technician install your new RAM. If you decide to do it yourself, invest in a static dissipation wrist strap (Belkin, about $7 at CompUSA) and follow the instructions in the RAM package and supplied by your computer's maker.

Bus

The *bus* is the path the information flows through, connecting all the peripherals (such as the hard drive, graphic card, and CPU) together. I like to equate the bus to a highway. The faster the speed limit and the wider the highway, the more cars will get through. The bus is usually tied to a specific type of platform. For example, the bus on a G3 Macintosh is slower than on a G4 Mac.

Clock Speed

Clock speed measures how fast your CPU can think, and is another component of speed and performance. A CPU running at 700MHz is slower than a 1.0GHz machine. What does that mean to you? If you are working on a 4 to 10MB file, it might take a few seconds more to rotate a file on a 700MHz than on a 1.0GHz. However, if you are working on a 100MB file, like I usually do, it could mean a few minutes. Another thing to consider is CPU series. A 1.0GHz Celeron is not as fast as a 1.0GHz Pentium III and an AMD Athlon XP 1700+ is just as fast as an Intel Pentium 4 2.0GHz.

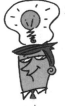

Say Cheese

Apple systems use processors from Motorola. The chips that Motorola makes are called RISC (Reduced Instruction Set Computer or Chip, depending on who you ask), which means that they understand instructions that are all the same length. Intel and AMD processors are CISC (Complex Instruction Set, well ... you know) based, which means they process instructions of different lengths. This approach allows RISC systems running at 1.0GHz to equal speeds of 1.5 and 1.7GHz RISC systems.

Hard Drive

The hard drive is like a filing cabinet; it's where you store all your information. The rule here is, again, the more, the merrier. Hard drives are cheap; the difference between a 20GB and a 40GB hard drive is not minimal; the 40GB drive is better and cheaper than the 20GB. How? The economics are simple when you understand the hard drive market. Prices are determined by the OEMs (Original Equipment Manufacturer, like Dell, Apple, or HP) because it's the OEMs that buy in bulk. When OEMs stop buying 40GB drives and start buying 60GB it becomes expensive to make the 40GB drives, so prices go up on the 40GB and down on the 60GB. This is why you'll see a 40GB drive for $99 and a 60GB drive for $119 at your local CompUSA. Look for this trend and buy wisely.

An external hard drive.

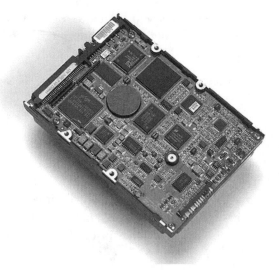

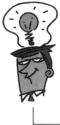

Say Cheese _____

On Windows platforms, you will probably see drives that plug into IDE connections on the motherboard. Most of these spin at 5,400rpm, but you might also see drives spinning faster, at 7,200rpm. Although the rpm is an important factor in how quickly you can access information, it is not the only one. Unless you are planning to do intense multimedia presentations, don't worry about access speed.

Ports

Ports are the outlets on your machine where you plug in all your cables. In addition to the monitor port, keyboard port, and SCSI port, you will find a port or two for your camera (if you can't find them, see whether your computer is using the same port for more than one task).

Behind the Shutter

SCSI (Small Computer System Interface) drives are also available on Windows platforms, but are more commonly found on Macs. SCSI drives are a little more expensive because of the added costs of a driver card, but they allow more drives to be connected.

You will also find FireWire (IEEE 1394) drives available for Macs as well as well as on some PCs. FireWire devices may be connected or disconnected while the system is running. Also, FireWire allows many more devices to be chained (connected) together than SCSI drives.

The following list describes the different types of ports:

◆ A *serial port* is the port you will probably use to attach your camera or other accessories.

◆ USB (*Universal Serial Bus*) *ports* are standard for most new computers—Macs and Windows—as well as on all cameras. They are fast, and more important, are universal to all new equipment. They also greatly increase your machine's capability to be *plug-and-play compliant*. I recommend that you think seriously before buying equipment that does not have a USB port on it.

◆ *IEEE 1394* (*FireWire*) *ports* are commonplace on current Macintosh computers and are rare on PCs. Many peripherals including most digital video cameras, DVD players, and even some MP3 players (most notably the Apple iPod) are coming with FireWire as a standard. FireWire connections are very fast and robust.

Flash

Both USB and FireWire devices can be "Hotplugged," which means that you can plug or unplug them while the computer is running. Plug a mouse into an Apple iBook and you will be able to use it right away. Plug in a FireWire-capable camera into that PC and transfer the pictures immediately.

Modems

With so much of our lives now revolving around e-mail and surfing the web, it is almost impossible to own a computer and not need a modem. All modems on the market today offer *56Kbps* (Kilobytes per second) speed; buying a modem that is any slower is a waste of money.

In Plain Black & White

56Kbps speed refers to the best possible download speed from your ISP (Internet service provider) via standard phone line connections. Poor phone lines, older switching technology, and sometimes your modem's mood will slow down the download. I find that during peak usage times (between 6 and 11 P.M.), the Internet gets very busy and your modem speed can get very slow. For night owls like me, this is not as much of a problem. Also, remember that the maximum upload speed on these modems is only 36Kbps.

Not all 56K modems are created equal. Some modems are generically referred to as "WinModems." Actually, they are not real modems at all, and only work with Windows machines. If you *have* to dial up, get a real 56K modem. It will cost you about $60 as opposed to $20 for a virtual one, but its value will pay for itself over time, in performance and less aggravation.

Say Cheese

Broadband, or really fast Internet access, is popular and growing. Check with your local phone or cable service provider to see if they offer broadband services in your area. Your telephone company will likely offer DSL. Your cable company pipes the Internet through the same cables that you watch HBO through. The best part is that you can usually get this service for about $40 a month, even less with a cable company when you already have cable TV. Don't let them charge you for the modem, though. There are plenty of deals that offer free modems. If you don't like what your telco or cable company offers, look into SpeakEasy at www.speakeasy.net. They have great deals and are in most metro areas.

Say Cheese

A lot of different video cards are available; many are geared toward 2D image graphics, whereas others include 3D graphics. The 3D cards greatly improve your video performance when it comes to viewing games. (You are going to play a few games, aren't you?)

Graphic Cards

Most very low cost computers (in the $300–400 range) offer video that is integrated into the motherboard. This is fine as long as you don't ever need more graphics power. Most machines, however, offer the graphic cards as stand-alone boards that take up one of the accessory slots. The benefit of stand-alone cards is that you can upgrade your video capacity without getting a new machine.

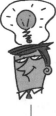

Say Cheese

The amount of VRAM (video RAM) on your video card determines how large a monitor you can use and what bit depth you see (for now, we'll define bit depth as the amount of color you can see). You don't want to cheap out here. Do not purchase a 2D card with less than 8MB of VRAM. With more VRAM available, you can get better texture and colors, and you will see a marked increase in video speed.

Monitors

Which monitor you buy might be the most important decision you make as far as image quality is concerned. If you can't see the image you have taken and its details, you will have a hard time editing it. However, there are so many CRT (cathode-ray tube) monitors on the market that buying one can easily become confusing.

Behind the Shutter

You can have the fastest computer in the world, but if your video card is slow, the benefits of that fast computer are counteracted. The faster your video card, the faster your screen redraws. This means you will see the changes you made to your images faster.

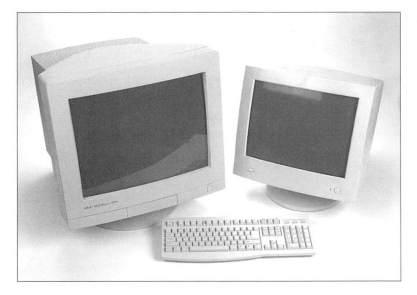

A 21-inch imaging monitor and 17-inch toolbox monitor.

Before you buy a monitor, it's a good idea to see what's hot and what's not. Pick up a computer magazine or visit a website that features tests and comparisons. Many of these reports will make it easier for you to compare monitors of similar size and with similar features. They might even rate the monitors as a best buy or editor's choice.

Behind the Shutter

Many professional photographers, illustrators, and graphic designers use two monitors with their systems. One monitor, which is run off the onboard video card, displays the imaging software's tools, such as the color palette. This monitor is referred to as the toolbox monitor. The other monitor, which is usually run off an in-slot monitor card, shows only the image. The benefit here is that the image can be viewed without the clutter of the software interface. Remember, each monitor needs its own graphic card.

Consider the following when buying a new monitor:

◆ **Size.** Monitor size is typically measured diagonally from corner to corner of the picture tube (the monitor's case might take a little off this dimension). Most computer systems come with 15-inch monitors, which are pretty small for imaging. (If you find that you are leaning into your screen or you are constantly cleaning off nose prints, your screen is too small!) If you can, buy a CPU without a monitor or try to trade up to a monitor that measures 17 inches—a great size for most imaging. Monitors should cost between $200 and $700, with most found in the $350 to $600 range (you will pay more for extra controls, higher resolutions, or faster refresh rates). The next size up from a 17-inch monitor is a 19-inch model, which ranges in price from $600 to $1,100. On top of the heap, king of the hill, and all-out huge, are the 21-inch monitors, which are primarily used by professionals and cost $900 to $2,500.

> ### Behind the Shutter
>
> Flat-screen LCD monitors are becoming more popular due to their size and relatively small footprint. They also weigh a lot less. As with most new technology, however, they are still a bit pricey compared to CRT screens (expect to tack on about $350 to add a mid-range 15-inch model). LCD monitors are sharper than CRT screens, but they have the disadvantage of being fixed resolution.

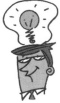

Say Cheese

If you want to save yourself a lot of eye, neck, and back strain, set your workstation up with your body in mind. Your keyboard should be on your desk or keyboard tray, resting at the level of your elbows when you are sitting in a chair (that is, if you are sitting in your chair with your arms at your side, the desktop should be at the same height as your elbows).

The next important thing is the monitor height. The monitor should be at your eye level when you are sitting in the chair. You should not have to look down or up at it. This will greatly reduce neck strain.

If you find yourself squinting at the screen, try to reduce the ambient lighting in the room. Put up a few shades or turn off some lights. I usually have a small desk light on my desk lighting up my paperwork or keyboard. Because you are sitting so close to the screen, especially for those of us who wear glasses, you might consider asking your optician to make you glasses that are set up for your computer monitor. You can also push your glasses down your nose a bit to shorten the focal length of your glasses.

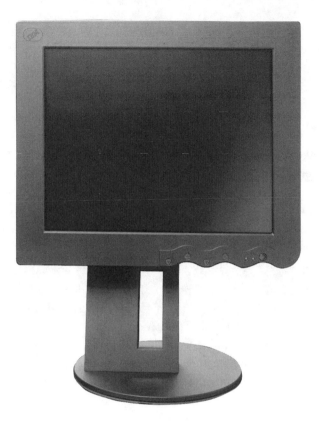

A beautifully designed IBM flat-screen monitor.

Peripherals

Many peripherals are available to enhance your computer. These gadgets take up much space in computer stores, and many pages in catalogs. Some of these peripherals, such as a zip drive, are pretty handy to have. Some, such as a coffee cup holder for your monitor, are not really needed. Take a few moments to think about what you are buying and how it will fit into your system "plan." Will your purchases enhance your system's capabilities or just look cool on your desk?

CD-R/RW

As discussed previously, you need a way to take data off your hard drive to store or transport. Graphic files can take up a lot of space, so reliable storage external to your computer. Compact disc recording drives are great for archiving information. The drives range from $100 for an entry level drive to $400 for a drive that records DVD-R. The medium is also incredibly cheap. A disk, which holds 650MB or 700MB, costs about a quarter. That's very affordable. I strongly recommend that you consider buying a CD-R. Besides it's cool to make your own CDs! With the faster 12× to 24× drives, you can record an entire CD in about eight minutes. CD-RW drives allow you to use special CD-RW discs in much the same way as floppy discs, and they're often as cheap as plain CD-R discs. Oh, and you can permanently burn a CD-RW as if it were a CD-R.

Printers

It is a lot of fun to take pictures and see them appear instantly on the LCD screen on the back of your camera. It is even more fun to see the images on your big new 17-inch monitor (you did get the 17-inch monitor, didn't you?). But what makes the whole process totally worthwhile is printing out the images on your own printer. You can make an image any size you want, and make as many as you want, just for the cost of the paper and ink! Your printer might well be as important a piece of equipment as your camera; a few extra dollars spent on the right printer is well worth it.

Finding the right printer can be a chore, though. There are dozens of consumer models available at local stores like CompUSA, Circuit City, Staples, and the like that come in at under $200. You'll find printers from HP, Epson, Minolta, Okidata, IBM's LexMark brand, Brother, Canon, Samsung, and many others. All printers in this range are ink jets, though Epson and HP have developed technologies that allow previously simple ink jet printers to output excellent images with great clarity onto special photographic paper.

While it would be impossible to test each printer, some displays at major retail chains do offer demonstration printouts. Give some of these a whirl and see which you like better, though avoid trying this if there is only one demo printer. You'll have nothing to compare it to. In the end, buy the best printer you can for the money you budget to spend. If you can afford a color laser (around $1,000 on the low end), by all means do so. Otherwise stick with ink jet. I have great luck with Epson products. Just make sure you can return it if it doesn't work out.

Behind the Shutter
Don't rely too much on the demonstration images that the manufacturers distribute or spit out automatically from the printer at the dealer. These images have been tweaked to make the printer look wonderful, taking advantage of the printer's capability to print some specific colors well. Additionally, an image might be chosen that has an "expanded" (very detailed) shadow or highlight area. I know; I've been paid to "tweak" a few in my time!

The image quality should be the paramount reason you buy a specific printer. However, there are a few more things to consider:

Inkjet Printers

Inkjet printers, ranging in price from $240 to $600, have become very popular. Inkjet printers spray ink through tiny jets, or nozzles, onto the paper. Pretty simple, huh? All in all, inkjet printers deliver great and affordable results, but there are some downsides:

◆ Inkjet printers can be very slow. It takes a lot of time for the print head to scan across the page and deliver ink. Pay close attention to the page-per-minute (PPM) specification when you are choosing a printer. (You'll have to spend more money to get faster PPM technology.) A printer that can print at two to three pages per minute is a good choice.

◆ While not always considered a downside, some printers cannot cover the entire page with ink. They will leave a small border of nonprinted paper. Some print-ers can print "borderless" images, but you may pay a bit more for this option.

◆ Many inkjet printers are four- and six-color printers. The first color is always black (K) and usually is in its own color ink cartridge. The next three colors— cyan, magenta, and yellow (CMY)—make up the needed colors to print color. The next two are specialty inks, usually an extra cyan and extra magenta, which really make the images sing. Some printers, usually the more expensive ones, will have separate cartridges for each color, while most will have a group cartridge for all the color. I highly recommend buying a six-color printer if you can.

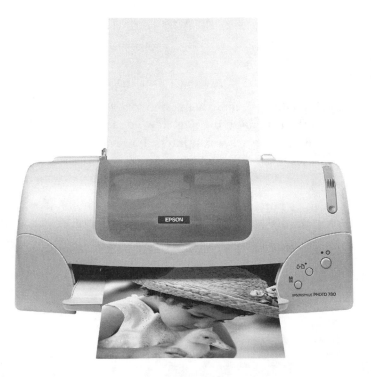

The Epson 780 printer shown here is a six-color printer and is also able to print borderless prints.

Although you can use "plain old" paper to get a quick draft image printed, a better paper grade, such as a good-quality laser paper, yields better results. For the best results use paper specifically designed for printing photos on inkjets. Some manufacturers, such as Epson, sell paper but you can also find papers by nonequipment manufacturers, such as Luminos, that work wonderfully. For you old darkroom folks, yes, that's the same Luminos that manufactured darkroom paper. The best thing to do is to get a sampler pack at a photo store and try out the various brands and surfaces and see what you like. I would use these papers for "final" images, using cheaper paper for working prints.

Dye Sublimation

Dye sublimation (dye-sub) printers deliver the closest quality to a photographic print. Dye-sub prints look and feel much like the drugstore color print you are used to looking at, delivering the best color clarity and sharpness. If I might put my bias in here, and I am going to, these are my favorite printers. I use a dye-sub, manufactured by Kodak, in my studio as a proofing device.

Behind the Shutter

Many dye-sub printers lay down one color of dye, push the print out, and then suck the print back into the machine to lay down the next color. Because the dyes bond with each other, this is a natural way to produce color, but I admit that the first time I saw this, I thought the machine was broken. When finished, the prints—whether they've been generated using multiple- or single-pass technology—emerge dry.

Thermal Wax Printers

Thermal wax printers, as you might have already guessed, deliver colored wax instead of dye. The wax sits on top of the paper. On the plus side, you can use the now-famous "any old paper"; the print quality of thermal wax printers, however, is not all that great.

Micro-Dry Printers

Micro-dry printers, which can be purchased for about $350, work much like dye-sub printers, delivering resin-based ink via thermal transfer from a ribbon. You can use any old paper with a micro-dry printer, but because the ink hits the paper almost dry, the colors do not blend as well as with dye-sub printers. For this reason, you will likely see dot patterns and banding (*banding* looks like striping in solid-color areas, such as in the sky).

Color Laser Printers

Laser printers work by magic. No, not really! A laser "exposes" a drum inside the printer. (Remember, a laser can produce a very small dot!) As a result, the drum is charged with static electricity. The drum picks up colored toner, which sticks to the static. The drum transfers the toner to the paper. The toner is then thermally fixed to the paper (this is why the paper is warm when you pick it up). Color laser printers produce a lot of heat—nothing dangerous, but it will warm your room up a bit—and consume a lot of electricity.

> **Behind the Shutter**
>
> Fargo makes a printer, called the Primera Pro, which takes advantage of both the dye-sub and thermal wax processes. It allows you to print out a draft print with wax and then produce a final print with dye-sub technology. This is a great blend of technology, quality, and budget.

Thermal Autochrome Printers

Thermal autochrome printers, which range in price from $450 to $600, do not use any ink or dyes. Instead, the color is already in the paper, and is "activated" by heat, somewhat like the process found in some fax machines. Although you don't have to replace ink or toner, you do have to use photo paper made especially for this process. The results are good, but not as good as a dye-sub print. Also, most of these printers produce only (give or take) a 4×6-inch print. This is not a widely used technology, but Fargo, Fuji, and Panasonic manufacture printers and supplies.

Scanners

Another accessory that you might want to consider for your digital darkroom is a scanner. A scanner can be a great way to add many of your old photos into your digital archive. You can use a scanner to reproduce or manipulate images you already have taken or images someone else has given you (my mom is always finding old prints that she wants me to scan in and reproduce).

Scanners cost anywhere between $300 for a basic one to $1,500 for a high-resolution one. I've even seen quite a few for the amazingly low price of $75. You will find many, many brands of scanners on the market; this is because scanners are the forerunners of digital cameras, and have been on the market for quite a while.

Agfa flatbed scanner.

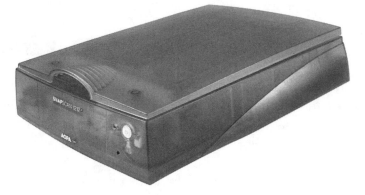

Two different types of scanners are available on the market:

♦ **Flatbed scanners.** Flatbed scanners are used mainly to reproduce reflective art, such as photographic prints or paper (also known as your kids' artwork from school). These scanners look like a rectangular box with a hinged cover; under the cover, you'll find a glass plate on which you put your image face down. The scanner head and mechanism are under the glass surface. You can lower the cover to hold the artwork flat, or simply to keep the glass clean when not used.

♦ **Slide scanners.** Slide scanners are made to scan 35mm (or larger) slide transparencies. Generally, these scanners cost more than flatbed scanners, starting at $800 and ranging as high as $2,000. These scanners cost a bit more because optics are usually involved, along with a light source, to illuminate the slide. Basically, with a slide scanner, the slide is inserted into a slot and the scanner does the rest. Some scanners even offer a transport mechanism, which allows multiple slides to be loaded up and scanned automatically.

Say Cheese

Speed is a definite factor to consider when purchasing a scanner, which is one of the advantages of a single-pass scanner. When comparing scanner speeds, be sure you are comparing scanners of similar resolutions.

Many flatbed scanners also scan slides. Techniques vary from manufacturer to manufacturer, but nearly all of them have found a way to illuminate slides and scan them. It is economical to buy one of these scanners as opposed to buying one scanner for each duty, but be careful when purchasing these types of scanners. Usually the slide-scanning technology has been an afterthought in the machine's development, so its quality might not be optimal. The best way to find this out is to test the scanner yourself or read an independent review of the machine.

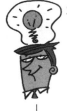

Say Cheese _____

Get your final image as close to correct as possible during the scanning process. For one thing, it is less time-consuming; you don't have to waste a lot of time in an image-editing program to get things right. Also, and this is important, every time you rearrange information in your image file, you are degrading it. If you resize your image, then brighten it, and then adjust the contrast, you have degraded your file

You are not going to get your scanner to budge one dot without some kind of controlling software. The software that comes with your scanner allows you to specify the size of your image, the contrast, and the white and black point, and to adjust for color. You might also be able to sharpen your image using your scanner's software.

Software, be it stand-alone or plug-in, comes *bundled* with your scanner. Stand-alone software, as you might have guessed, works independently of any other software (other than the operating system, of course). Plug-in software works from within other software, such as your photo-imaging software or an illustration software. In some cases, you might even be able to control your scanner from your word-processing software.

You will probably think of your scanner software as an "acquire" module that enables you to scan images and save them as a file to your hard drive or view them onscreen. However, this doesn't mean that you shouldn't think about what features you want in your scanner software. For example, your scanner software should allow you to perform a preview scan—a quick screen resolution scan that gives you a good idea of what the image will look like as well as whether it's correctly set up in the scanner. You can also crop a preview-scan image, saving you time if you want to scan only a small section of the image. The most important thing your software needs to do is let you see your preview scan as large as possible on your screen—not just a tiny image that you can't see any detail in. Also, you need a large preview image to select points to apply your adjustments, such as selecting white and black points, contrast, brightness, and the like.

The Least You Need to Know

- If you buy a Mac or a Windows machine, both will perform well.
- Buy the biggest monitor you can afford.
- Buy a removable storage device or some way to back up your treasured data.
- Watch out for consumable costs when buying a printer.
- If you buy a scanner, get one that can be as versatile as possible.

Chapter 6

Software: What You Want to See Is What You Get

In This Chapter

◆ Image-editing software

◆ Improving composition and image quality

◆ Storing your images

◆ Using tools like IrfanView

◆ Creating photo albums

All the fun in taking digital photographs is in being able to control and manipulate them. You can accomplish this and more with the many image-editing software programs that are available on the market. You will also find software that allows you to store and retrieve images just like a photo album. Small and home office software can help you create a brochure or newsletter.

Although you can transfer, or *download*, your images from your camera to your hard drive via the "on camera" controls, image-editing software is the primary way for you to move your images from the camera. Also, image-editing programs are needed to *acquire* (open) the images from your camera.

Let's take some time to overview what image-editing software can do.

Improving Composition and Image Quality

There are many ways to improve your image's composition and quality:

- **Cropping.** The first major duty of image-editing software is to help improve composition. With little trouble, you can crop your images, enabling you to reframe them or change their proportions.

- **Resizing.** You might also want to resize your image, enlarging it or reducing it. If you were not holding your camera perfectly straight and your horizon line is sinking to the left, no problem. You can rotate your image and straighten up the skyline.

- **Adjusting brightness and contrast.** If your image looks a little flat, you can increase the contrast. Suppose the photo you took of a house was a little dark because it was in the shade; no problem, just brighten it!

- **Changing colors.** You can change your image's color, adjust the contrast, lighten or darken it, and saturate or desaturate the color—all with your image-editing software. You can reshape reality!

- **Cutting and pasting.** With a little skill and practice, you can cut and paste images from one photo into another. If Uncle Joe was late showing up for the family group photo, you can take a separate photograph of him and paste him into the group shot. Here's another example: I recently took a picture of a bunch of irises. I wanted a photo just filled with the flowers but I didn't want to take the time to arrange three dozen flowers. I copied a few of the flowers and pasted them back into the shot in different places.

- **Applying filters and special effects.** You can apply many special effects to your images using your image-editing software. You can make your photo look like an oil painting, or add a texture to your backgrounds. Just as you could put filters over your camera lens, you can apply filters to your image. For example, if you choose a distortion filter, you can spherize your image and add reflection to it to make it look like you were looking into a crystal ball.

As you can see, there is almost no limit to what you can do to a digital image. If you can imagine it, you can do it. Remember all you are doing is manipulating pixels by using image-editing software. Also remember that the phrase you've been hearing all your life—"A picture never lies"—no longer applies. Ever since a photo editor at a magazine moved the great pyramids of Egypt closer together to fit them onto the page, photography has never been the same.

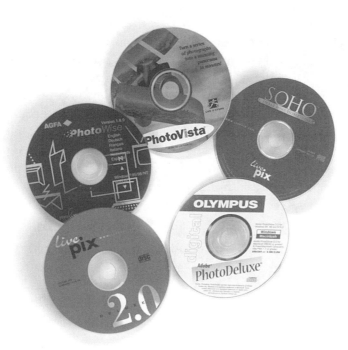

A sampling of bundled software. With good, easy-to-use software, digital photography can be very accessible. Test drive your software!

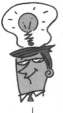

Say Cheese

The most important piece of software to be bundled with your camera is an image-enhancement program such as Photoshop or Photoshop Elements. After that, cataloging or "shoebox" software is a big help. Special effect software is great to have also, but a lower priority if you are counting "freebees." Web design software can also be found bundled. Remember many of these programs are "light" versions and may not be fully functional.

Proprietary and Third-Party Software

Most cameras come bundled with free software. This is handy, because it means you won't have to go out and immediately buy software. Some cameras come with software designed by the manufacturer, while other cameras are bundled with third-party software. We'll take a look at both.

Proprietary Software

Some camera manufacturers bundle their own proprietary image-editing software with their cameras. Most proprietary software packages more than cover your basic image-editing needs. The software enables you to download the images from your camera; adjust color, lightness, and contrast; and perform most of your basic image-enhancement tasks. You can also cut and paste, crop, enlarge, retouch, and make selections. These software packages also usually help you print your images as single photos or grouped on a contact sheet. Proprietary software can even help you access the Internet and e-mail your images. If all you are interested in is basic image manipulation, a proprietary software package is all you need.

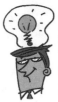

Say Cheese

Most of the software distributed with cameras will work on either a Mac or a Windows platform.

Agfa PhotoWise

One example of proprietary software is PhotoWise, which Agfa packages with some of its cameras. PhotoWise will enable you to download images from the camera and create photo albums to help you store and organize them. PhotoWise will also help you improve your image quality by letting you adjust color, contrast, brightness, and sharpness. You can also resize, crop, and rotate your images. PhotoWise is a good basic image-editing program.

Adobe Photoshop

Photoshop is a robust image-editing program and, by far, one of the most popular on the market. It is used by virtually every imaging professional—professional photographers, art directors, designers, illustrators, and even the motion picture industry use Photoshop. Photoshop is also the core of most image-enhancement at printing presses. It would not be a long stretch to say I owe a lot of my career to Photoshop.

Behind the Shutter

Adobe System was founded in 1982 and is the father (mother) of all imaging software found today. Photoshop, the original imaging software, is the basis of all photo and image manipulation software. Adobe made digital photography possible, even before digital cameras were commercially acceptable. Although there have been many challengers to Photoshop, it still stands as the premier model for all image programs. Additionally, Adobe Illustrator has contributed and is the model for all digital illustration. Many, if not all, professional photographers and illustrators, owe their current careers to Adobe. I certainly do!

It's a good idea to get used to the Adobe way of doing things, because Adobe has a major share of the imaging and illustration market. As you get more serious about imaging, which I know you will, you will find Adobe Photoshop a natural step up from PhotoDeluxe.

Photoshop can used to make complex image manipulations such as collages and multiple-layered images. It can also be used for complex color corrections and color management, and to help make images press ready. Although Photoshop is a complex and in-depth program, it can be mastered with a little practice. If you decide to use Photoshop, which is available for all platforms, be aware that it needs a lot of RAM (at least 128MB) and a quick processor to run. Before buying Photoshop, you should master Photoshop Elements.

Third-Party Software

Many cameras come bundled with third-party software—that is, software from third-party vendors that the camera manufacturer is licensed to distribute.

> **Flash**
>
> Be aware that some third-party software might be "light" versions that do not have all the functionality of a full version. You might also find software that is set to work for only a short period of time; after that, you'll have to pay for a fully working version. You might even find demo software that lets you do everything except save or print the image. This can be especially aggravating.

Adobe Photoshop Elements

One of the most popular nonproprietary software programs you will find bundled with a camera is Adobe's Photoshop Elements. Photoshop Elements, baby brother to Adobe Photoshop, can perform all the functions that the proprietary software can and more. For example, using Photoshop Elements, you can save the selection you made to be used again or as a mask, and you can apply filters and special effects to your images. I will be using Photoshop Elements for many of the demonstrations in this book, and I highly recommend that you use this program as your image-editing software of choice. Besides, it's inexpensive and demo copies are available for download from Adobe's website and may even be distributed with some of the more recent cameras.

LivePix

Another popular image-editing program that you might find bundled with your camera is Live Picture's LivePix Deluxe. LivePix performs all the common image-editing chores, and also lets you apply your images to templates—supplied with the software —to produce calendars, cards, and photo stationery.

Paint Shop Pro

Paint Shop by Jasc Software has the added bonus of being both a bit-mapped and vector-based graphics program. This means that you can edit photos and illustrate with the same program. This is the best of both worlds. Paint Shop also offers some web graphics goodies including compression and the ability to slice images.

Managing Your Images

Once you've begun collecting all these photographs, you'll soon realize that your previously unlimited hard disk space has now become a precious commodity. With the promise of freely reclaimable picture media that incurs only the cost of time, you'll take more and more pictures, and with a high resolution camera, this can build up fast. These files must be stored somewhere, or posterity is only a joke. That's where CD-R/RW and other removable media come in. Now, how to work with them and organize them logically? The answer comes in the form of a free tool for Windows called IrfanView.

Using IrfanView for Windows

IrfanView is the brainchild of Bosnian programmer and Viennese student, Irfan Skiljan, and he maintains the application regularly. The current version at the time of this writing was 3.75 and it includes all of the tools you need to manage your growing collection of visual memories. Primary among its skill set is the ability to read and display nearly every single graphic file type ever created. It also has the ability to convert the vast majority of these formats to others. As part of this ability IrfanView is capable of dithering colors to make the output remain as visually appealing as possible.

Of course, it's the batch processing and thumbnail views that you want to assist you in managing your photographs. First, a brief explanation is in order. Batch Processing allows you to process a large number of files in the same way without having to do each by hand. This comes in handy when you set the exposure too low, forget to set it back up again, and then shoot an entire card full of dark pictures. IrfanView is very good at this kind of thing. The thumbnail feature makes it easy to examine and organize a large number of images in one place. First, though, we need the application.

Downloading and installing IrfanView should not take very long, even if you have a 33.6 modem. IrfanView is available for free download at www.irfanview.com. Try to use the available mirrors (sites that contain the same files in an attempt to relieve the main server from a lot of users at one time) and select the link to the Self-extracting file. It's a small file of less than 1MB. Double-click the file (something like "iview375.exe") and follow the installation instructions.

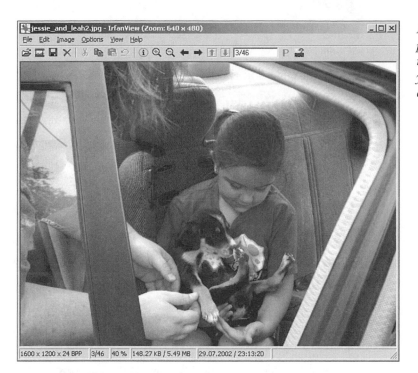

IrfanView for Windows is a powerful free application that can help you manage your images. There is no free equivalent for the Mac OS.

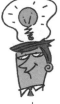

Say Cheese

Note that during the installation, you will be asked which file formats you want IrfanView to handle. I'd generally say click the Select All button, but that will cause IrfanView to take over other programs file formats. Instead, go through the list and check any file formats that are not familiar to you and leave the ones that you know are handled by another application. IrfanView is capable of displaying Windows Media (WMA, WMV, AVI), QuickTime (QT, MPG/MPEG, PICT), and RealPlayer (RAM, RA) audio and video formats, so watch out.

Once IrfanView is installed, an icon for the program will appear on your desktop. The easiest way to view any image is to drag it onto the IrfanView icon. The program will automatically open the image. If there are errors or if the file is mislabeled IrfanView will try to repair it, and it commonly can. Of course, it's batch processing that's the most helpful when dealing with images from a digital camera. When you take a series of pictures with a digital camera, it stores each image using a generic filename (for example, /DCIM/100NUCAM/PICT0001 on a SiPix SC-2100). This is usually a little too generic for most people, since we don't say things like, "Gee, that ECGx001DF00234 was a really great shot!"

This figure shows the Batch Rename/Conversion dialog, which will get a lot of use in IrfanView.

To change a collection of filenames using IrfanView, do the following:

1. Open IrfanView by double clicking the icon of the red cat on the desktop.

2. Open the File menu and select the Batch Conversion/Renaming option. This will open a new window.

3. In the Batch Conversion window you will see the familiar File Open/File Save group of controls in the top right. Navigate to where your pictures are being stored.

4. Add the images that you want to process. If you only have a few, select each one and then click the Add button to the left. If you want to process all of them, click the Add All button. If you want to process most of them, I suggest you Add All and then remove the ones you don't want processed.

5. In the Output Directory section (middle right) select where you want the processed images to end up. One limitation of IrfanView is that you cannot create a folder here. You must have one already made, but don't quit IrfanView to do it. Just go make the folder and come back. It will appear.

6. In the Work As section, select the Batch Rename option. The other options will become unavailable. Click the Set Rename Options button that remains active.

7. In the Batch Rename Settings dialog box, modify the filename as you prefer. Leave the Copy Input Files To Output Directory (recommended) option selected. Remember, in Windows you can have file names that are 255 characters long, so use them if you need them. When you have the form you want, click OK and return to the main dialog.

8. Run through all of your settings one more, even two more, times just to make sure everything is correct. Only when you are sure should you click the Start button (top left).

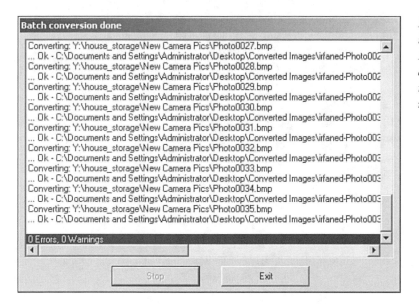

IrfanView is finished processing a large set of images. Here we see that I have caused IrfanView to add the term "irfaned" to the beginning of each image's filename.

Now that you have batch processed a number of images (not that you have to, mind you) you can now look at them in Thumbnail view. Select the Thumbnail option from the File menu or just press the "T" key while in the main IrfanView screen. If you have an image open when you open Thumbnail view, all of the images in that directory will appear in the new Thumbnail window.

As you can see in the above figure, a number of images are shown in small, easily viewable renderings of the original image. To load another set of images, use the Folder Tree on the left side of the window to locate it. I suggest you spend some time in the File and Options menus and see what can be done with images and the powerful Thumbnail view.

IrfanView displays all images in a directory in the Thumbnail view. Images can be moved, renamed, deleted, and more from here.

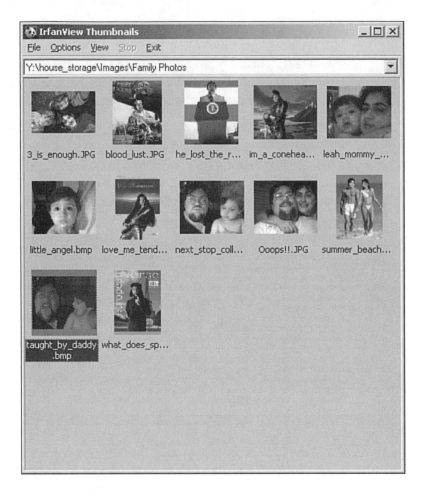

Album Software

Many imaging software programs include album software, but in case yours doesn't, you can always buy stand-alone album software such as Kodak's Picture Easy, Microsoft's Picture-It, Ulead's Photo Explorer, Extensis Portfolio, and Live Picture's LivePix Album.

The techniques and technology used in the various albums differ in complexity and abilities. It would be difficult to review each album software here, as they are constantly evolving in their capabilities. If you are shopping for a cataloging software, my suggestion is to test drive a few packages; download demos from the software developers' websites.

When deciding what type of album software to buy, keep your current and future catalog and retrieval needs in mind. Although it will be hard to do, try to estimate how many photos you are going to need to store. You will need to ask a few questions when deciding which software to purchase:

- What are the capacities of the program?

- How many images can it store?

- Will the program keep track of multiple disks?

- How good is it at retrieving images?

- Can you use simple searches, such as looking for keywords in the image's filename or description?

- Does the program create its own image formats, or can you use your own?

- Will it compress your files?

- Will it alter your images?

- Can you re-create a catalog description file if the original files get lost or damaged?

The easiest way to evaluate software (of any type) is to check out the advertising. You can learn a lot about specific software by what is said and—more important—what is not said about it!

The Least You Need to Know

- Image-editing software helps you download your images from the camera.

- Image-editing software will help you improve and manipulate your images.

- Camera manufacturers and third-party developers make image-editing software.

- Catalog software will help you store and retrieve your images.

- How to use IrfanView for Windows to process large numbers of graphic files.

Part 3

Let's Take Pictures

It's easy to pick up a camera and take a picture. All you do is look through the viewfinder and press the button. But to make a photograph, that's another story altogether.

The difference between taking a picture and making a photograph is control. It is not meant to be a difficult task or hard work. The more fun you have making a photograph, the more satisfying and creative your results will be.

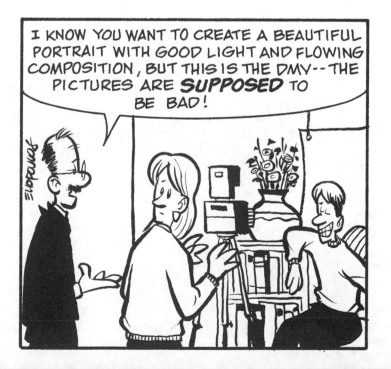

Chapter 7

Exposure Made Simple

In This Chapter

- ◆ F/stops
- ◆ Shutter speed
- ◆ Film/chip speed
- ◆ Creative controls
- ◆ Depth of field

Taking a photograph that will reproduce what you saw through the viewfinder involves correctly exposing the film or chip. Too much light produces washed-out images. Not enough light reproduces images as dark and murky.

The Lens

Let's explore, for a moment, how the light gets to the film or digital chip. Providing that the lens cap is off and your fingers are out of the way, light enters your camera through the front of your lens. It then passes through a series of lenses that bend the light and send it on its way to be focused on the film plane (where the film or chip is found). The lenses are usually found in groups of two or three, and are cemented together to form optical groups, or *optics*. Depending on what type of lens you have and its quality, you might find two to five sets of optics in a lens.

Inside your lens, usually somewhere between the groups of optics, is an *iris*, also called the *aperture*. The iris regulates how much light passes through the lens. Your finger, lens cap, and camera strap might also accomplish the same effect, although the results will not be desirable.

The iris, which is located between the groups of elements in the lens, is made up of tiny blades that can be opened and closed.

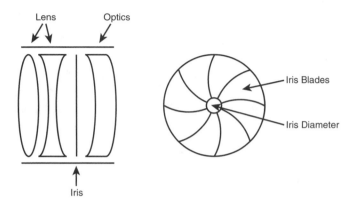

The Shutter

Next, there must be a way to limit the amount of time that the light strikes the film plane; this is where the *shutter* comes in. The shutter is usually found behind the lens; on a 35mm SLR camera, the shutter, called a *focal plane shutter* or *shutter curtain*, is usually part of the body of the camera.

A focal plane shutter works in a two-part motion. During the first motion, a metal or rubber curtain travels across the shutter mechanism to expose the focal plane to the light traveling through the lens. After the proper amount of time, another curtain travels in the opposite direction to close the shutter and cut off the light. When you advance the film, you reset the shutter.

The focal plane shutter starts out as a closed curtain, and travels to the right of the shutter until fully open. It then travels back to the left until closed.

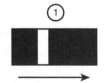

Direction of curtain travel,
curtain opening

Shutter all the way open

Direction of travel,
curtain closing

With some cameras, the shutter is incorporated into the lens itself. This is accomplished by incorporating the shutter into the iris. The iris remains closed until the shutter release is pressed; it then opens to the desired diameter. The iris closes when the proper amount of time has passed.

F/Stops

So what is an f/stop? The *f/stop*, or *f/number*, refers to the diameter of the iris and how much light it lets through the lens. To make it sound mysterious and confusing, f/stops are not enumerated in a clearly logical fashion. The f/stops progress in a series of numbers, each of which lets in half as much light as the number before or after it. The higher the f/number, the smaller the diameter of the iris. The progression goes like this:

- ◆ f/1.4
- ◆ f/2.0
- ◆ f/2.8
- ◆ f/4
- ◆ f/5.6
- ◆ f/8
- ◆ f/11
- ◆ f/16
- ◆ f/22
- ◆ f/32
- ◆ f/45
- ◆ f/64
- ◆ f/90

An f/stop setting of f/8 lets in twice as much light as f/11, but half as much light as f/5.6 (remember: the higher the f/number, the smaller the diameter of the iris). This can be a little confusing, so try to think of it as a fraction. One sixteenth of something is less than one eighth of it.

Lenses are referred to by their focal length, such as 135mm or 35mm (we'll get to focal length in Chapter 8), but you'll also see a second number associated with the description of the lens, such as 2.0 or 3.5. These numbers refer to the maximum iris opening of the lens, also called the *speed* of the lens or how *fast* the lens is. A 2.8 lens lets in twice as much light at its maximum iris as a 3.5 at its maximum iris. The 2.8 lens also costs more than a 3.5 lens of the same focal length. You will also see 1.2, 1.4, and 1.8 lenses; these are pretty quick lenses—twice as fast (or more) than most consumer-level cameras' lenses, which are usually f/2.8 or so.

In Plain Black & White

Of course, there are also half stops. **Half stops** are f/stops between the "regular" f/stops. These will enable you to fine-tune your exposure.

Shutter Speed

The shutter controls how long the film is exposed to light. Shutter speeds are measured in fractions of a second starting at 1 second. Each increase in speed is twice as fast as the shutter speed before it. So if you start at 1 second, the next shutter speed will be ½ second, and the next one will be ¼ second. The progression is not perfect after that: The rest of the shutter speeds are ⅛, ¹⁄₁₅, ¹⁄₃₀, ¹⁄₆₀, ¹⁄₁₂₅, ¹⁄₂₅₀, ¹⁄₅₀₀, and last but not (well, actually, I guess it is …) least, ¹⁄₁,₀₀₀. Some really fast, expensive 35mm cameras have shutter speeds as fast as ¹⁄₄,₀₀₀ of a second.

Behind the Shutter

Undoubtedly, a few of you tech heads want to know the formula for determining an f/stop. Remember: The f/stop indicates the diameter of the opening in the iris; it's the ratio of the diameter of the iris opening divided by the focal length of the lens. So if you are using a 100mm lens and you select f/4, the diameter of the iris will be 25mm. I hope I've made you happy!

Putting It All Together: The Relationship Between f/Stops and Shutter Speed

You might have noticed that both the shutter speeds and f/stops work in increments of a half or double. This works out well because the shutter speed and f/stop are used in conjunction with each other to obtain a proper exposure. (Remember again that a proper exposure is made when the film or chip is exposed to a specific amount of light.)

For a moment, however, let's forget about f/stops and shutter speeds. Let's play ball. Say you have a team of eight players that have arrived at the stadium on the team bus. All eight players need to be on the field to start the game. Between the team bus and the field is a gate, which is open only two feet wide. For all the players to get on the field, they must disembark from the bus and walk through the gate. So one by one and slowly, they walk through the gate.

The coach of the team is upset about how much time it takes the team to get on the field. "Let's show a little hustle, boys!" He orders the players back onto the bus and tells them to do it all over, but this time twice as fast. The players are dumbfounded. They cannot figure out how to get onto the field any faster. From the back of the bus, a small voice is heard; it's the water boy. "Open the gate four feet wide. That way, you all can go through the gate two by two and get onto the field twice as fast." Such a smart boy!

Okay, back to photography. As you have seen, there is a direct relationship between the f/stop (the gate) and the shutter (the speed of the players). Each time you open up the f/stop (make it wider), twice as much light can get to the film to expose it. You therefore need to increase the shutter speed to get a proper exposure. If for some reason (and there will be) you decide to use a smaller diameter aperture (higher f/stop number), you must slow down the shutter speed. Remember, the longer the shutter stays open, the more movement will be recorded—also known as blur!

Let's get a little more specific. Say your light meter (or, if you don't have a light meter, your best experienced guess) indicates that you need to use the f/stop f/11 at $\frac{1}{125}$ second to expose your film properly. You decide, and rightly so, that the soccer player you are photographing is running down the field at a quick pace, and you'll need a faster shutter speed. Well, if you open your f/stop up to f/8, you can shoot at $\frac{1}{250}$ second. That works, but what if you want to freeze the action of the players? You decide that you should set your shutter speed to $\frac{1}{5,000}$ second. What would your f/stop need to be? Time's up: f/5.6!

Behind the Shutter

Modern light meters work because as light strikes a photosensitive cell, called a *photo-electric cell,* voltage is produced and is registered by a meter arm or LED. Before these modern conveniences were invented, however, photographers still needed to know how much light they were dealing with. What was a photographer to do? Well, the answer was to bring a cat along on a photo shoot. A photographer of old would look at the iris in the cat's eye to determine how much light was present. If the cat's eye was very dilated, or wide open, then a longer exposure was needed. If the iris was very small, then a higher shutter speed could be used. Of course, to be totally accurate, the same cat had to be used every time!

The following figure further illustrates the relationship between shutter speed and aperture. Notice that the proper exposure line runs through f/stop and shutter speed "sliders" (for this demonstration, we will keep the sliders locked in position). When the proper exposure line moves to the left, a proper exposure still results because as the f/stops are increased (the aperture is made smaller), the shutter speed slows down. When the aperture is made smaller, less light gets in to the film; therefore, the shutter must stay open longer. If you move to the right, and the aperture size is made larger, the shutter speed must speed up. Of course, you can also see this relationship from the point of view of shutter speed: If you move the exposure line to the right or left, the shutter speed increases or decreases and the f/stop setting follows.

The relationship between f/stop and shutter speed is locked for a proper exposure.

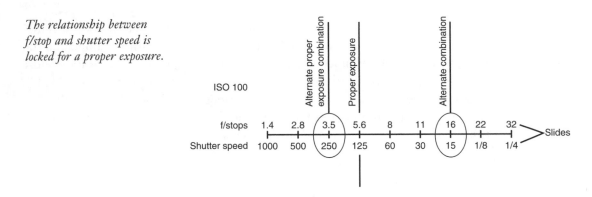

In all these examples, the relationship between the f/stop and shutter speed has been fixed. We've been picking arbitrary "proper exposures"—f/16 at $\frac{1}{125}$ of a second or f/16 at $\frac{1}{60}$ of a second. Have you been wondering what sets up this exposure relationship? Read on!

Behind the Shutter

The EV (Exposure Value) system, which is found on light meters, is determined by the amount of light present and the speed of the film. A higher EV value means that more light is present or that a higher speed film should be used. In the examples used in the previous figures, the relationship between the sliders was determined by an EV rating, which provided the original positions for the shutter speed and f/stop sliders. After the EV was set, the proper exposure settings (f/stop and shutter speed) can be determined. The EV rating is the same anywhere on the slider scale, as long as the relationship between the two slider cameras stays the same. Some cameras, such as Hasselblads, actually have levers built into their lens that would keep the f/stop and shutter speed locked to the EV. Because the shutter is built into the lens on a Hasselblad as you move the f/stop on the lens, the shutter speed will follow.

ISO/ASA

ISO and ASA are not leftover NASA acronyms! The ISO enumeration is the rating given to a film, or chip, that describes how sensitive the film or chip is to light. ASA ratings are seldom seen these days, but they are equivalent to ISO ratings. The higher the ISO rating, the more sensitive or faster the film is. If the ISO speed of film A is double that of film B, then type B film will be twice as fast as A. Generally, you will find ISO ratings between 50 and 400 on film (slide films are usually slower than negative films). On digital cameras, where the chips are given ISO ratings, you will find ISO ratings as high as 1600.

The one drawback to using higher-speed films is that film grain, which looks like tiny dots, is more apparent. This can appear as a texture in your film and affects the sharpness of your images. The general rule is to use the slowest film you can get away with. On a sunny day, an ISO 100 film serves well. Inside, however, you should use an ISO 400 film, because it is more sensitive to light.

One of the benefits of using a digital camera is that you can change, or *push*, the ISO rating of your chip. Digital cameras have an optimal ISO setting, which is determined by the manufacturer of the camera. You get your best results by using the optimal ISO rating for your digital camera, but this rating can usually be altered. Of course, just as with film, digital cameras suffer with excessive ISO speed. Higher than optimal ISO ratings produce noise, which is usually most apparent in the dark or shadow areas (it looks like a blue/black or blue/red dot pattern).

This is not to say, however, that cameras designed to work optimally at ISO 400 are noisier than cameras designed to work optimally at ISO 100. Nonetheless, you can be sure that if you push the ISO 100 camera to ISO 400, the image it produces will be noisier than the "optimal" ISO 400 camera.

We can now begin to unlock the relationship between the "exposure sliders." Let's assume that in the following figure, the optimal ISO rating is 100. If you push the ISO 100 chip to 400 or use an ISO 400 camera, you would move the top and bottom sliders apart from each other, two spaces in opposite directions (one space for the jump from ISO 100 to 200, and another space for the jump from ISO 200 to 400). The benefit of this jump is that you can use a faster shutter speed than before if you kept the f/stop the same, or a smaller f/stop than before if you kept the shutter speed the same.

Say Cheese _____

If you get into a dimly lit situation, try turning on some lights or using a flash before you push your ISO rating.

Flash _____

Digital cameras are inherently slow compared to film-based cameras; it takes more light than with a film-based camera to take a good shot. Plan on carrying extra lights with you. Some cameras, such as the Olympus DL620, allow you to hook up an additional flash to the camera.

ISO affects film speed.

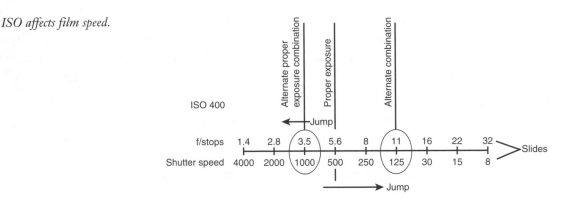

Creative Control

The advantage of all the give and take of the exposure system is the creative control you gain. This is your camera, you are making the photographs, you have the control. Just don't let it go to your head!

Shutter Speed

The first control you gain is the ability to pick your shutter speed. With a fast shutter speed, you can capture and freeze action. With a slow shutter speed, your images can blur a bit. (After all, what better way to show a speeding car than to have it blurred a little?) You can also slow down your shutter speed to use a higher (read: smaller) f/stop.

Depth of Field

Your second creative control is created by the optics of your lens. It is called *depth of field* and has nothing to do with the height of grass. Depth of field is the area that will be in focus between two distances from the lens. If all the objects between two and five feet from your lens are in focus, you have a depth of field of three feet. With a shallow depth of field, you can, for example, take a portrait of someone and have them in focus and have the background be out of focus or blurred. With a deep depth of field, you can take a picture of your family and have all the mountains in back of them in focus. Very nice creative control!

A few things affect the depth of field, and you can control all of them:

 ◆ **The closer an object is to your lens, the shallower your depth of field will be.**
  If you find yourself on your hands and knees, trying to take a full-frame close-up
  picture of the first spring crocus, you will have a hard time getting all the flower
  in focus. (By the way, this is not necessarily a bad thing; you can tell all your crit-
  ics you were being creative!) If you are taking a picture of your family, who are
  standing 15 feet away from your camera, you can be sure that the background
  behind them will also be in focus. (This all hinges on the fact that you got your
  family in focus in the first place!)

 ◆ **Depth of field can be controlled by which f/stop is used.** This is a lot more
  practical than moving the crocus back and forth in front of your lens; this is also
  going to make all the exposure control contortions worthwhile. Without going
  into a long technical dissertation, please believe me when I tell you that the
  higher the f/stop (the smaller the diameter of the iris), the greater the depth of
  field, so you can creatively control the focus of your subject by choosing which
  f/stop you use (along with how close or far that subject is from you). Note, however, that if you want to alter your depth of field by choosing which f/stop you
  are going to use, you have to let the shutter speed fall where it may (remember,
  the f/stop and shutter speed are closely related).

Try to retake that photograph of the crocuses, but this time, back up a little and get a
group of the flowers in focus. Let's say that your exposure indicates you should have
an f/stop of f/8 (forget about shutter speed for now). So what is in focus? If the whole
group of flowers is in focus, that's fine. But is the grass behind the flowers also in
focus? Is that a little distracting to you? Well, it is to me, so I'm going to open up the
f/stop to f/3.5 or so. Now the flowers are in focus, but the grass is out of focus.

Suppose your flower plot is three feet deep from back to front. Suppose, too, that the
depth of field at f/3.5 is three feet. If you focus in the middle of the flower plot, all
the flowers will be in focus and the grass behind them will be out of focus. What happens if you *shift* your focus so that you are focusing on the space in front of the plot
of flowers (keeping the same f/stop as before)? Anything that is 1½ feet in front of
the flowers will be in focus, as will all the
flowers in the first foot and a half of the
plot. All the flowers behind that first foot
and a half, along with the grass behind
the plot, will be out of focus. This might
be a nice effect, especially if the flowers in
the back of the plot were looking a bit
shabby or thinned out.

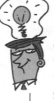

Say Cheese

Don't take boring photos. This
demonstration has shown you
that you have the control you
need to take wonderful photographs!

A wider or lower number f/stop yields less depth of field.

A smaller or higher f/stop yields more depth of field.

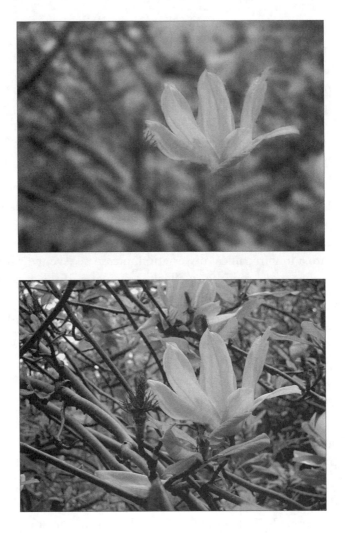

Suppose, however, that some wonderful gardener has ripped up all the grass and replaced it with a sea of flowers! This time, you want to get them all in focus. All you need to do is focus somewhere in the middle of the group of plants and close down the f/stop all the way to f/22 (or more), and everything will be in focus.

Manual or Automatic Exposure

If after all the explanation about exposure you would rather not deal with any of it, relax. Many cameras, especially the lower-priced (point-and-shoot) cameras, come with fully automatic exposure control. You'll find these easy to use and, as long as you don't get yourself into an exposure pickle (this is a nontechnical term), you should make great photos.

The mid- and upper-priced cameras give you more creative control over your f/stops and shutter speeds. A few cameras give you the option of picking which aperture to use; the resulting shutter speed is determined by the camera itself. This is called *aperture priority exposure*. Other cameras offer the opposite, letting you pick the shutter speed and extrapolating an f/stop. This is called *shutter priority exposure*. Some cameras will offer both shutter and aperture priority settings. As you can see, there are pros and cons to both systems. You will not see a totally manual digital camera until you are using semi- or fully professional equipment

In Plain Black & White

A few of the more expensive digital cameras employ **center-weighted** and **matrix-based** exposure systems. A center-weighted metering system bases 90 percent of its exposure setting based on what it reads in the center of the image. This is a very good system, because the exposure will not be adversely affected by a difficult background, such as in a backlit situation. Matrix-based metering systems read specific spots in the image's frame. This comes in handy when, for example, you photograph the interior of a room with an open sunny window. If the meter were to take an average reading, the window light would cause the aperture to close down and the room would be too dark. With a matrix system, the window light and the interior lighting are taken into account. The system would know that the window light is a small part of the photo and would give more emphasis to the interior, making it brighter.

Digital cameras might not have shutters or apertures at all. You will find this especially true on lower-end cameras. These cameras replace the shutter on the camera by turning on or off the chip for the same duration as a true shutter might work. They replace the aperture by adjusting the sensitivity of the chip. Different manufacturers achieve the results in different ways. Don't be disappointed. If you didn't pay a lot for your camera, you still will get excellent results.

Say Cheese _____

Even if you don't have shutter or aperture control over your camera, you might be able to force your camera to "think creatively." If you can adjust the ISO rating of your camera, you can make your camera change shutter speeds or pick a different aperture. Let's assume, for example, your camera is set to shoot at $\frac{1}{60}$ second and the ISO dial is set at 100. If you were to change the ISO to 400, making your camera two stops faster, your shutter speed would be increased to $\frac{1}{250}$ second. The same effect can be had on the aperture. It depends on the camera system as to which will be affected by your change. Bear in mind that you might suffer the effects of noise if you mess with the ISO speed too much.

Another way to fake out your camera is to put a neutral density filter (ND) over the lens (a neutral density filter can be purchased at a good camera store). ND filters are neutral gray tinted filters that darken the image without imparting color to it. This forces either the f/stop to open up more or the shutter speed to slow down, depending on your camera. Note: If you want to use ND filters, you must be sure that your camera is taking its meter readings from behind the lens and not externally. If your camera is not metering through the lens, you must cover the meter up, also.

The Least You Need to Know

◆ It is important to understand the basics of exposure and the creative control you can gain by manipulating the variables.

◆ Depth of field can be controlled by your aperture choice.

◆ Shutter speeds will control how you capture movement.

◆ You can control your exposure or have the camera set the exposure for you.

Chapter 8

I Can See Clearly Now: Lenses

In This Chapter

- ◆ Focusing
- ◆ Wide-angle lenses
- ◆ Telephoto lenses
- ◆ Zoom lenses
- ◆ Lens choices

In Chapter 7, we talked about focus in relation to depth of field. But how, exactly, does "focus" work? Here's the skinny: Rays of light travel in a straight path through a transparent medium, such as air. When the light rays travel from one medium to another, for example from air to glass, they bend. This bending of light is called *refraction*. As the light rays pass through the lens, they refract and converge, or meet. This convergence point is called the *focal point* or *focal plane*. (The focal point is a great place to locate the *film plane*, which is where your film or CCD chip is located.)

Say cheese.

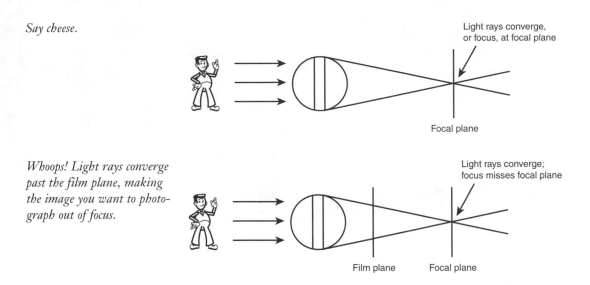

Whoops! Light rays converge past the film plane, making the image you want to photograph out of focus.

If the distance between the lens and the film plane is not correct for the distance between you and the subject you are photographing, the convergence point will not fall at the film plane. You are out of focus!

You can focus your image by adjusting the optics in the lens (or the lens itself) so that the convergence point falls on the film plane. Have you have ever held an SLR (single lens reflex) camera and twisted the lens barrel? If so, you were, in reality, moving the lens groups and adjusting the convergence point to fall on the film plane.

Types of Lenses

Different types of lenses can be used:

♦ A fixed-focus lens is a simple lens that has no moving parts. The lens is designed to focus on an average *taking* distance from the camera—usually anywhere from 12 feet to infinity. Fixed-focus lenses, which are usually found on low-end, point-and-shoot cameras, don't deliver sharp images.

♦ Lenses that can be focused have multiple optics in them. These optics are usually found in groups. When you twist the focusing ring or knob on your lens, you are moving the optics to direct the light to the focal point. You will find these types of lenses on midrange and professional cameras; they are almost always mounted on an SLR camera body.

Some digital camera manufacturers make their lenses out of plastic optics because, historically, CCD chips were not good enough to hold the resolution that glass could provide. These days, however, CCD (charged couple device) chips are vastly improved; if you're looking for clear pictures, you should buy a camera with a glass lens. Also, quality lenses have antireflective coatings (usually blue or purplish in color) on the front optic, which will increase the contrast of your image and reduce glare.

Even the very best lenses don't work very well when dirty or scratched. Here are some good ways to keep your lens in good shape.

- If your lens has dust or grit on it, the first thing you should do is try to gently brush it off or blow it off with your squeeze bulb. The best bulbs are the kind used to suction mucus from a baby's nose (really!). You can also try lightly swiping at the lens with your soft cloth. Do not blow on your lens with your own mouth—you will end up spitting on your lens.

- If you have smudges on your lens, you'll have to work a little harder. Put a few drops of lens-cleaning fluid on your cloth or lens-cleaning tissue, and then gently wipe the lens with the cloth. After you remove the gunk, you can try polishing the lens gently with a dry cloth. Never put the cleaning fluid directly on your lens; it will seep in between the lens and lens body and you will end up with fluid inside your lens!

- A great way to keep your lens clean and safe is to cover it with a clear filter. If your lens has screw threads on its front barrel, you can buy a filter to fit on it. The best filters to buy are UV (ultraviolet) filters, which are clear and also provide the added benefit of reducing UV haze. These filters are cheap protection, and if you scratch one, you can just throw it away (recycle!).

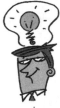

Say Cheese

Nose prints, fingerprints, and other assorted muck and dust do not make for great optical coatings. All photographers, great and small, must carry lens-cleaning materials in their camera bags. Your kit should include lens-cleaning paper or a soft cloth (be sure the paper or cloth is not full of dirt!), lens-cleaning fluid, and a soft lens-cleaning brush (I like the kind that have a small bellows or squeeze bulb built into them). You can buy all these items at a camera or photo supply store.

Auto-Focus Lenses

Unless your camera has a fixed-focus lens, it probably employs some sort of auto-focus mechanism. The advantage of using an auto-focus lens over a fixed-focus lens is that your lens can be precisely focused for the correct subject-to-camera distance. Your images will look much crisper than they would if they were taken with a fixed-focus (or, as most professional photographers say, a Coke bottle) lens. There are a few different types of auto-focus cameras:

◆ Many auto-focus cameras measure the distance between them and the subject by sending out a pulse of sound, called *sonar*, or by transmitting a beam of infrared light. Both systems work similarly: The camera measures the time it takes for the sound or light beam to leave the camera, bounce off the subject, and return. It then calculates the distance and adjusts the lens. Although you can't hear the sonar pulse, you might drive a few nearby bats a little crazy!

Some auto-focus cameras measure distance by using sound or infrared.

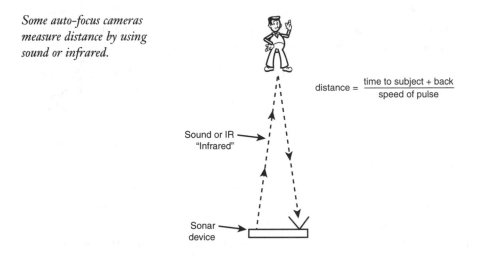

$$distance = \frac{time\ to\ subject + back}{speed\ of\ pulse}$$

Sound or IR "Infrared"

Sonar device

◆ Passive auto-exposure systems, which are found on higher-end cameras, focus a lens by assessing the contrast of the image. If you compare an out-of-focus image to an in-focus image, you will see that the in-focus image has much more contrast.

Auto-focus systems have a few weak points:

◆ If something—such as a fence—comes between the camera and your subject, the camera's focusing system might set the focus for the fence instead of your subject.

◆ If your subject is near a large object, that object can reflect the measuring beam instead of your subject, skewing the distance measurement your camera uses to focus.

◆ If you are photographing a group of people who are at various distances from the camera, the camera might have trouble determining the correct focus.

Focus Lock

Auto-focus systems that offer a *focus lock* are a good way to get around these problems. With a focus lock, you can prefocus the camera, lock the focus, and then move the camera to get the image you want. For example, suppose you want to photograph your kid standing on a stone wall, with a beautiful sky behind him, but you want to compose the image so that he is to the side of the viewing frame instead of smack in the middle of it. Odds are that if you simply snap the picture, your auto-focus will focus the camera to a distance of infinity (and beyond) instead of on Junior, because auto-focus lenses typically focus on the middle of the viewing frame. To rectify this, do the following:

1. Frame the image so that Junior is more prominent (that is, closer to the middle of the viewing frame).

2. Let the camera focus.

3. Lock the focus.

4. Reframe the image to get the composition you want.

5. Shoot the picture.

Behind the Shutter

If you point your camera at someone but have to wait for it to focus, they'll probably figure out what you are trying to do, and you'll lose your candid shot. If, however, you use the focus-lock feature, you can focus on someone or something else (be sure the dummy subject is about the same distance away from you as the intended subject), lock your focus, and swing your camera back around to take your candid shot.

If you have your camera set up to take wide-angle pictures, you might be able to take candid photos without even looking through the viewfinder. Most professional photographers are very good at this technique, especially sports and news journalists.

Close-Up Shots

Taking close-up shots drives your camera and its lens into contortions. If you look at a good 35mm camera lens, you'll notice that it *racks*, or *extends*, way out when focused on a close object. Many auto-focus cameras have a *macro* setting, which adjusts the lens for close-ups. Sometimes the optics inside the lens are adjusted; other times, some other special arrangement is made to allow for close-ups. When you take close-ups, try to use the macro setting as much as possible. Not only will it help you focus your close-up image, it will also help increase your depth of field (which is almost nonexistent when you are close in).

Focal Length

Focal length is important because it tells you how big your image will be on the focal plane. It will also help you approximate the visual angle and area of coverage of the lens (I'll explain this in a second). The focal length of a lens is the distance, in millimeters, from the optical center of the lens to the focal plane when the lens is focused at infinity. Don't worry; you don't have to do this yourself. The manufacturer does all the testing of the lens design well before you ever see the camera.

Taking Angle and Area of Coverage

The following diagram describes the two important features of a lens:

◆ The first thing to look at is the *taking angle* or *visual angle* of the lens. Both describe how wide the lens can "see." Sometimes this might be referred to as the *field of view* (*FOV*). Lens #1 sees a small portion of the image because it has a small visual taking angle; lens #2 sees much more, or a wider angle, of the picture.

◆ The second thing to look at is the area of coverage, which is the area that the image covers on the film plane. (Note: Because the lens is round, the area of coverage is circular.) Notice that on lens 1, the coverage is much larger than the size of the chip or film frame, meaning that only a tightly cropped portion of the full image will be captured by the chip. Lens 2, however, has an area of coverage that is about the same size as the chip, meaning that this chip will capture most of the image.

Angle of view determines how wide an area a lens can see and area of coverage indicates how much of the image will show up on the film plane.

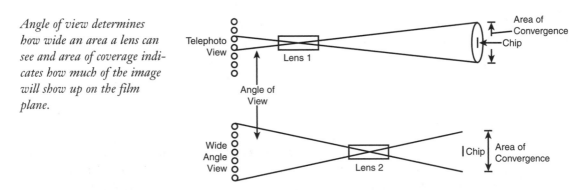

The visual angle and lens coverage usually work in conjunction with each other. However, it is not uncommon for a lens to have a wide angle of coverage *and* a wide visual angle. Actually, depending on the lens design, any combination of coverage and taking angle is possible.

So What's Normal?

The taking angle and area of convergence are much more important on large-format cameras where large film areas come into play; a normal lens has a visual taking angle that is approximately the same as your visual taking angle (that is, close to what you see without turning your head). A normal lens also has an area of coverage that is close to the same size of the diagonal measurement of your chip (see the following diagram to see how the chip diagonal is the same as the diameter of the area of coverage).

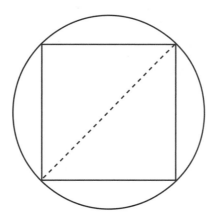

A normal lens will have a field of view approximately the same as your vision.

On a 35mm camera, a 55mm lens is considered normal. Although it is slightly tele-photo, it is closest to the human field of view. (The diagonal measurement of a 35mm piece of film is 44mm, which would make a 44mm lens truly normal, but I've never seen a 44mm lens!) On a typical digital camera, the CCD chip is much smaller than a piece of 35mm. Therefore, a normal lens on a digital camera is much smaller. Because the CCD chip sizes vary from manufacturer to manufacturer, a normal lens on one digital camera might not be a normal lens on another. Also, as the chips become larger, such as on the new 2Mp (megapixel) cameras, what was normal last month might not be next month. Typically, a normal lens for a digital camera ranges from 4.5mm to 7mm.

The Telephoto Lens: A Long Story

Telephoto lenses have *long* focal lengths, which is why they are called *long lenses*. Telephoto lenses have a very narrow angle of view; they might also have a matching coverage circle, but not necessarily so. Wide film coverage will decrease the telephoto effect and introduce lens aberrations. Aberrations, which are errors in the lens design such as color distortions or soft focus, usually show up at the edges of the picture. Because the chip area is smaller than the lens coverage and the chip is located in the center of the coverage, lens aberrations are minimized. On view cameras, where the lenses are designed to swing and tilt (see Chapter 3), wide coverage is very important. It also makes view camera lenses very expensive. My 150mm (normal for a 4×5 view camera) cost $1,500!

Behind the Shutter

To confuse the "normal" issue even more, some manufacturers label their lenses as *equivalent* to 35mm camera lenses. I reviewed one camera whose lens was marked as 9.2mm to 28mm (zoom). This would be a "fisheye" lens on a 35mm camera. This camera lens was marked as a true measurement. Another lens was marked 28mm to 110mm (zoom). How can this be? Either the second camera has a huge CCD chip array, or its manufacturer is giving the camera's focal lengths in 35mm equivalents.

I actually feel that using the equivalent method is fine. As I said before, chip sizes vary from camera to camera, and unless you know what size the chip is, you will have no idea what the normal lens is. Also, most of us are familiar with 35mm cameras, and are comfortable with the idea of using that marking system. As long as you know what system is being used, all should be well. The only problem lies in being able to compare one camera to another—it makes for great confusion!

Most commonly, a telephoto lens is used to photograph objects that are far away to make them look bigger. Conversely, because of the angle of view, you can photograph an object that is near and fill your frame with only part of the subject—such as when you want to photograph one person in a group of people. A slightly telephoto lens makes a good portrait lens, and enables you to get a nicely filled frame without standing too close to your subject.

One characteristic of a telephoto lens is called *visual compression*. Because you can get objects that are far away as well as objects that are close by in the frame at the same time, the objects look like they are compressed in space. To add to this, remember that objects that are close to the camera look very big in the frame.

A good example of compression can be seen on your TV set. If you have ever watched a baseball game, you have been a victim of compression. The shot from the center field camera that shows the pitcher throwing the ball to the batter is a great example. Notice how big the pitcher looks in relation to the batter; they also look like they are right next to each other. It seems like the pitcher spends an awful amount of energy to throw the ball such a short distance! Take a look at the following photograph to see how the buildings look compressed and stacked one next to the other.

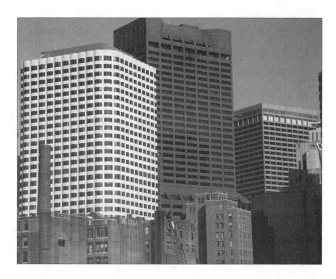

A long telephoto lens brings the object closer and also "compresses" the image.

Because you are photographing objects that are at different distances from each other, and with the added effects of compression, depth of field can be shallow when you use a telephoto lens. Be aware of the depth of field fall-off, and focus carefully—you might even be able to use this shortcoming to your creative advantage. Also, because of your narrow angle of view, camera shake is much more apparent. Your margin of error when holding a camera with a telephoto lens in your hands, especially in dimly lit situations, can be small. Brace yourself against something to steady yourself, or prop your camera up on something to steady it.

Wide-Angle Lenses: A Short Story

Wide-angle lenses are basically the opposite of telephoto lenses: They have a short focal length and a wide angle of view. They also have a small area of coverage on the film plane, meaning that your film or chip captures nearly the entire image.

Wide-angle lenses are used to photograph large areas, especially if you cannot get far enough away. Some of the most wonderful skyline shots and mountain views would need to be taken from three states away if you used a normal lens! Wide-angle lenses have a great depth of field, which means that you can photograph objects that are relatively close to you and still have other objects in the background stay in focus, as shown in the following photograph. On the downside, you see a lot of distortion in a wide-angle shot; your horizon line might even seem to bend! However, this can lead to some interesting effects.

A wide-angle lens allows you to get more view in your image.

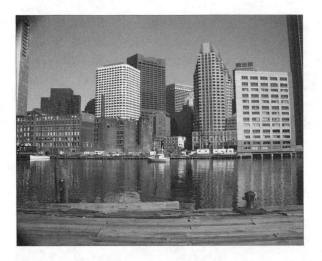

Zoom

A *zoom* lens is a lens that has multiple focal lengths, which can come in pretty handy—especially if you have only one lens bolted to your camera. A zoom lens has many groups of optics in it, which are shifted internally to provide the different focal lengths.

Typically, a good zoom lens won't zoom all that much—you won't find a lens that zooms from wide to long telephoto. Mostly, you will find lenses that start just shy of wide and zoom to a moderate telephoto. For example, talking in 35mm speak, zooms that range from 35mm to 100mm are a good bet.

Because of all the shifting of elements, zoom lenses are not as sharp as *prime* lenses, which are of fixed focal length. Additionally, because of all the glass involved in zoom lenses, they are usually a stop or so slower than a prime lens. Zoom lenses are also harder to keep in focus; you should check the focus after you zoom. Having an auto-focus camera that refocuses after or as you zoom is a good idea—thankfully, most do.

All in all, unless you are using a high-end professional camera and can interchange lenses, buying a zoom lens is a great idea.

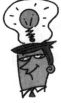

Say Cheese

Have you ever put your hand over your eyes to shade them on a sunny day? If so, did you notice that your vision improved? Well, guess what? If you do the same for your lens, your picture will look better, also.

Always try to use a lens shade when taking pictures outside, or any time that a lot of glare or stray lights are hitting your lens. It is the easiest thing you can do to improve your shots!

True Zoom Versus Electronic Zoom

Many manufacturers give a specification for their zoom lenses, such as 3×, 4×, and so on. Basically, this tells you that your lens zooms in a range that triples or quadruples itself. An example of a 3× zoom is a 25mm to 75mm zoom. When you see a specification for your zoom lens such as 3×/2×, you are in for a ride! This type of specification indicates that you are getting a true 3× zoom lens, and your camera can zoom in two more times electronically.

So how do you suppose the extra zoom is accomplished? Time's up! Your camera is going to interpolate the image, also known as enlarging it, to simulate the zoom. This is not a great idea unless you really need it, because as soon as you start electronically enhancing an image, you invite pixelization (image distortions) and color errors. Do not buy a camera based on the extra electronic zoom; you can do the same, if not better, in any image-manipulation software.

The Least You Need to Know

- Focus is the meeting of the rays of light, after they pass through the lens, on the film plane.

- Your camera's lens can auto focus, or be focused manually.

- Wide-angle lenses let the camera "see" a wide field of view.

- Telephoto lenses make the image look closer to the camera and have a narrow field of view.

- A zoom lens has a variable field of view.

Chapter 9

Composition: No Snapshots Here!

In This Chapter

- ◆ Balancing your composition
- ◆ Creating visual interest
- ◆ Point of view
- ◆ The use of color
- ◆ Texture and patterns

Even with all the tools you have at your disposal, you can still take terrible pictures if you don't compose them well. A good composition is a careful arrangement of all the objects in your photograph. Take a look at photographs you see in magazines and books. What makes them interesting? What makes them sparkle? Recording the moment is a good use for photography. But why not tell a story at the same time? A photograph should challenge the viewer to imagine what is happening in the picture. It should be inviting. Instead of taking a picture of your family on top of a mountain, take a picture of them standing next to the signpost that says how high the mountain is. Now the viewer can see how much you accomplished.

If a picture is worth a thousand words, let it speak for itself. Before you take a picture, think about why you are taking it. What are you trying to say? What is the story? How do you feel about where you are? Can you make the viewer feel the same way? Ask yourself, "How can I make this a better picture?"

Make your photos visually interesting. Don't just use the viewfinder as a targeting device. A good photographer (and by the time you finish reading this book, you will be one) frames the picture in her mind's eye before taking it. Take time to look at what you are shooting. Enjoy the moment! Have fun!

Not in the Center, If You Please!

The subject in your photo should be the interest point, and the story line of your photo should revolve around your subject. All the artistic elements in the photo should lead your eye toward the subject. Draw in your audience; involve them.

One way to involve viewers in your photograph is to guide their eye through the photo—in other words, their eye should start somewhere in the photograph and travel across it. Imagine a photograph of a line of people waiting; at the end of the line is a clown making a balloon animal for your child. When you view that photo, your eye travels across the group until it gets to the end. And not only have you made the viewer's eye travel across the photo, you've also told a story at the same time.

The longer a viewer looks at a good photo, the more interesting it becomes. You can enhance a viewer's visit to your photo with color, shape, and subject. Keep the viewer's eye moving. If you put your subject dead center in your photograph, you quickly kill the viewer's interest. The viewer looks at the photo, looks at the perfectly centered object, and leaves. Next!

So where do you put the subject in your photo? Take a look at the following figure for a classic composition diagram. Begin by imagining a tic-tac-toe game in your frame. The areas where the lines cross are your *hot spots*. Try to center your subject on one of these spots.

The following two photographs illustrate the difference between placing your subject smack in the middle of your frame and placing your subject elsewhere; don't you agree that the second photograph is much more compelling than the first? Notice that its subject is on the lower-right hot spot.

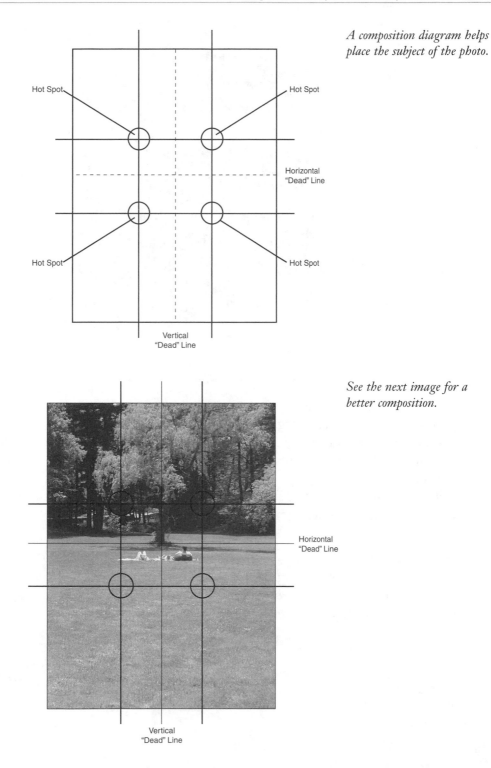

A composition diagram helps place the subject of the photo.

Hot Spot

Hot Spot

Horizontal "Dead" Line

Hot Spot

Hot Spot

Vertical "Dead" Line

See the next image for a better composition.

Horizontal "Dead" Line

Vertical "Dead" Line

*Notice how much more com-
pelling this image is than the
first.*

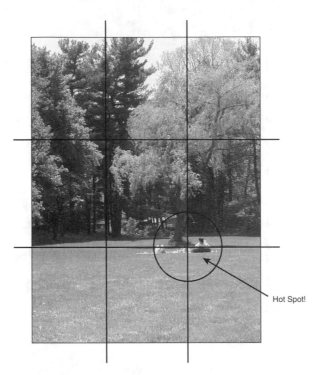

Hot Spot!

Of course, this doesn't mean you have to leave an empty space in the middle of your photo. Imagine you are taking a picture of a sailboat on the harbor. The sun is shining on the water, and birds are soaring through the air. Where do you put that boat? You could put the boat on the horizontal dead line and slightly to the right, and the image looks okay. But try placing the boat in the lower-right hot spot. Doesn't that feel better? Maybe you can get the birds to fly through the upper-left area or put the fluffy clouds or the setting sun there.

Let's take another mind's-eye photo. Your darling daughter has a new kitten sitting in her lap. (If you don't have a darling daughter or a kitten, you can substitute freely. It's your mind.) Put your daughter's face in the upper-left hot spot, and put the kitten in the lower-right hot spot. Nice picture. Composing your picture this way gets nice viewer involvement, as their eye travels from the girl's face to the kitten and back again.

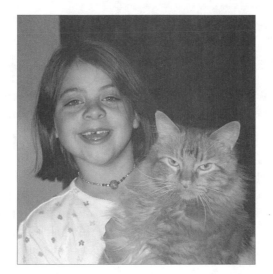

The cat's face balances out the face of the little girl.

Balance

Your photos should use balance to make them exciting. In the picture with the little girl and the kitten, the kitten served as a balancing object for the little girl. In our imaginary photo of the sailboat, the balancing object was the birds or the setting sun.

The balancing object and the subject don't have to be the same size; a small object can balance a large one. The idea is that your eye travels from the subject to the balancing object and back. The balancing object should be a clearly defined object or action.

Let's take a few more mind's-eye photos. On the right side of your photo, imagine a big beautiful flower. On the left, maybe coming in from the lower-left corner, is a bumblebee. Obviously, the bee and the flower are not the same size, but look how each balances the other.

Try another one: Your two-year-old son has just built his first tower out of wooden blocks. He is so proud of himself; he's smiling from ear to ear. But next to him, coming into the frame, is the puppy, headed directly for the tower. Click! You've got a great photo. You're telling a story, your composition is exciting, and the small puppy balances out the boy.

You don't need two objects to have balance in your photograph. Suppose you just baked an apple pie, and you want to take a picture of it. How can you compose your shot? Try taking a wedge out of the pie to show the contents of your pie, and also to give your pie some dimension. You'll find that the missing pie piece, or the space it leaves, balances the rest of the pie. Then put the pie off-center in the frame—the missing pie space should be slightly over the center line. Notice how the space and the pie balance each other.

Horizon

The horizon line can be a powerful composition tool; the sky, the water line, the roofs of buildings, clothes hung on a line, a fence, or a tree line can be used as horizontal elements, and can also set the horizon in your shot. As a general rule, the horizon line should not divide the picture exactly in half; a shot with the horizon line neatly dividing the sky and water is stagnant and boring.

If you take another look at that composition diagram I showed you earlier, you'll see the horizontal lines that run through the hot spots. These lines divide the frame into thirds. It's a good idea to place the horizon line in your photo so that it divides the frame in a like manner. Another rule I try to follow is to keep my horizon line parallel to the bottom of the frame. Take your time and be sure things look straight in the viewfinder. There is nothing more disconcerting than having a boat sailing uphill in a photo!

This photo shows the water line and horizon over Boston harbor.

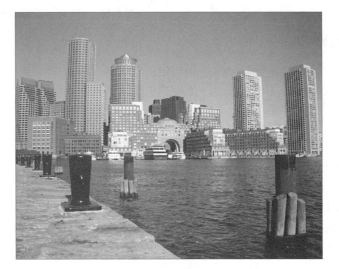

Cropping: Be Frugal!

The frame in your photograph should contain only your subject and its balancing object. Don't get sloppy. If you don't crop out unnecessary objects or people in your shot, your image becomes *diluted*. The viewer will get confused about the subject of your photograph. Are all the objects in the shot important? If you are photographing a scenic view, such as a skyline, don't include more than you need to. Also remember, especially with a digital camera, that resolution is a premium. If you use software to crop an image after you take it, you affect the optimal resolution of the image. Be frugal. Get everything you need in your image, and nothing else!

Use your telephoto or wide-angle lens to help you fill the frame, and be creative by using the effects of compression and distortion. If you need to move a little closer to your subject to fill the frame, do so. Take a few extra moments to compose your shots.

Here are a few guides to follow when deciding when to take an image in a horizontal or vertical mode:

- ◆ Use your camera in a horizontal mode when you need to fill your shot with a landscape. Group shots, scenic views, and crowd shots all work well horizontally. A horizontal shot emphasizes the width or breadth of your photo.

- ◆ Vertical shots are a great way to emphasize height. They make wonderful portraits. Also, photographing a small object and a tall object in a vertical frame is a great way to show height comparisons.

- ◆ When photographing for a newsletter or magazine, be sure you photograph your subject in both modes if you can. Your art director might have a layout that calls for only one or the other. Chances are that if you don't ask beforehand, you will use the wrong mode. (That, folks, is one of "Murphy's Laws" that professional photographers hate!)

Take your time to fill your frame. Make every pixel count.

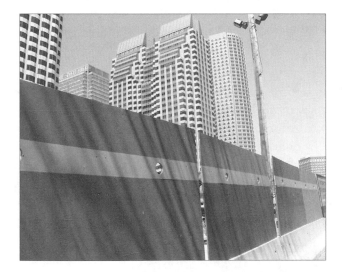

This is an example of a poorly cropped photo.

This is an example of a tightly cropped photo.

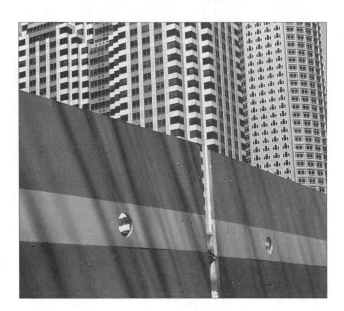

Color

Color can be a wonderful compositional tool. A vividly colored bed of tulips can be an interesting photograph; an old red barn can tell a wonderful story. Frame your image so that the barn is predominate in the image; this allows you to use the color of the barn to your advantage. Of course, too much of a good thing can be a disadvantage; be careful not to get too carried away with color. Just as you would not wear a suit of clothes with many different colors in it, you should try to avoid shots that suffer from the same. A shot, for example, with a lot of red and a few other colors works well, because the reds hold the composition together and the other colors add balance.

You can use saturated colors to aid your composition. In addition, contrasting colors can work well together, setting one another off. For example, instead of photographing a red rose with the sky in the background, try to frame it so the green leaves of other flowers form a background. The contrast of the red and green colors makes your photograph vivid. Monochromatic colors also work well as compositional tools. A stand of green trees in a forest or a pool of blue water with a child floating in an inner tube are good examples. If you fill your frame totally with sand dunes, all the same color, the lines and shapes of the dunes jump out at you, making an interesting composition.

Color can also be used to set the mood in a photograph. The subtle colors at dawn or dusk help you feel as if you are there, or involved in the photo. An image featuring objects that are predominantly red exudes energy and excitement. An image with pastel blue or green tones makes you feel cool and calm. *Lack* of color also can help compose an image. Imagine, if you will, a foggy harbor, devoid of all color except the gray mist. A lone red boat floats at the dock. The red boat adds interest and brings a little life to the image. Another good example is a snow-covered field with just a hint of color from a child in a snowsuit.

Contrast

Contrast can be achieved in many ways in a photograph. Color can be used to create contrast, or contrast can be created by the use of lighting. Deep shadows and well-lit areas can create wonderful contrasts in an image. Textured objects, when put on or adjacent to a smooth background, can set up image contrast—for example, a beautifully detailed piece of tree bark with an out-of-focus soft background.

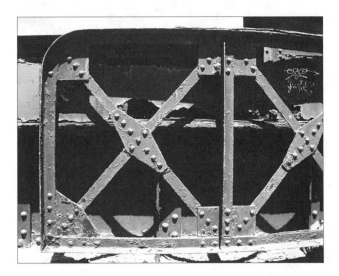

Strong light and shadows can create an interesting composition.

Negative and Positive Space: The Final Frontier

The space that your object takes up in your frame is called *positive space*. The space that is not used, such as the background, is called *negative space*. The positive and negative space in a photograph work together to reinforce each other. Imagine you are taking a picture of a tree branch with a blue sky in the background. If you look at the pattern formed by the interweaving branches, you see that the blue sky plays an important part of the image, supporting the pattern. The sky is as important to the composition of the image as the tree branches are.

In the collage image of a lamp in the following figure, the spaces between the lamp structures (that is, the negative spaces), which are colored, begin to form an image all their own. The contrasting colors also help support the image.

The colored background space works as negative space to help "set up" the lamp parts in the positive space. Both are compositional elements.

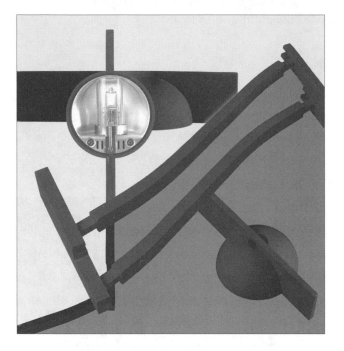

Movement

One of the most important attributes of a modern camera is that it can freeze motion. Speeding cars, children on bicycles, and kites flying through the air can be frozen in time. Stop-action photographs can hold a viewer's attention for quite a while.

Behind the Shutter

Early photographs by Edward Moybridge were a massive study on movement. He would shoot a series of photographs of a person jumping using, what was then, a high-speed camera. His series on animal locomotion was used to prove a bet about whether a horse has all four feet off the ground when galloping. Much later, Doctor Harold "Doc" Edgerton of the Massachusetts Institute of Technology (we Bostoners call it MIT) made many studies of high-speed movement, such as the famous photograph of a bullet being shot through a playing card.

Speed doesn't always need to be represented by stop action. A little blurring of an object is just as effective, if not more, to show how quickly an object is moving. Slow down your shutter speed to help create the illusion of movement. Alternatively, if you have an automatic camera, you might try putting neutral density filters over your lens to trick your meter into slowing down the shutter speed. Another good way to show speed in a photograph is to employ a little trick I call "action panning" (also called a "drag-shutter effect").

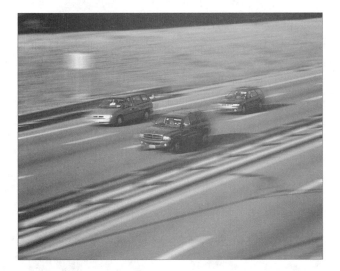

Panning the camera helps create the illusion of action.

Say Cheese

To create the illusion of movement through action panning, begin by setting your shutter speed at about 1/30 of a second or so. The exact speed isn't important, but it will alter the results of the effect. To enhance the effect, use a telephoto lens. (Note: This technique works best when your camera is in a horizontal mode.)

1. As your subject, let's say it's a racecar, comes into frame, start panning your camera in the same direction in which the car is traveling, and hit your shutter while continuing to move the camera.

2. Your results should be a combination of stop action and motion blur. The background is almost all blur, because it is put into motion by your camera motion. The car, however, which remained relatively in the same spot in your frame, has a bit of stop motion effect to it, but not completely.

Viewpoint: Low, Different, or Political

The point of view (or POV) that you use to photograph your subject can greatly add to its visual appeal. If you can avoid it (and you can), don't shoot an object straight on; doing so can make your shots boring. Instead, look at your subject from different angles. Will shooting partially from the side enhance the image? Will a total side view look even better? Shoot from a low angle looking up, or a high angle looking down. If you are shooting a scenic view, consider where you are going to put your horizon line. Consider using your wide-angle lens to create an interesting distortion.

Of course, you should be careful not to go overboard. If your point of view distracts too much from your subject, your photograph won't work. Don't let your fancy footwork rob from your subject its reason for being photographed in the first place. Confusing your viewer because you fell in love with a point of view will not help your image.

There are no hard and fast rules about point of view; just try to remember the composition guide and place your interest point on the hot spot.

Explore different points of view to make your subject look interesting.

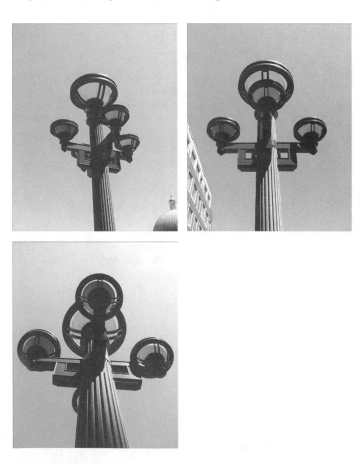

CAUTION **Flash** _____

Your safety should always be a prime concern when taking photographs. Years ago, I was photographing a high school basketball game. I was intent on following the action through my viewfinder. As the ball got bigger and bigger in my viewfinder, I got more excited about what a great shot I was going to get. Finally, reality—and the ball—struck me! There is no feeling like having your camera smashed into your face.

So be careful when taking photographs. Don't hide behind your camera, thinking it is a special magic shield. Many professional photojournalists have been injured and a few have died because they forgot they were mortal. Watch where you are stepping when you are taking photographs. Don't go out on a limb, literally, to get a great shot. Think safety!

Perspective

Many photographs suffer from a lack of dimension. They look flat and unrealistic. Adding an element in your photograph that creates perspective can often help. Usually, featuring two lines that start out separate but converge somewhere in the photo (the point where the lines meet is called the *vanishing point*) helps create the illusion of perspective and depth. The human brain knows that when two lines that are normally parallel meet, the vanishing point is in the distance. A good example of this is a railroad track or highway, but look for roof lines, fences, and even power lines to help create perspective.

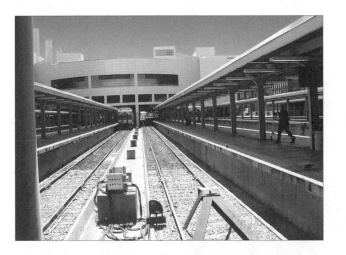

Perspective caused by receding lines of railroad track add depth to a shot.

Another way to create perspective in your photograph, especially if a railroad track or a road is not handy, is to twist your object or shoot it slightly from the side. As you can see from the following photograph, the objects not only show their size and shape, but as the images recede into the background, they create depth.

Receding lines created by the side of the box and the chess pieces add perspective and depth to the photo.

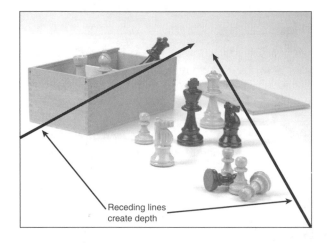

Receding lines
create depth

Foreground/Background

If you have a familiar object in your foreground and another in your background, you can create a sense of depth. For example, let's say you have two adults in your photograph. The adult closer to your camera appears bigger in your image, and the adult in the background appears smaller. Your brain certainly knows about this phenomenon and associates depth into your photograph.

Overlapping images also help create depth in your photograph. Say you photographed your cat—okay, anybody's cat. Directly behind the cat, but in the distance, is a sofa. In the photograph, the sofa looks smaller than the cat. The viewer's brain, when looking at the photo, associates distance in the shot, because it knows that the cat can't possibly be larger than the sofa. (Although I have seen a few cats that are as big as chairs!)

The field and goal net add depth to the photograph.

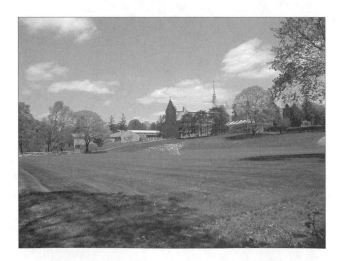

Line and Imaginary Line

An object or series of objects can create a line or visual path through a photograph. This helps engage the viewer and deliver the photograph's message. You can also use an imaginary line to create interest and help your composition. Sometimes objects in your photography can be used as strong compositional tools to lead the eye toward your subject. These real or *regular* lines can be as obvious as the pipes in the following photograph.

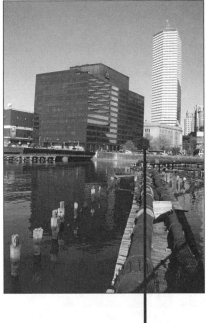

Old pipes add direction and line, drawing your eye toward buildings in the background.

Line as element
of design

Let's use our mind's eye again to create a few examples. Say you have a photo with a child pointing up in the air and crying. Above the child, a balloon sails away into the sky. With this photograph, you have told your viewer that the child is upset by the escaping balloon, but you have also created an interesting visual. The viewer's eye follows the imaginary line between the child's outstretched arm and the balloon. This is a successful image. Congratulations!

In another mind's-eye shot, a dog stares at a spot on the floor with great intensity. In the photograph, a tiny spot can be seen just beyond the dog's nose. Could it be an ant or a tiny morsel of food? Whatever it is, the viewer's eye travels back and forth from the dog's nose to the spot on the floor.

Try to keep the imaginary line contained in the image; that is, do not offer an "end point" to the imaginary line that exists outside of the composition. If the dog was intently staring at something outside of the frame, the viewer's eye follows. After the eye leaves the image, it probably won't come back.

Watch Your Background

Distracting objects always find their way into your shot, but that shouldn't give you the right to have tunnel vision! Don't get so involved in your subject that you forget to look at what else is in your viewfinder. The quickest way to ruin a photograph is to have a distracting background.

A messy desk is the sign of a brilliant mind!

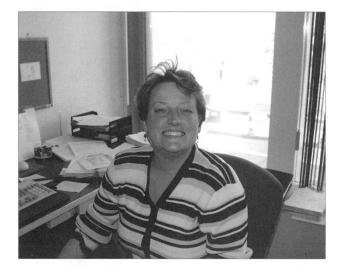

Sometimes it is unavoidable—you cannot prevent someone from walking through your photo … or can you? If I have a friend with me when I'm taking a photograph in a public place, I ask my friend to be sure no one walks in front of me while I'm taking the shot.

Look around the area you're about to shoot, and pick up any stray pieces of paper or litter. A white piece of paper can be a distracting object in your shot. (Besides, people will think you are really cool if you pick up litter!) Look in the background behind your subject; remove stray coffee cups and dinner plates. Don't photograph someone with the company bulletin board behind her. You are in control of your photograph; take the time to look at what is going on in your image before you hit the shutter.

The most criminal act you can do when taking someone's picture is to have something behind them appear to be growing out of their head! Watch your background. Be sure no trees, poles, books, door trim, and so on, are lined up behind your subject's head.

Watch out for power and telephone lines when photographing outdoors. Sometimes you can change your point of view to avoid a power line, and sometimes you can't. Of course, with a little bit of digital imaging, you can erase those power lines—but it still takes time and effort to do so.

Texture

Texture can be a wonderful aid to composition. An image made completely of a textured object, such as an old piece of weathered wood, can be wonderful. Of course, you should be sure to balance a textured object with something else in the frame that has no texture. Even a smooth background works to balance your subject. Take the time to explore the textures of wood, stone, paper, and even water. By exploring the nature of these objects, you can learn much about yourself and how you view your world.

Texture can also be created by patterns. The pattern in the weave found in cloth is an example of texture. The small ripples in a pool of water, the cells in a honeycomb, and even the patterns in clouds, are all wonderful forms of texture.

An intricate pattern of colors can form texture; for example, the delicate purples and yellows of a field of wildflowers can create a wonderful blanket of color and texture. Take a good close look at an old piece of painted wood. Find a piece that might have been painted a few different colors over the years, and you will discover wonderful textures.

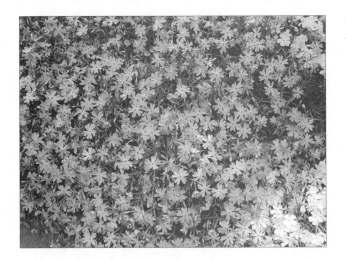

Colored flowers create a wonderful repeating texture.

You can use your texture as a background element or in the foreground. It can be the entire subject photograph, such as a beautifully weathered old tree stump, or it can be used as a background, such as a piece of crumpled newspaper with a delicate flower or piece of pottery in its center.

Scale

In a portrait or even a landscape, the scale of the objects is not important. We know how big the average person is. With a few visual clues, such as a tree, we can generally get an idea of how large our landscape is.

Many still-life photographs, however, can suffer from a lack of scale. If there are no visual clues to help identify the size of an object, the image can become confusing. For example, in the following photo of the nuts and bolts, we would have no clue as to their size without the pen being in the shot. Even if we used a wrench or a screwdriver as a scale reference, the size of the bolt might still be in question.

The pen helps clarify the size of the bolts in the shot.

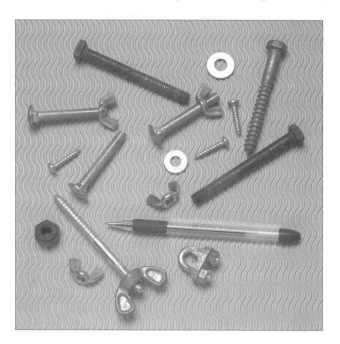

The Least You Need to Know

- To keep your viewer interested, create a story with your composition.

- Balance the objects in your photo.

- Don't place your subject in the center of the frame.

- Draw your viewer's eye into the shot using "line" and perspective as composition tools.

- Color and texture can also be used as composition tools.

Chapter 10

Lighting: It Makes or Breaks a Shot!

In This Chapter

◆ Available light, use it or lose it

◆ Flash, make your own light!

◆ Lighting setups that can make your pictures shine

Now that you can create beautifully composed images, you need to start thinking about lighting. Lighting is as important to your image as the composition, and can add mood, create depth, and emphasize form.

Using Available Light

Using available light, such as sunlight, is often the easiest way to take a photograph. The light is believable and natural.

The time of day influences the angle of the light. In the morning and just before sunset, the sun is low on the horizon, and casts a beautiful sidelight on your subject or scene. At "high noon," the sun is well overhead; the shadows it casts are short, but intense. At 3 P.M., the light is much more angled and casts very different shadows (go look for yourself!).

The *color* of light can also be affected by the time of day, and even the season. During most of the day, when the sun is high in the sky, the light is neutral. When the sun is low on the horizon, especially during the summer months, it picks up a warm yellow tone. This can be dramatic and beautiful.

Weather affects light, too. Whereas a clear day proffers brilliant, intense light, an overcast day tenders soft, diffused light. In some situations, this can be pleasing; other times, it takes away your shadow detail and makes your images look flat.

Behind the Shutter

There is nothing worse than showing up to take a picture and finding the building you want to shoot completely in shadow; that's why most professional location photographers carry a compass in their camera bag. After all, we all know that the sun rises in the east and sets in the west. By paying attention to what direction the camera will be facing and what time of day the shoot will occur, a photographer can predict where the sun will be and how the lighting will look in a scene. If you miss a shot because the sun is in the wrong place, figure out a good time to come back and grab a quick shot.

Backlighting

The general rule to using sunlight as a light source is to try to position your body so that the sun is behind you (the photographer), or over your shoulder. That way, the light falls on the front of your subject. Of course, you can't always depend on the light being exactly where you need it. Many times, it comes from behind your subject, casting it in shadow. This is called *backlighting*.

When an exposure meter reads a scene, it expects to find bright areas and shadow areas. The meter assumes that if all these areas were totaled up, the average light would be a middle gray. So when a meter detects a bright area behind your subject, it shuts down your aperture to compensate in an attempt to render an average exposure. Unfortunately, that leaves your subject in the dark. What's a meter photographer to do?

Behind the Shutter

A bright area behind your subject, such as a white wall or pool of light, also creates backlighting. You should be aware of these types of light sources in addition to that great bright orb in the sky.

Well, if your camera has an exposure override, allowing you to open up the aperture or slow down the shutter, you can easily correct for this. Give your subject a few more *stops* of light, and your image will be properly exposed. Many consumer cameras now come with a backlight feature in their menu. As an alternative, many cameras enable you to spot read and lock in an exposure. Spot reading allows you to gather a reading in a smaller area; you could, for example, measure only the shadow area, and then lock in the exposure settings. The camera then automatically opens the aperture and ignores the backlighting.

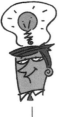

Say Cheese

The only drawback to overriding backlighting by adjusting your exposure for the shadows is that the brighter areas in the image will be overexposed. One way to avoid this overexposure is to add some light to your subject by filling the shadow area with reflected available light. A large white card or a white bed sheet can be used to reflect the light back at the subject.

Nighty Night!

Shooting photographs at night is not as hard as it used to be. With your fancy preview LCD screen, you have a good idea of what your exposure should be. When shooting at night, definitely use a tripod; also use a cable release or fire the camera using the self-timer.

When photographing at night, try using various shutter speeds. You can get a nice effect from the streaks of lights from a car's taillights if you use slower shutter speeds. If you are trying to photograph fireworks, try varying your shutter speed to capture different types of bursts. Some cameras might even enable you to hold the shutter open as long as you like; this is called a *bulb* setting. With the shutter left open, you can record as many firework explosions on one frame as you want. Of course, you can always manipulate your images by using image-editing software to make your own fireworks!

Say Cheese

Another way to avoid overexposing the bright areas in your backlit image is to leave your settings alone, but use a *fill flash*. You'll learn more about this technique later in this chapter, in the following "Fill Flash" section.

Flash

Gone are the days of flashbulbs and flashcubes. All consumer-level cameras, digital and film-based alike, come with built-in flash. These built-in flashes generally provide enough light to take a picture indoors, provided that the subject is within 10 to 12 feet of the camera. Built-in flashes will allow you to take photos in low-light situations, but will not render a natural lighting effect (the flash will usually look a bit harsh).

Don't expect that tiny little flash to light up the entire room; it is just not strong enough. In the same regard, don't expect a flash to even reach a subject that is more than 20 feet away from the camera. I always have to laugh when I watch a televised sports event and I see flashes going off in the stands—those flashes will never reach the field!

To use your flash effectively, do the following:

- Keep your subject 10 to 15 feet from the camera.

- Light from a flash does not spread well. This is called *fall off*. Keep your subjects in an area no wider than six to eight feet.

- Keep your flash higher than your lens. Don't have it lighting from an angle lower than the lens, or pointing up.

- Avoid cameras with tiny flashes or flashes mounted very close to the lens.

Fill Flash

Some cameras have a "fill flash" setting, which enables you to add light to your image without affecting your exposure settings. This is because your meter is working with the available light, and not accounting for the light that will be provided by the flash. A fill flash simply adds lighting to the backlit (shadowed) areas, *opening* them up. You can also use the fill flash in normal sunlight to fill in (and, as a result, soften) the shadows on your subject. Don't be surprised if your subject seems to pop out a bit when you use a fill flash; the flash might be just a bit brighter than the available light. Of course, all this works only if your subject is within a reasonable distance from you, the photographer.

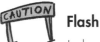

Flash

I almost always use a flash when photographing outdoors, especially when photographing people. Be aware, however, that this practice drains your camera batteries a lot faster than normal. Be prepared! Carry extra batteries.

Bounce Flash

Many times, using an on-camera flash can make your subjects look like deer in headlights. One way to correct for this is to bounce your flash off a wall or ceiling (this might not be possible with some low-end cameras). If you can point your flash at the ceiling or a wall and still keep your lens pointed in the right direction, you can greatly soften the output of your flash. When the light bounces off the ceiling, it both diffuses and lights your subject more from above.

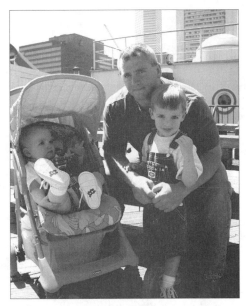

Fill flash helps overcome backlighting.

Before

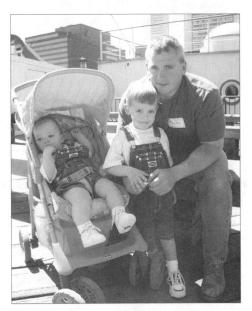

After

Using an Extra Flash

One way to add more flash power to your exposure is to get an extra flash. Stand-alone portable flashes are not very expensive—you might already have one for your old film-based camera. You can preposition your second flash so that it is aimed at your subject, or set it up so that it bounces off the ceiling to provide a nice, soft fill light.

Your flash needs to have a *slave eye* on it so that it knows when to flash. A slave eye detects the on-camera flash going off, setting off the auxiliary flash at the same time. (As an alternative, many professional photographers trigger the slave flash via a radio signal to prevent the slave flash from activating when someone else in the room takes a picture with a flash.) You can buy a slave eye for your flash if it does not have one built in.

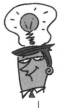

> ### Say Cheese
> Remember that when you are bouncing the flash off a wall or ceiling, you are sending the light on a far longer journey. Its apparent output might be greatly diminished.

Be sure to keep track of where your additional flash is and where it's pointed. You don't want to end up photographing your flash as it goes off, or having it send its light directly into your lens. Also, don't be fooled into thinking that the second flash must be close to your camera! When I am shooting at a party or during a family event, I generally carry a spring-loaded clamp so I can rig a second flash up somewhere high in the room.

Get a Bracket!

To avoid red eye and reduce harsh shadows, you should place your flash as far away from your lens as possible. To aid in this, many photographers mount a second flash on a *flash bracket*, which is basically an L-shaped handle that attaches to your camera. The bottom of the L attaches to the base of your camera, and the leg of the L holds the auxiliary flash over the camera and to the side. You can aim your flash at the ceiling to diffuse the light, or you can aim it directly at the subject. If your camera has a PC (patch cord) socket, you might think about blocking the light from the on-camera flash with some opaque tape and using only the bracket-mounted flash as a light source.

For the flash to operate, it must be connected to the camera body through a *PC* (*patch cord*) socket. That way, the flash goes off at the same time as the shutter. Counting on an optical slave is not a good idea, because the sensor will be behind or above your built-in flash and might not detect when the built in flash goes off.

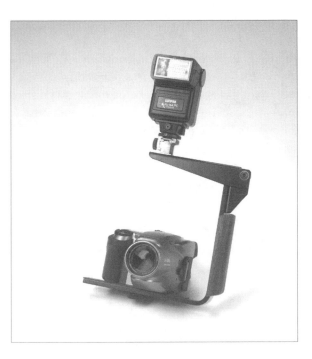

A flash bracket helps keep the flash away from the lens. Note that the bracket can swivel so that the flash can be reoriented when the camera moves from horizontal or vertical positions.

Say Cheese _____

Because most auxiliary flashes are powerful compared to the tiny on-camera flash, consider putting diffusion material, such as a small white handkerchief or a piece of cheesecloth, directly on your flash. Alternatively, go high-tech and buy some plastic diffusion material, lighting filters, or gels at a camera store or even a theater supply store. The major manufacturers of lighting filters and gels are Rosco Filters Co. (www. rosco.com) and Lee Filters. Rosco also manufactures wonderful set paints. Another good source for almost all things photographic is *Photo District News*, which is a magazine published for professional photographers. Their website (www.pdn-pix.com) has a wonderful resource section.

Adding Lights

If you don't want to be securing auxiliary flash units all over a room, there is a simpler way: Turn on a few lights! Try setting up a few clip-on lights and using brighter bulbs in some of the lamps and fixtures in the room. Reflectors can be used to concentrate and focus the light; typically bowl-shape metal reflectors work well. The shape and size of the reflectors determine how wide a beam of light is *thrown* and how *hard* the light will be.

Color of Light

We've all heard the phrases *white hot* and *red hot*, and we've all seen heated metals glow and emit light. Many years ago, a system was devised to determine what *color* light was using during these observations. A piece of metal was heated and observed under daylight at noon. As the metal changed color, its temperature (measured in Kelvin) was taken, and the color of the glow was noted. It was observed that the hotter the metal got, the closer the color came to white. White hot metal, when observed under daylight, was measured at 5,500° Kelvin; interestingly, average daylight at noon is rated the same. We now use the Kelvin scale to describe the color temperature of light (see the following table).

Color Temperature of Light Sources

Source	Color Temperature
Candles	1,950° K (how romantic)
Dawn	2,000° K (also romantic)
Household incandescent	2,800° K
Fluorescent tube	3,000° K (yucky color!)
Photo incandescent	3,400° K (sold at camera stores)
Noon sunlight	5,000 to 5,500° K
Sunny day with some clouds	6,500° K
"Incredible" blue sky	11,000 to 18,000° K (wear sun block!)

Behind the Shutter

Commercial photographers often use soft boxes to produce an even, diffused source of light. A soft box is a box made of flameproof, lightweight material, the front of which is translucent. The light source is mounted inside the soft box, so the light shines through the diffusion material.

If you don't want to buy a soft box (and I wouldn't blame you, they can be expensive), you can rig a simple substitute. Hang a white cloth sheet from a stand or a clothesline, and shine your light source through the sheet in the direction of your subject. Although this method doesn't pass as much light as a professional soft box, it delivers a soft, diffuse light. Be careful not to burn or overheat the cloth; keep your light source a safe distance from the cloth.

If you look at different light sources, such as a standard light bulb or sunlight, you will notice that they are different colors. A standard tungsten light bulb, such as a household light bulb, burns at about 2,700 to 2,900° Kelvin. In relation to sunlight, this appears yellowish. Tungsten photographic lighting equipment "burns" at 3,400° Kelvin; daylight-rated photographic light bulbs burn at 5,500° Kelvin.

When your camera detects light falling on a subject, it must determine the color of the light source. Most cameras (or their software) automatically adjust for the correct color temperature; this is called *color balance*. If your camera (or its software) does not adjust for color temperature, the images carry a color cast (an overall tint of color). Imagine your camera is set to work only at 5,500° Kelvin. If you brought your camera inside to photograph under household lighting, everything would have an unpleasant yellow cast. Alternatively, if your camera were set to see tungsten lighting, then all your outdoor shots would look very blue. If you want proper, or neutral, colors in your pictures, be sure your camera is set for the color temperature of the main light source.

> **CAUTION**
>
> ### Flash
>
> Be careful when adding light to your subject. Use similar types of sources in the same environment. If you mix lighting, such as using a flash (which is 5,500°) and tungsten lights, you end up with a strange and unwanted color cast. Your camera adjusts for one of the sources or the other. If it decides to average the color temperature, you will see blue and yellow light in your image.

Of course, you might decide not to correct for the light temperature. For instance, if you were to take a moody candlelit picture, it would be a shame if the warm light of the candles were overcorrected to a neutral color. If you can turn off the color balance correction, try to do so. If you are setting the color balance using software, try leaving it off. Experiment and practice; remember, you are not shooting film and you have nothing to lose.

Lighting Setups: You're a Pro Now!

Whether you are setting up lighting for a portrait or a product shot, it is easy to control your lighting. Start off by deciding what the important part of your photograph is and then decide how you want to light it. Try the following:

1. Add the first light, which is called a *key light*. The key light delivers the main and brightest light. It can come from directly in front of the subject, but it adds more dimension if it comes from the side. As you can see in the following figure, a key light casts a harsh shadow.

A key light casts a strong and abrupt shadow.

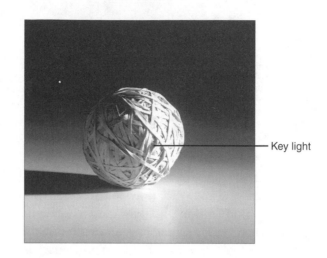

Key light

2. Before adding another light, see what a fill card will do. Place a white card opposite the key light. It bounces light back onto the object, and fills in the harsh shadows.

Use a fill card to fill in the harsh shadows.

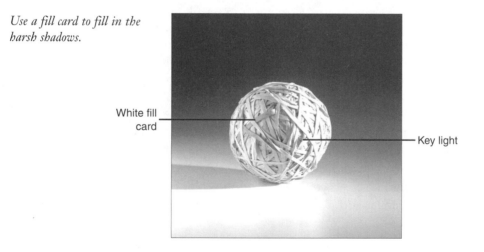

White fill card

Key light

3. If you need more light to fill your shadow, you can replace the fill card with another light source (I'll call this a *fill light*). To keep some of the shadow detail, this light should be dimmer than the key light. If the key light and fill light are the same intensity, move the fill light farther away from the subject, or try diffusing it. In the following photograph, note the shadow thrown by the fill light to the right of the ball.

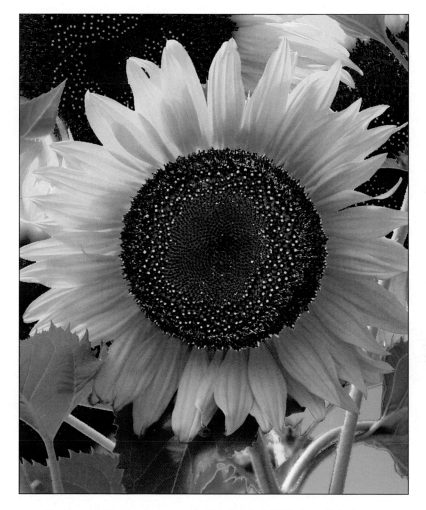

Sunflower. Sometimes you can't get that "perfect" photo. See if you can identify the "elements" I used to put this image together.

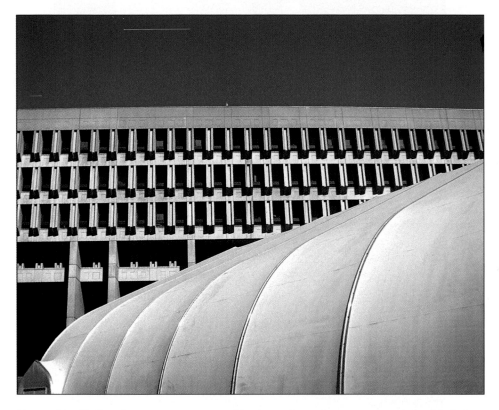

Boston City Hall and temporary structure. It's always fun to keep your eyes open and look for unusual shapes. Don't be afraid to crop using your eyes and camera frame.

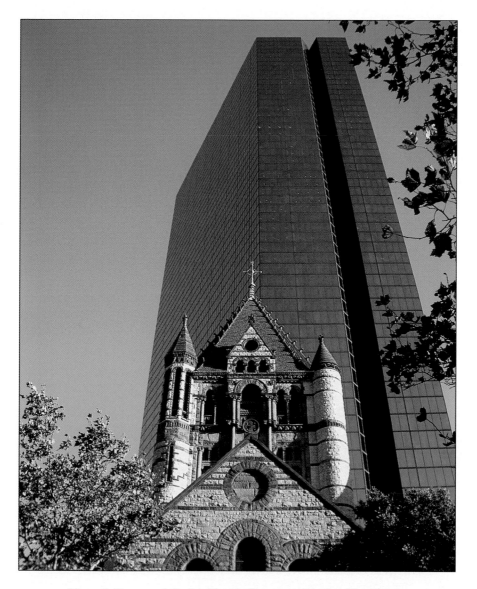

*Hancock Tower and Copley Church. By contrasting the old and new,
you can emphasize the uniqueness of both.*

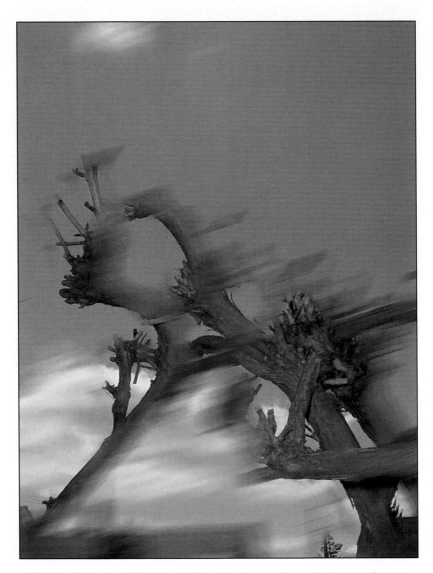

By using Selections, filters and color corrections can be applied to specific areas.

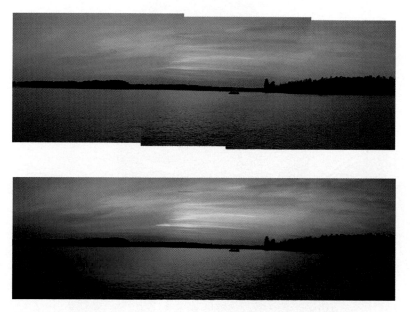

Photoshop Elements 2.0 can make panoramic images from several composite shots. In the top figure, you can see how three images have been combined into one. There are some distinct lines of demarcation between shots after using the panorama feature to combine the shots.

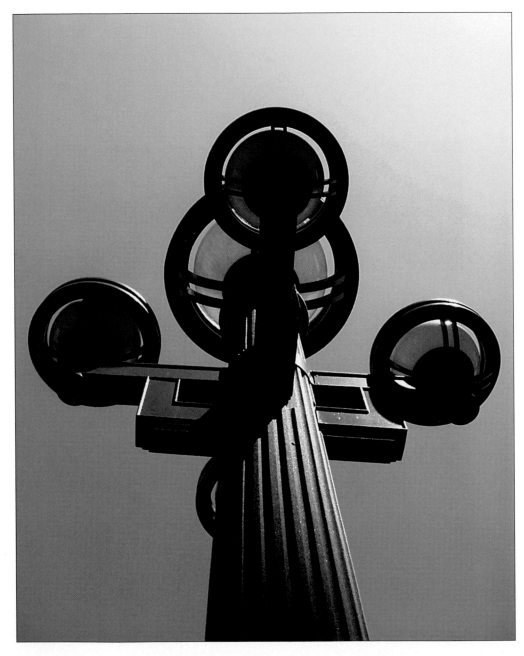

Unusual or creative angles make for great compositions.

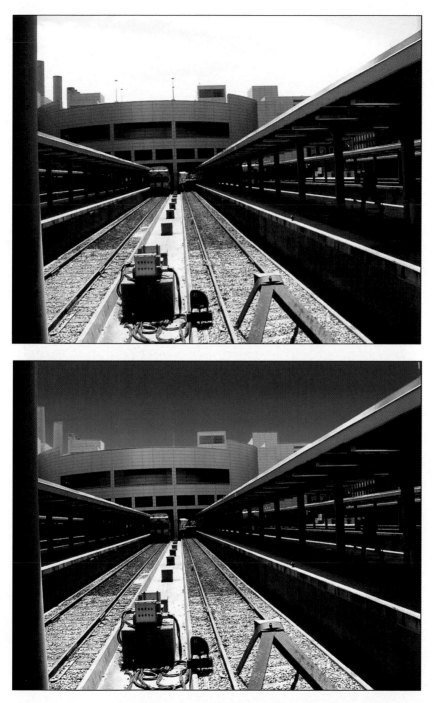

An image can be enhanced with a little retouching and color correction.

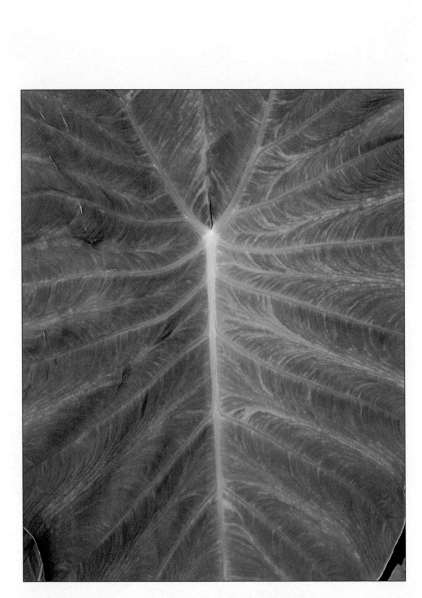

Leaf, Boston Garden. Don't be afraid of using only one color. Here, it helps bring out the leaf's texture.

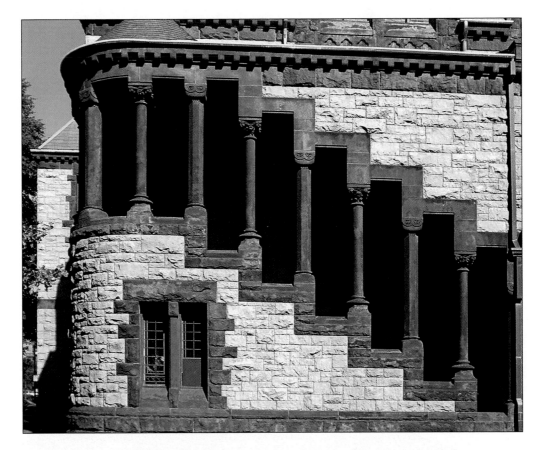

Stairs, Copley Church. By careful adjustment of shadows and highlights, this fine architectural detail is brought to life.

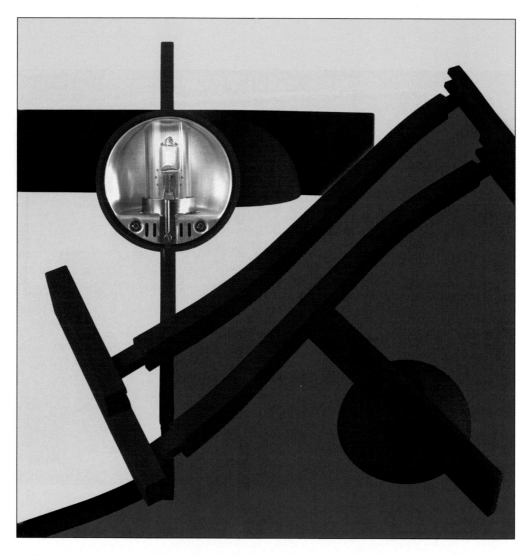

Strong colors and abstract shapes help to define negative (colors) and positive spaces (lamp parts). This is a great compositional tool.

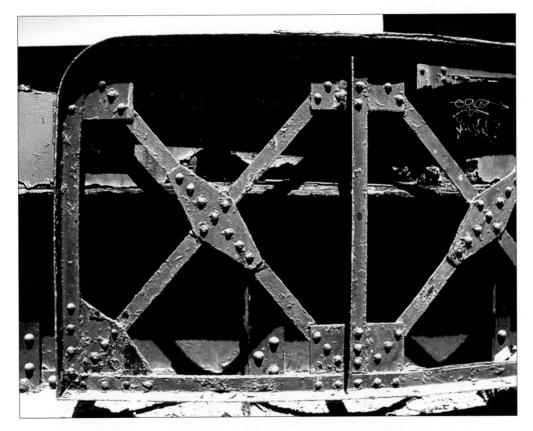

Texture, light, and shadow help make this an interesting photo.

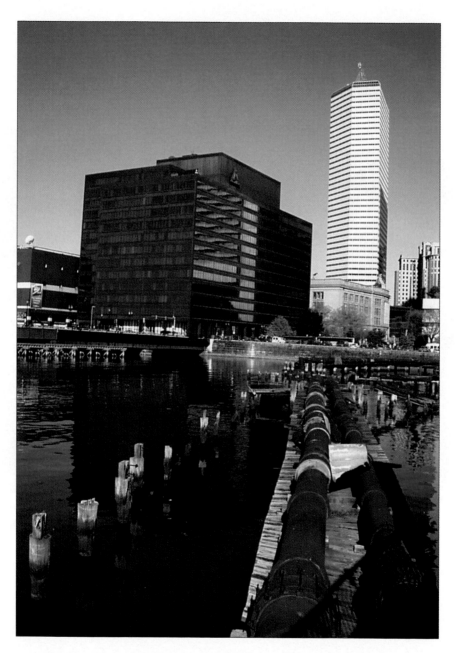

Compositional tools, such as line (the pipes in the foreground), help draw the viewer's eye into the photograph.

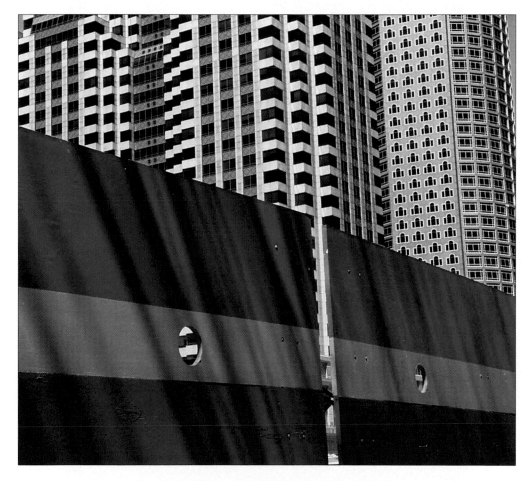

Use color and texture to create wonderful compositions.

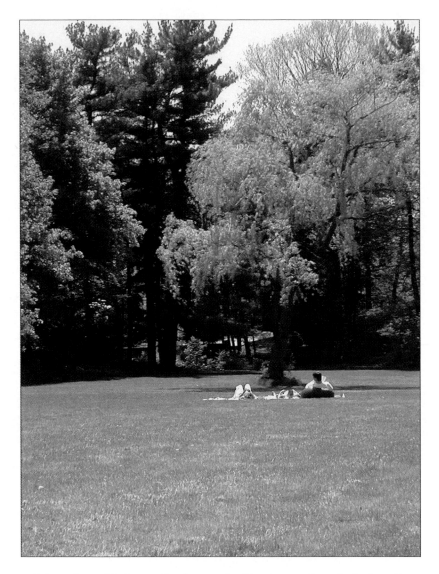

Balance is a critical part of a photograph. Always try to keep the horizon line from running across the middle of the image.

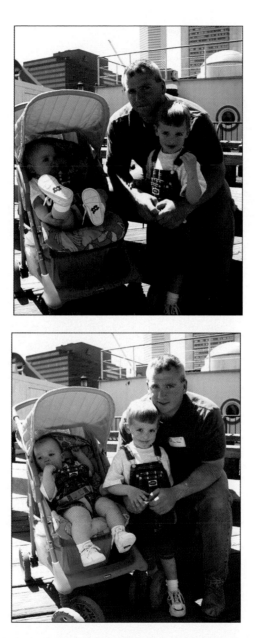

*Here is good example of using a fill flash outdoors. The shadows have
been lightened, allowing important details to show.*

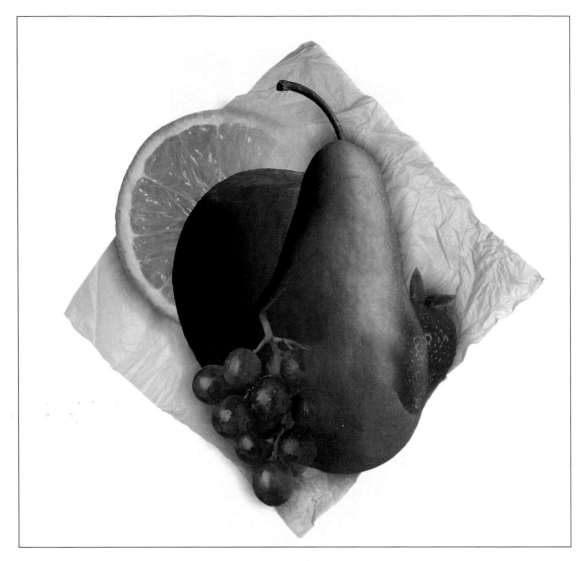

Each element in this photo is on its own layer. The transparency between each image is accomplished by using the Erase tool with various opacity settings. This is a wonderful example of using layers effectively.

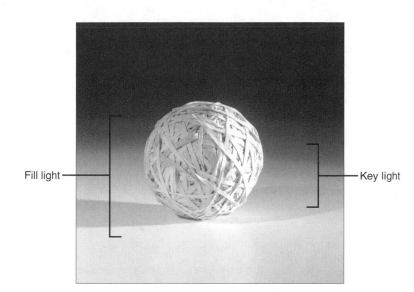

A fill light can throw a secondary shadow. This can create an unnatural lighting situation.

Fill light

Key light

4. Product shots might need a top light, which should be placed above the object. You can place the light slightly behind or in front of the subject, depending on the effect you want to achieve. This light also should be diffused—be careful not to cast a heavy shadow on the product! When photographing a person (or when photographing an object that is very textured, like the one shown here), using a hair light can add a nice effect. Place the hair light above and behind the person; it picks up the texture of the hair and adds some nice highlights. Be careful not to shine the light into your lens.

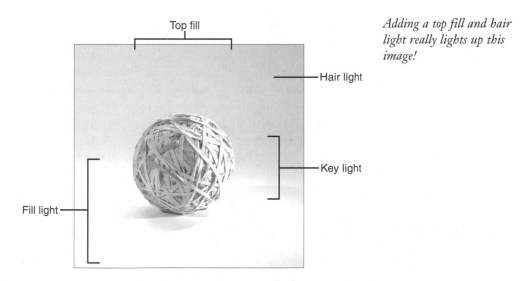

Top fill

Hair light

Key light

Fill light

Adding a top fill and hair light really lights up this image!

Practice your lighting techniques! Try out different types of light sources, and experiment with different placements. If you really want to get fancy, try coloring your light sources. Red lights add a sense of action to your shot, whereas blue light often gives the feeling of calm or coolness. Experiment with different colors and color combinations to get the mood you want. Creative lighting can produce exciting and pleasing results.

Lighting Safety Tips

As with all things in life, you should consider the safety hazards of using lighting:

- Don't overload your electrical circuits when using lighting.

- Use heavy extension cords.

- Place your electrical cords carefully to avoid creating a trip hazard.

- Weigh down your light stands so they don't tip over. You can make inexpensive weights by filling one-gallon plastic bottles with sand.

- Be careful of the heat the lamps produce. You can easily burn your subject.

- Don't touch the bulbs, they're really hot even when off for a few minutes. Also the oil on your hands will effect the longevity of the bulb.

- Be careful when using colored gels on your lights. If they get too hot, they might melt. Also, and this is extremely important, use only photographic gels or theater gels on your lights. They are designed to be used near high-temperature lighting.

- Do not move a light when it is on! Light bulbs are very fragile when they are hot—especially when lit. They might shatter or explode when moved. Turn lights off before you move them!

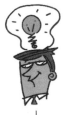 **Say Cheese**

If you have forgotten your tripod and find yourself in need, here is a good trick: Hold your camera to your eye, and relax your arms and body. If you stiffly brace yourself, you are going to shake. After you take several deep breaths, exhale slowly. At the end of the exhale, trip the shutter. This not only reduces shake in your body, it will calm you down, also. If you find this technique helpful, you might consider signing up for a yoga class!

Stand Still: Working with a Tripod

When your camera's shutter speed falls below $\frac{1}{60}$ of a second, you will not be able to hold it without shaking it—especially if you drink coffee! In a low-light situation, such as with an interior, you can be sure you'll need a tripod.

When you buy a tripod, be sure to get a sturdy one. Better tripods will have a Teflon-like surface on the legs to aid them in movement. The taller the tripod and/or the more compact it is, the more you will pay for it. Pay close attention to the pan head, which attaches your camera to the tripod—it should be sturdy and have smooth movements.

Most professional cameras will have a screw-like socket to attach a cable release. A cable release, which is a long spring-loaded cable, allows you to trip the shutter without shaking the camera (after all, it doesn't do you much good to put your camera on a tripod and then shake it when tripping the shutter). If your camera doesn't have a cable release socket, use your self-timer! Set the timer, trip it, and your camera takes the photograph vibration free.

The Least You Need to Know

- ◆ Use available light for your basic exposure.
- ◆ Don't let your meter be fooled by bright or dark backgrounds.
- ◆ Use a flash to add light to your photos.
- ◆ Use your flash as an indirect source of light.
- ◆ Use reflector cards to fill in your shadows.
- ◆ Use additional light sources to add creativity to your images.
- ◆ All light sources have their own color.

Chapter 11

Resolution: Is Bigger Better?

In This Chapter

◆ What we see and what we get?

◆ Getting it all on paper

◆ Get the skinny on how ink jet and laser printers print images differently

We all remember Goldilocks and the Three Bears. One bed was too soft, one bed was too hard, and one bed was just right. Resolution behaves a lot like our friend Goldie. Too little resolution causes your images to lack detail; too much resolution clogs up your computer and printer and robs you of speed; and the proper resolution is just right.

Image Resolution/Monitor Resolution

Your camera can produce images at various resolutions. As a general rule, the larger your file is, the more you can do with it. If your file size is too small, you won't be able to reproduce large images and still have detail. The drawback to large images is that they take up a lot of storage space on your camera's onboard hard drive.

The resolution of your monitor is measured in pixels, just like the resolution of your images. Monitors can display your images at various resolutions, which affects how those images look onscreen (however, it doesn't affect the resolution of the images themselves).

Demo: Calibrating Your Image Resolution and Monitor Resolution

Both the screen resolution and the size of an image affect how that image is displayed on the monitor, but don't take my word for it! Humor me by performing the following steps, which illustrate how your monitor resolution and image resolution work together:

1. Click the **Start** button, click **Settings,** and choose **Control Panel.**

2. Double-click the **Display** icon (**Monitors and Sound CP** on a Mac).

3. Click the **Settings** tab, and look for the **Screen area** slider at the bottom of the panel. Drag the slider to set your screen resolution at 640×480 pixels. You can see the change in the small view monitor or by hitting apply. If you decide to select apply, be sure you write down your current settings so you can change them back if desired.

Changing the screen resolu-
tion changes how the onscreen
image is displayed.

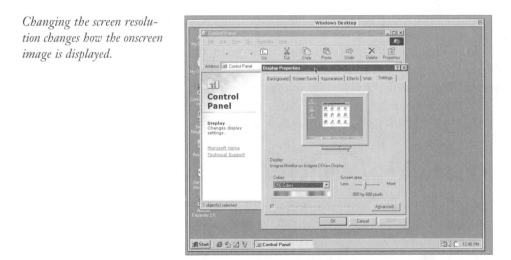

4. In PhotoDeluxe, open the **File** menu and choose **New** (alternatively, press **Ctrl+N,** or **Command+N** on the Mac).

5. In the New dialog box, shown in the following figure, type 9.4 in the **Width** field (don't worry about adjusting the **Height** field), and 72 in the **Resolution** field. (You'll understand why you're entering those particular numbers in just a moment.) Be sure to select **inches** as the measurement for the width and height (note that you can change this to **pixels, centimeters, points, picas,** or **columns**), and that **pixels/inch** is selected for resolution. Click **OK.**

New
Name: Untitled–1   OK
Cancel
Image Size: 434K
Width: 6.667   inches ▼
Height: 4.278   inches ▼
Resolution: 72   pixels/inch ▼

Select the width and resolution in the New dialog box.

Look! The image's window fills the width of your screen when viewed at 100 percent. So how did I know to enter 9.4 in the **Width** field in step 5 to make the image fill the whole screen? Here's a hint: Your monitor is set up to *display* images at 72ppi (pixels per inch). Give up? Okay. Divide 640 pixels (remember that you set your monitor's screen resolution, or the total number of pixels available on your screen, to 640×480 in step 3) by 72ppi, and you get 9.4 inches!

So what happens if the image is 9.4 inches at 100ppi instead of 72ppi? Well, the image will no longer fit on the screen at 100 percent—you're out of screen pixels! You can display it at 100 percent and scroll the screen to view the image in its entirety, or you can increase the screen resolution. If you increase the resolution to 1,024×768 (or thereabouts), you will again be able to see the image at 100 percent—with a little screen to spare. (9.4 inches × 100ppi = 940 pixels to display. We set the screen to be 1,024 pixels wide, so we can see the entire image.)

To see the entire image onscreen without changing the resolution, begin by specifying that the screen display only some of the total pixels available. So instead of specifying that you want to see 100 percent of the pixels in the image, you can tell your software (in this case, PhotoDeluxe) to show a smaller percentage of pixels. For example, if you choose 25 percent, you'll see

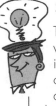

Say Cheese

To keep things simple, just worry about the width of the image, and likewise the width of the screen. Don't worry about adjusting the height of the image.

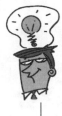

By the way, when you first open an image in PhotoDeluxe, it opens the image at the largest zoom size that fits, in full, on the screen.

only one in four of the pixels in the image (thus, losing some detail), but you won't have to use the scrollbars to view the image in its entirety.

Just as you can zoom out to view more of the image on your screen (thus, making the image appear smaller), you can zoom in to make the image appear larger to view more of its detail, as shown in the following figure.

You can zoom in and out to see the detail of your image.

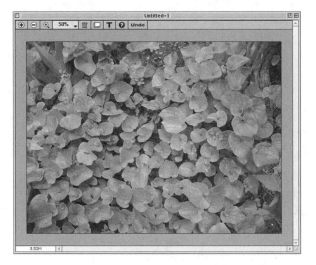

Printer Resolution

Printers usually have a fixed resolution at which they best reproduce an image. For most laser and dye-sublimation printers, this is usually 300dpi (dots per inch). So what happened to the ppi (pixels per inch)? Printers don't print pixels; instead, they lay down tiny dots of ink or dye to produce an image. The printer should, at the very least, print one dot for every pixel.

To get the best image reproduction from your printer, you should maximize your image size. Also, the resolution of your image should be the same as your printer resolution, if you can swing it. If your printer has a resolution of 300dpi, then your images should have a resolution of 300ppi (pixels per inch). Note, however, that this need not be the same as your monitor's screen resolution (probably 640×480 pixels), which is why the printed image will not be the same size (in inches) as it was on your screen.

If your image is too small or has less resolution than your printer, one of two things will happen:

♦ Your printer might just leave a space between each dot when it prints. As a result, your image will lack detail and sharpness.

♦ Your printer might interpolate information to fill in the gaps between the pixels. As we know, interpolated information is not as good as original information. Your images might still not look sharp, and might lack detail.

The moral of this story: If you want great detail and print quality, start out with enough image data.

The Inkjet Exception

There, on the side of the box that contains a shiny new inkjet printer, is a label proclaiming, "This printer capable of 1,200dpi!" Wow! That's a lot better than the 300dpi quality of my laser printer!

Well—it is, but it isn't.

Inkjet printers can reproduce a very tiny dot, much smaller than the dots that laser and dye sublimation printers can produce. Also, inkjet printers can move their inkjet heads in very fine increments. By using this technology, the inkjet printer can lay down many dots when printing. Instead of printing one dot for each pixel as a laser printer would, an inkjet printer can lay down two, three, or even four! That means your 300ppi file can be printed at 1,200dpi, because the printer lays down four dots for each pixel. The benefits to this can be finer detail and better color blending. Don't confuse this with interpolation, however. The printer is not making up information to go between the missing pixels. Instead, it is repeating the information it already has. That is, the printer is printing your 300dpi file at the same resolution, except it is using more dots to do it.

A high-end laser printer will produce as good an image at 300dpi as a 1,200dpi inkjet. A laser can produce a very tiny dot, but because of the way the toner is spread to the paper, the dot will appear to be bigger. Because the dots are bigger, they might overlap or blend into one another. This will render a natural color effect.

You will need to do a side-by-side comparison to decide which printer gives you the more pleasing result. It is almost like comparing apples to—well, more apples!—each printer has its pros and cons. It is very difficult to say that a 1,200dpi inkjet printer produces a better print as compared to a 300dpi color laser. But the point is that a 1,200dpi inkjet is not four times better than a 300dpi laser printer.

In any case, if you plan to use your printer at a high dpi resolution, be sure you are using good-quality paper. Also, remember that it takes a lot longer for your printer to cough up a print. You might want to proof your image out at a lower resolution before you go the high-resolution route.

How Big a File Do You Need?

With small and lower-end digital cameras, you will probably not run into the problem of having too large a file size. Again, whatever size you decide to make your print, the dimensions of the print and its resolution should match the printer's settings.

If your image *is* too big, however, your printer will throw away information—think of this as *reverse interpolation* or *downsizing*. You should make the image smaller before you ship it to your printer, but be sure you never resize the original image. Instead, copy it, and then resize the copy. You might find that you need to make a few "variations" of your print, depending on the printer and paper type.

If your printer gives its specifications in lpi (lines per inch) instead of dpi, fear not. To determine how much resolution you need, double the lpi required; the resulting number will be your dpi/ppi setting. For example, if your printer wants an image at 133 lpi, your image should be 266 ppi.

It's always a good idea to call a commercial printer and ask them at what line screen they will be printing. Line screen, "printer talk" for lpi, refers to the mask that is used by a printer when exposing the negative, which in turn will be used to make the printing plate. The lower the line screen, the "coarser" your image looks. The line screen is also determined by the type of paper you are using. A newsprint type of paper doesn't hold a lot of detail. A low lpi is used so that detail will not be "clogged" up as the ink soaks into the porous paper. Glossy paper holds detail much better because the ink won't soak into the paper as readily.

The Least You Need to Know

- Monitors display images at 72dpi. An image that has the same amount of pixels in it as the monitor can resolve will display at 100 percent.

- You need to have enough resolution in your images to print properly. A printer has a higher resolution than a monitor.

- The size of an image onscreen might differ from the size it prints out at, depending on the onscreen pixel ratio.

- Enlarge your image size to get a better reproduction.

Chapter 12

Learning Compression Helps Avoid Image Depression!

In This Chapter

- The lowdown on resolution and quality
- Learning the ins and outs of compression
- Clearing up confusing file types

To reduce storage size, your images can be *compressed*. Compressing images enables you to store more on your camera's and computer's hard drive, but unfortunately, compression might (and often does) destroy information.

Getting Quality Images

The best image quality that you can have is from a noncompressed original image (what I call a *straight* image). If image quality is important to you, you should try to find a way to get your images from your camera without compressing them. Unfortunately, many (if not all) mid- to low-end cameras don't give you the opportunity to download your information before it has been compressed. How, then, can you be sure you end up with the best possible image file—especially for those once-in-a-lifetime shots?

Well, it's confusing. Determining what the quality of your image will be requires an understanding of image size, resolution, *and* compression—and each camera manufacturer describes its options differently:

♦ **Image size/resolution.** Your camera might give you anywhere from two to five options on what size your finished image will be, usually presented in pixels (for example, 1,152×864 pixels, 640×480 pixels, and so on). The lower the *resolution*, the smaller the *file size* and, consequently, the less *compression* required. If you simply intend to put your images on a website, you don't need a lot of resolution. If you intend to print your images, select the highest resolution available.

♦ **Compression.** One would think (or at least I would) that the *quality* of the image would have to do with how much image information is available, but that's not what the manufacturers are talking about. Instead, your camera's quality setting represents how much the image is *compressed*. The more compression an image undergoes, the more quality is lost. If given the option, choose the highest quality possible.

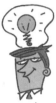

Say Cheese

You might think that taking a smaller image and compressing it only slightly would give you a better image than taking a larger image and compressing it a lot, but that's not true. The problem is that the smaller image has started out its life with less detail; the larger file, when uncompressed, still holds more resolution (it might, however, suffer from interpolation).

Some cameras do not give you the option to pick the resolution and compression rates; instead, you'll see Good, Bad, and Ugly settings, which determine the compression and resolution at the same time. The camera either shoots at a low resolution and compresses less, or shoots at a high resolution and compresses more! The only way to get a clue as to what's going on is to look at the final image size. For example, suppose you applied the Good setting to one copy of an image, and applied the Bad setting to another copy of the same image. If both the images end up the same size, then you know that the compression rate was varied. If the images end up sized differently, then you know that the resolution was changed. As you can see, this type of blind quality control is not the most desirable.

Lossy Versus Lossless Compression

Lossy and lossless might sound like Vegas streaks, but instead they refer to types of compression schemes:

♦ **Lossless compression.** A compression scheme in which no information is lost during compression or retrieval (also called *run-length encoding*).

◆ **Lossy compression.** A compression scheme that loses or throws away information in order to compress your file. Lossy compression relies on your brain and eye to "fill in" the information it threw away when you look at the file after it has been retrieved.

Lossless Compression

Instead of saving all the color information in your file pixel by pixel (which would offer no compression at all), lossless compression keeps track of the location of each pixel of color. For example, the compression process logs the color green, noting all the places in the photograph where that color is located, and then saves that information. So instead of saving 1,000 pixels of green, it saves 1 pixel of green and a directory of the locations in the photo where that color resides. This takes up a lot less space than saving each individual pixel and its location. When the file is uncompressed, the process happens in reverse. The compression scheme rebuilds the file using the colors it has stored and the directory that outlines where they should be located. There is very little visual difference between the original and the restored files. Because the "logging" process is not perfect, it cannot exactly reproduce the original file.

Using lossless compression is a safe way to save your files, but the drawback is that the compressed file doesn't end up being that much smaller than the original file.

Lossy Compression

Take a close look at any two objects that are adjacent to each other in a photograph—for example, a shiny red Porsche against a deep blue sky. Now look at the edge where the car ends and the sky begins. Notice how the pixels begin to *tween*, or blend from red to blue? This tween information is exactly the information that lossy compression software is going to chuck. It relies on your brain to detect where there should be tween information and to put it in for you when you look at the photo. One additional disadvantage of using lossy compression is that every time you resave an image, you lose even more information. Eventually, your image is going to look like a pile of mush.

The benefit of using lossy compression is that you can compress images to very small sizes. This aspect comes in especially handy when you are sending images via e-mail or posting them to a website (besides, website images usually are so small that most of the detail is lost anyway). The smaller size greatly speeds download time.

Archiving Programs

After a while, you will find your hard drive brimming with hundreds of images you just can't throw away. You will need to back up your hard drive onto portable disks, such as a floppy or zip disks. Simply copying files off your hard drive onto a disk is an easy and quick way to store images and files. The problem with this is that you will need many disks to back up all your files. What do you do?

Archiving programs are designed to help solve storage problems. These programs will help you store your files and keep track of them. The archiving program will compress your files, without losing any data, so you will use far fewer disks than if you were just copying them onto a disk. The programs will also keep track of your files creating catalogs or disk file directories. Some programs will simply compress your files and offer simple file directories. More elaborate programs will create backup logs and might offer file histories.

PKZip/WinZip

PKZip (used primarily on DOS platforms) and WinZip (used on Windows platforms), both of which can be found as shareware and as commercial programs, are lossless compression programs. PKZip and WinZip (found at www.winzip.com) can reduce image files about 20 to 30 percent; text documents (such as Word documents) and computer program files compress up to 60 percent.

In Plain Black & White

Shareware programs are developed by private individuals or small companies, usually to help fill the gaps left by large software companies. These programs are offered at a low cost or free, and are usually downloadable from user group bulletin boards or websites. If a fee is involved, it is usually small—$25 to $50—and generally goes to the programmer to help defray his costs in operating his website or developing the program code (although some shareware programmers derive their sole income from developing shareware programs).

Not only can PKZip and WinZip compress many files at the same time, they can *archive* the image files into one single file. You can usually tell when a file has been zipped, because it has the extension .zip in its filename (as in File.zip).

To restore an archived file back to its original form, run the file back through the zip program. Typically, you will use a program such as Un-Zip, or something similar sounding, to restore the file. Usually this requires little more than dragging and dropping the file onto the archiving programs icon. Zip files can also be archived as self-extracting archive (SEA) files, which do not require the use of the un-zip program to be unpacked. SEA files might be a bit larger than ZIP files, because they contain a small amount of computer code to run the extraction. SEA files are useful if the computer that is doing the unpacking does not have the zip program installed on it.

WinZip compressed these files with an average savings of 35 percent.

StuffIt

StuffIt, which is manufactured and sold by Aladdin (www.aladdinsys.com), also employs a lossless compression scheme; however, this scheme has been developed to work on Macintosh platforms (although Aladdin also provides an expander program for Windows platforms). StuffIt works similarly to PKZip and WinZip, except that files are compressed and labeled with an .sit (StuffIt) extension. StuffIt compresses an image file about 25 to 30 percent, and a document or code file up to 60 to 70 percent. In addition, StuffIt can archive many files into one group folder.

StuffIt also supports a self-extracting format, SEA; as mentioned previously, SEA files are larger than SIT files because they also contain the code needed to perform the extraction. Note: Because SEA files generated by StuffIt can be opened only on a Macintosh, it's a good idea to save your files as SIT files so that they can be read by both Macintosh and Windows machines (besides, the files will be smaller).

StuffIt saved 43 percent with lossless compression.

File Formats: Acrimonious Acronyms

So many file formats are available that it is often confusing to figure out what they all do. Some formats are specific to a program or manufacturer, although others indicate industry standards. We will look at only those formats that relate to pixel-based images.

Some formats are used to compress images, others are used to reduce color information, and still more have been developed specifically for web usage. Not every format can be read by every computer (some formats can be read by Macs only, and others only by PCs). Let's take a few minutes here to look at some important image formats.

JPEG

JPEG (short for Joint Photographic Experts Group and pronounced *jay-peg*) files are lossy compressed files. The JPEG format can be read by all computer platforms; because JPEG files are small in size and extremely portable, they are an excellent (and the pre-ferred) way to deliver images over the web.

When you save a file in your photo-editing software, you are given the option to save your file in the JPEG format. If you do, you are then asked how much compression you want applied; play around to find out how much compression you need. When you want to reopen the file (no matter what program you use), the image is automatically restored.

JPEG is the primary lossy compression format used.

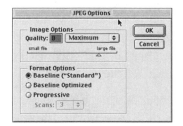

Say Cheese

For those of you who want to know the who, what, where, when, and how you took a picture, you're in luck! This data, which is called "metadata" is stored along with your image data in the JPEG EXIF (Exchangeable Image Format) format. Many higher-end consumer and professional cameras can store data in this format.

If your camera can write files in this format, a "Picture Information Extractor" software program will probably be bundled with the camera. If not, a quick search on the Internet will find you plenty of them.

This info can help you learn how your camera, or you, are making exposure decisions. It will also help you remember when you took them!

Save It Once!

I was walking my dog the other day and one of my companions stopped me and asked, "Hey Mister Photo Book Wizard (I prefer to be called "Smart Pants"), how come when I send picture to my friends via the Internet, they look grainy and all messed up?" After a quick thank you (the wizard part) I asked her how she was opening, editing, and saving her images to determine my answer.

To start with, her camera was saving the images in a lossy compressed format that she couldn't control. Then as she was editing them and resaving them, the images were again compressed. Additionally, her e-mail program was compressing them once again. It was a wonder that there were any original pixels left at all!

As her camera offered no control over compression (there's a reason to buy a camera that does), I suggested that she import the images directly off the storage media, then open them in PhotoDeluxe and then save the original image in a TIFF or PDD format and to keep using this format until she was done. Both of these formats offer lossless compression. After she was done editing she should save a copy of the file into a JPEG file with as little compression she could afford. This way she has already saved a few rounds of compression. I also suggested that she turn off the compression in her e-mail program and send the JPEG file she made.

This was a few extra steps more than she had intended on, but the image quality was greatly increased.

TIFF

TIFF, which stands for *Tagged Image File Format,* is one of the most universal formats for pixel-based images, and can be opened on Macintosh and Windows-based machines. Although TIFF uses a lossless compression scheme, TIFF files retain their original file size and offer no standard compression. TIFF images are not welcome on the web, because they are large, bulky, and slow to open.

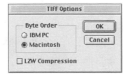

TIFF files must be saved in a byte order specific to the platform that will read them.

To compress a TIFF file, you must save it using the optional LZW compression scheme. However, most people do not take advantage of the LZW compression, because the compression it affords is minimal. (I once tried to use the LZW compression algorithm, and it took forever and a day to close the file. I don't know how long it took to open the file, because I got tired of waiting and opened the original file and threw out the LZW file.)

GIF

GIF, short for *Graphic Interchange Format*, was developed by CompuServe as a compressed graphic format. GIF files are still widely used on the web. Because the LZW compression algorithm, which is incorporated in the GIF format, was designed mainly to handle text formats, GIF files support only 8-bit color and best handle icons, text, and line drawings.

> ### Behind the Shutter
>
> Both Windows and Mac platforms save files differently from each other. They differ in how they order, or arrange, the data bits in a file. Using a platform-specific byte order is an efficient way to store data.

GIF files can be delivered over the Internet, and support interlaced graphics (which allow the image to be displayed partially as the web page downloads). An interlaced image file displays, for example, every eighth row or line of the image, and then fills in the other rows afterward. This way, the image can be seen quickly—although not in great detail until it is fully loaded. In addition, simple animation can be delivered via the web using animated GIFs, which consist of a batch of GIF files that are delivered "flip book" style.

EPS

EPS (*Encapsulated PostScript*) files can be huge, because they incorporate the PostScript language and the original file. *PostScript* was invented by Adobe as a language to tell printers how to print a file. A PostScript file tells any printer that supports the PostScript language how big a file is, which font or fonts it uses, and other information about the file. This enables the printer to print the file as it was intended to look.

EPS files contain a few lines of code in the *header* of the file that enables the images to be inserted into word-processing and other documents. This makes EPS files portable, but also large and slow to work with. This slowness is compounded by the fact that the image-processing program must process the PostScript instructions in addition to the image, which slows the computer down quite a bit. For these reasons, EPS files are not a great format for the web.

PDF

PDF (*Portable Document Format*) is a modern version of the EPS format. Like the EPS format, PDF contains instructions for the printing device such as font, size, and color descriptions. The PDF file is not a single file, but an entire document that contains page-layout, image, and color-management information.

Using PDF files is an excellent way to distribute large documents, especially over the Internet. Because PDF *readers* are freely distributed by Adobe and other companies, many software programs are being distributed with PDF manuals instead of actual printed instructions. This allows software developers (and anyone else who needs to distribute manuals) to save a lot of money by not printing and shipping books.

Many government organizations, corporations and even small businesses are increasingly relying on PDF as a reliable format to route important documents both internally and externally. The upshot being the professional sector is now incorporating PDF into their normal everyday operations.

To write a PDF file, you need a PDF *distiller* such as Adobe Acrobat, which allows the page layout to be *published* into PDF format. PDF files are very small, because many of the layout and type specifications are contained in code that *describes* the layout or file instead of containing the actual file.

FlashPIX

FlashPIX, developed by a group of software and imaging companies (including Kodak, Hewlett-Packard, Live Picture, Inc., and Microsoft), is another modern file format, and is excellent for the web. FlashPIX uses lossy compression to store the complete image and multiple lower-resolution versions of the file.

As the user calls for an image at a specific resolution, the FlashPIX format delivers the specific resolution to fill the section of the screen called for. Remember, when you enlarge an image, you will be filling the entire screen; you don't need to load file information into RAM that will not appear on the screen. If the user calls for a higher or lower resolution, that file is quickly *swapped* in. This allows for a very speedy change in onscreen resolution. Also, because only the information needed for the specific resolution is loaded into the computer's RAM, more RAM is left over for other duties. For example, instead of loading all 20MB of information for an image that requires only 100KB to display the image, FlashPIX enables you to download only the 100KB you need; thus, much less RAM is used. Also, a FlashPIX image can be downloaded into a web page at a low resolution, with a more detailed version of the image ready and waiting to be loaded into RAM if needed. This decreases the download time and increases image detail.

BMP

BMP files are a standard bitmap file format used by Windows. You will see these files associated with Windows programs. BMP files offer out-of-date compression schemes and do not resize well. Don't use the BMP format if you can avoid it.

PICT

PICT-formatted images, which work similarly to TIFF files, can be read only by Macintosh computer programs. PICT files are lossless, and can be compressed by programs such as StuffIt.

Because PICT files cannot be used on Windows or DOS machines, it is better to store files in the TIFF format if you can. If you find a Macintosh program that lets you save files in the PICT format only, you can reopen the file and resave it as a TIFF file.

So Many Choices!

If you are storing finished images and you are pressed for space, use the JPEG format. Make a copy of the original image and try a few different compression ratios until you find the right file size you need. Unfortunately, you can't predict the file size beforehand.

If you can afford the storage space, save your files in a lossless format such as StuffIt, PKZip, or WinZip. If you plan on storing a lot of images, it might pay to purchase a CD recorder and store your images on recordable CDs (CD-R). CD-R discs are inexpensive.

TIFF and PICT formats are great formats in which to store your images if you plan to do more work on them. They are lossless, but not compressed. They also open quickly. If you plan to store your images later, you can compress the files with StuffIt or PKZip. Your system determines which programs to use. TIFF files are the most universal, and are a safe bet. They can be opened on a Mac or *Wintel* machine.

> **Behind the Shutter**
>
> With some files, you see a .tif file extension instead of the .tiff extension, but fear not; these files are indeed TIFF files. In the old days, before Windows, DOS machines allowed only three-letter extensions, such as .tif, .doc, or .let.

If you have an image that will be placed on a website, JPEGs are the way to go. Also, if you plan to deliver your image via a modem and it will be viewed on a monitor only, go JPEG! JPEG files can be made very small and can also be *interlaced*, meaning that they will open on a web page at a low resolution at first, and then "fill in" their resolution as the remainder of the file is downloaded. The benefit is that the web viewer can get an idea (albeit a bit blurry) of what the image will look like, and not feel frustrated waiting (and looking at nothing) while the image downloads. If the viewer is not interested in the image, he can move on to something else. This speeds web pages along.

GIF files are an excellent format for logos, line art, and solid-color images. They are quick, can be compressed, and can be interlaced. Do not use a GIF format to save or deliver an image unless it is part of a logo.

The Least You Need to Know

- ◆ You can compress your files to save space.

- ◆ Lossless compression does not change the file; lossy compression throws away some information. The files will be changed in appearance.

- ◆ There are many file formats, some specific to each platform.

- ◆ Choosing the right format will preserve your image data and make it readable for other users.

Part 4

Let's See It: Imaging Techniques

You can manipulate exposure, shutter speed, and focal length to draw attention to your subject and add life to your images. Your point of view and use of lighting can create mood or just add detail to your subject. And when you download your images from your camera to your computer, you can enhance and manipulate your images in ways you've never dreamed!

Scratches, errant telephone wires, and missing teeth can be fixed. Perspective can be controlled, color can be enhanced, and images can be sharpened or blurred. You can combine elements from many photos to create a brave new world. Images that existed only in your imagination now can come to life on your screen and in print.

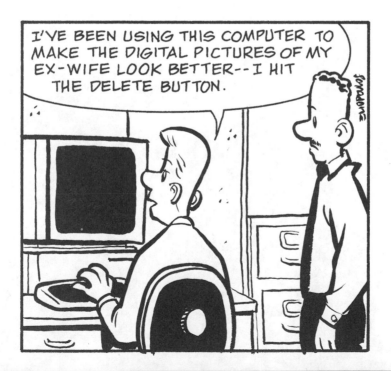

Chapter 13

Go Get It: Downloading Your Images

In This Chapter

- ◆ Download images via the manufacturer's software
- ◆ Download images using Photoshop Elements
- ◆ The fastest way: download images directly from a removable disk
- ◆ Getting images off CDs

You have been running around all day. Your pockets are brimming with hard drive cards, stuffed with wonderful images. Your friends are driving you crazy asking for prints. You have all these fancy and wonderful toys at your ready.

It would be impossible—not to mention boring—to cover the details of using each individual camera and software package on the market. Fortunately, in the process of reviewing cameras and software packages, I found many similarities in the ways cameras operate and the ways software is formatted—many programs work the same way, even though their interfaces look different.

If I happen to be demonstrating how to use the exact type of camera and software you are using, you're in luck. If, however, I am not using your specific setup, just try to understand the basics of what we're trying to accomplish, and apply it to your situation. When all else fails, read the instruction book that came with your camera. Believe it or not, some of the instructions actually work. Also, don't be afraid of making mistakes; you won't learn otherwise.

> **Flash**
>
> The demonstrations that follow do not in any way reflect an endorsement of any one product. I've picked software that I hope is readily available and will have a common interface and functionality. I've also tried to review software that I think will be fun to use and add enjoyment and creativity to your photographic experience. But as always, my advice to you is to get out there and experiment!

Hooking Up the Camera

Before you download images from your camera to your computer, no matter what type of software you are using, you must connect the two. Following is a general procedure for hooking up a camera; most cameras and cables work in the same way. Check your instruction manual before connecting any cable just to be safe.

1. Both USB and FireWire (IEEE-1394) were made with the express intent of using them while the devices are turned on or "hot." Although you could choose to turn off your computer and camera before connecting them, you could save yourself the trouble and time waiting for everything to reboot each time you plug in a new device.

2. If you're using an older Windows machine, find the serial port on the back of your computer. You might find one or two ports; they are labeled COM1 (port 1) and COM2 (port 2). Line up the serial connector on the cable, insert it into COM1, and tighten it down with the screws. Definitely think about adding a USB card if you have a slot available on your machine. Look on the back of your machine and if you find a "slot cover" still there you probably have room. On newer Windows machines look for the USB port, sometimes found on the keyboard, and attach the cables. If the USB ports are taken and you have several USB devices, get a USB hub! They are inexpensive and very useful. USB connections are goof proof!

Say Cheese

Don't shove a cable into a port. If it doesn't fit easily, be sure you have the right cable. Before you connect any cables, inspect them. Check to see whether your cable has any bent pins or foreign objects stuck in the connections.

If you're using a PowerMac or 68K series Macintosh, locate either the modem port or the printer port on the back of your Mac. You can connect to either port—your choice! If you are using a camera and G3, G4, or iMac just connect them using any USB port on the computer and the USB connection on the camera body. FireWire equipment is connected in a similar fashion.

3. Find the other end of your cable. Take a look at the pin setup, and check the sockets on the camera to help you align the cable properly. Gently insert the cable into the serial socket on the camera.

> **Behind the Shutter**
>
> One of the first computer hardware problems was actually caused by small insects living inside the machine!

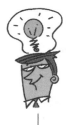

Say Cheese

Many times camera equipment and other peripherals do not connect and are not recognized by the computer as prescribed. If you are lucky you won't be the first user to find this disparity, more commonly called a bug. Take a trot over to the camera manufacturer's website and look for a newer version of the software driver or control panel. Download it, install it, and carry on.

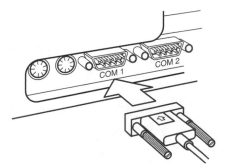

Connecting to a Windows machine is easy.

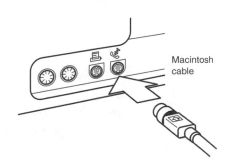

Connecting to a Macintosh is easier.

Downloading Via the Camera Manufacturer's Software

Every camera will have a different way to connect to the computer. Many will have more than one way to access the onboard photos. Camera manufacturers typically include their own proprietary software, or some variation or adaptation of canned software, that has been designed specifically to work only with their cameras. This software is called *OEM* (original equipment manufacturer) *software* (it might or might not have been developed by the manufacturer, but they like us to think it was, so we will). This does not include brand-specific software such as Adobe Photoshop Elements or Photoshop, although they also might have been supplied with your camera.

Before you start, be sure you have the correct version of software for your operating system. Nothing is more frustrating than trying to shove a square peg into a round hole! Also, and this is really important, *back up your hard drive* in case something goes awry during the process of loading new software. Follow the instructions in your software manual *exactly*. After you've finished backing up your machine, go ahead and install the software that came with your camera (refer to relevant documentation that came with the camera as needed).

I am using Image Expert, which is supplied with the Epson Photo PC 750Z. Image Expert allows users to preview images on the camera, to select certain images to be downloaded individually, and/or to download all the images at once. You can store your images in a photo album, and perform simple editing for color, contrast, and brightness.

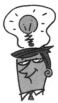

Say Cheese

Many software packages distributed with cameras work on both Windows and Macintosh machines; I have chosen to work with programs that work on both platforms, and that have only minor interface differences. I will note any important differences as we go.

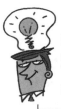

Say Cheese

If you are using Windows 95 or 98, you will see the Quick Tour Screen. Skip the tour for now, and close the window.

After your camera is hooked up to your computer, you can begin transferring images (assuming, of course, that you've already installed the downloading software, as mentioned earlier). Follow these steps to transfer images:

1. If you're using Windows 95, 98, ME, or 2000, click the **Start** button, choose **Programs,** select **Photo PC750Z,** and click **Image Expert.** For Windows XP click the **Start** button, choose **More Programs,** select **Photo PC750Z,** and click **Image Expert.**

   However, if you're using a Macintosh, find the Photo PC 750Z folder on your hard disk, double-click **Image Expert** to open the Image Expert folder, and then double-click the **Image Expert** icon.

2. You should see the window shown in the following figure. Click the **View Pictures in the Camera** button.

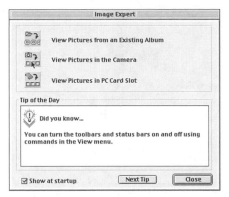

Click the View Picture button to start the downloading process.

3. A window displaying a "filmstrip" of your images appears, as shown here. Click **Get All** to transfer all the images to your hard drive; alternatively, click an individual image (or multiple images) to select it, and click **Get Selected** (the **Get All** button will change to **Get Selected** when only some of the images are selected).

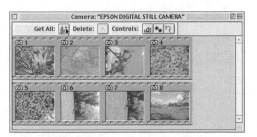

You can choose to download all your images by clicking "Get All" or by clicking on the individual images, select just a few.

4. After you choose your images, Image Expert automatically creates an album (folder) for your pictures with the current date as its name. You can change the title if you like by overwriting the title, or you can choose an existing album and add the images to it.

5. Click **Open** (**OK** on the Mac) to begin transferring your pictures; the progress of the transfer is indicated in the progress window that appears. Note: This might take a while. Go get a cup of coffee, walk the family pet, or visit with your family.

After you have chosen all your images, click OK to start downloading to your album.

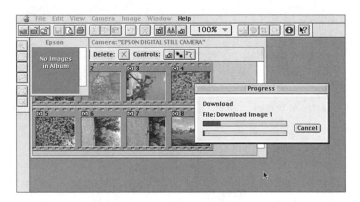

The progress bar can give you a good idea of how long it will take to download your images. This is a good time to take a stretch!

6. When the transfer is finished, close the filmstrip window.

7. A message appears asking whether you want to delete all the images on your camera. If you want to make room for more images, delete the images by clicking **Yes.** If you are a chicken like me, wait until you are sure they really exist on your computer by checking your directory!

Be sure your images have transferred to your computer before you delete them. Check your directory!

8. You can double-click an image to open it.

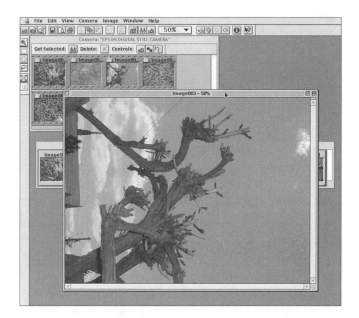

When you double-click on one of the images in the album, it will open on your screen.

9. I suggest you save a copy of the image before you begin to "play" with it, preferably using another name. This way, if you really mess up, you will have a backup of the original image. To save your image, just click the **Save** button. To save a duplicate of your image, open the File menu, choose Save As, and save the file with a different name such as Filename**copy.tif,** or Filename**2.tif.**

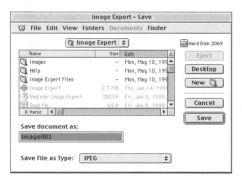

Before you start to make changes to your image, make a copy of it and then save it.

10. You might want to rotate the image using the drop-down menu or the **Rotate** menu button if you took your image in a "vertical" mode.

11. With the image still active or selected, open the **Image** menu and select **Corrections.** A screen appears that allows you to make various corrections to color, contrast, and the like. I won't go through these corrections here, but do note that the screen is split so that you can see the effects of the corrections before you apply them.

Color corrections and image enhancements can easily be made using the Image Corrections menu.

Downloading Via Image-Editing Software

As we discussed previously, many cameras come with their own software. These imaging programs, on average, do just enough to get by. They offer color correction, resizing, cropping, and the like, but with few options. If you want to do more with your images, you need to use different image-editing software.

Behind the Shutter

TWAIN drivers allow software, especially image-editing programs, to communicate directly with the camera, and are distributed with many cameras and scanners by their manufacturers. The TWAIN driver is installed into your imaging software when you install your camera software onto your system. A camera that can use a TWAIN driver is called *TWAIN compliant.* TWAIN drivers are written in a universal language and can be used by most computer platforms and operating systems (OS). You will almost always find the TWAIN access option in the *File* menu; depending on the imaging software, you need to select either *Acquire* or *Import* to download the image via the TWAIN driver (you might also have to pre-select the TWAIN device). You might not even realize you are using a TWAIN driver because many are transparent to the software you are using.

Adobe Photoshop Elements is one imaging program that is written for nonphoto professionals. It can handle all the basic photo imaging, and much more. I will be using Adobe Photoshop Elements for most of my demonstrations; it is widely distributed and bundled with some cameras at no cost. It works much like its big sibling, Adobe Photoshop, featuring many of the same options and features.

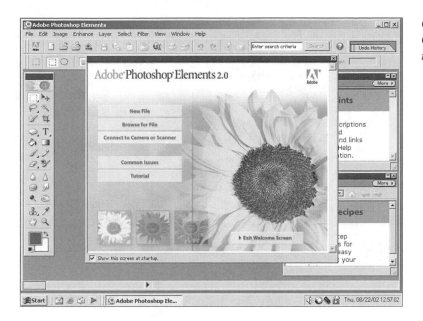

*Click on the **Connect to Camera or Scanner** button to begin to open your photo.*

Before you can download images using Adobe Photoshop Elements, you must first install it on your system. Read the instructions thoroughly before you start to install the program. As always, be sure to back up your hard drive before adding any software; you won't be sorry!

After Photoshop Elements is installed, you can get to work downloading images:

1. In Windows 95 or 98, open Photoshop Elements by clicking the **Start** button, choosing **Programs,** and then clicking **Adobe Photoshop Elements 2.0.**

   (Or use the icon that is on your desktop that was installed during the installation process.)

   On a Mac, double-click the **Adobe Photoshop Elements** folder in your hard drive window, and then click the **Adobe Photoshop Elements** icon.

2. Be sure your camera is connected to the computer and is turned on before proceeding if you're not using a USB connection.

   Click the **Connect to Camera or Scanner** button on the Welcome screen.

3. The "Select Import Source" dialog opens on your screen. Be sure your camera is connected to the computer and is turned on, and then select your camera's driver from the list.

4. When you click **OK,** the TWAIN driver for your device will open and start connecting to your camera.

The Pretec camera TWAIN software connecting to a DC620 digital camera.

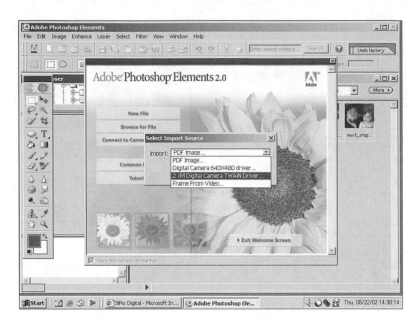

Flash

Remember: All TWAIN drivers are not alike. Each manufacturer builds its drivers a little differently from the rest. It's impossible to describe how to use every driver for how every camera works! It would take hundreds of extra pages to do that!

Most drivers follow a common course of action, but don't worry if your driver does not exactly follow my demonstration. Try to find buttons that perform similar tasks, and look for patterns in button operation. Use your intuition, follow your gut, experiment, and stay calm! You won't damage your software, camera, or files.

Say Cheese

The download interface, which is specific to your camera, allows you to access some or many of your camera's functions, possibly including the ability to adjust the camera's settings and defaults. The Pretec TWAIN driver is very simple and does not offer much in the way of options.

6. You now see the **Digital Camera 640×480 Driver** screen. Your driver display will likely look different. This one scans the camera that it is connected to and loads thumbnail images of everything stored in memory.

7. Click the **Select All** button or highlight individual images to select them, and then click the **Save to Folder** button.

8. Choose which folder you want to put the images in; you can create a new folder or use an existing one.

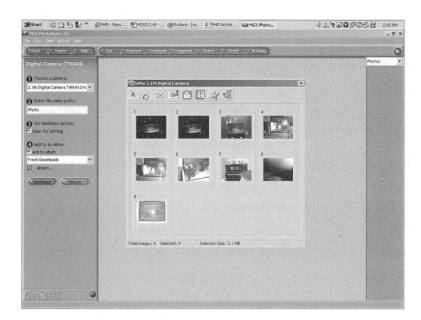

You can begin to acquire your images by clicking on individual image icons or the Select All button.

9. The software begins to download the images. This process can take a while. The Pretec DC620 is able to connect with a standard serial port or through a direct connection with USB. The USB option is far faster, but this camera requires a special cable that is not easy to find.

10. When the file transfer is done, click the **Close** button to exit the download interface and return to Photoshop Elements. You can now open your images and begin to manipulate or improve them.

The Fastest Way: Downloading Directly from Disk

You do not have to directly download from your camera. If you have a pocket full of smart disks or compact discs, you might want to use an adapter of some sort—such as a floppy disk adapter or an external hard drive. That way, you can download images to your computer while you continue shooting with your camera. (Obviously, you need to have at least two disks to work this way.) This is the fastest way to transfer images from your camera.

Many adapters are available for each type of removable storage disks. Some adapters are supplied by the camera manufacturers, and others are after-market devices. (Before you buy an adapter, be sure it will work with your system.) I use a reader, called the Iread by Ariston, on my Mac. This accepts a PCMCIA type card that can read both SmartMedia and Compact Flash. There are also PCMCIA type readers, which make an excellent choice for you laptop owners.

For this demonstration, I am using the FlashPath floppy disk adapter, which came with my Olympus 620 camera. This adapter allows you to download SmartMedia cards via the floppy drive. Just follow these steps:

1. Follow the manufacturer's instructions to hook up the adapter. Install the adapter software driver, which is supplied with the adapter, by following the supplied instructions for your platform. In this example, the software driver is named *Read FlashPath*—simple and descriptive! Remember, this demo is using my software settings, platform and product version. Your results may differ. Just follow along and follow my drift!

2. Open and start the software (click the **Start** button, choose **Programs,** and find the software in the list).

3. Open the **File** menu and choose **Import from FlashPath.**

4. You are asked to insert the adapter into your drive. Be sure the media card has been inserted in the adapter, and then insert the adapter into the drive.

Insert the FlashPath into your floppy drive when prompted to by the software driver, not before!

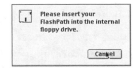

5. A screen appears that shows the name of your FlashPath card. (Don't be confused by a goofy filename that you don't recognize. The disk names are assigned during the disk-formatting process; you might or might not have a choice in naming the disks.) Click **Open.**

The FlashPath card might display a goofy name (which was assigned by the software). Don't worry about it here, just roll with it.

6. You should see a directory of all the image files on your card. If you want to select just one (or a few) file(s), select the image(s) and then click **Open.** Otherwise, click the **All Files** button.

All the images on your disk are shown on the directory at this point. Notice that they are all in the JPEG (JPG) format.

7. You are asked where you want to store the files on your hard drive; you can select an existing folder or create a new one. After you select your destination, click the **Select "FlashPath"** button.

I've selected the FlashPath folder to store my images. You could choose a different folder if you want.

8. The downloading process begins. Depending on how many files there are, you might want to find something to do to keep yourself entertained.

9. When the download is finished, the floppy adapter ejects. Go to the location on your hard drive and verify that your files are where you expect them to be. Congratulations!

The Least You Need to Know

◆ You can download your images by using the software supplied by the camera manufacturer.

◆ You can also download your images by using a TWAIN driver and your imaging software.

◆ The fastest way to download is by removing the storage card and downloading directly using an external card reader.

◆ FlashPath card adapters are great for older PCs that do not support USB.

◆ You can typically use your camera's TWAIN software to delete all of the images stored on your camera once you've downloaded them to your computer.

Improving Your Images

In This Chapter

- ◆ Getting started
- ◆ Reshape your image
- ◆ Resize your image
- ◆ Reorient your image
- ◆ Correct perspective of your image
- ◆ Understand brightness and contrast

One of the most important reasons to shoot pictures with a digital camera is the control it can give you over your images. You no longer have to settle for poor-quality photographs! With the use of imaging software, you can control and manipulate the color, contrast, size, and even the sharpness of your image. Of course, reality dictates that not all pictures can be fixed to perfection, but digital pictures make it much easier to try.

Getting Started ...

Before you get down to the business of improving your images, you should, of course, start Photoshop Elements (see Chapter 13 if you're not sure how), and either use the Welcome window's **Connect to Scanner or Camera**

Say Cheese _____

In many instances, Photoshop Elements's menus and controls are the same for Macintosh and Windows platforms. Note, however, that in certain instances, Macs use different keys from Windows to perform certain tasks. For example, Windows uses the Ctrl key and Macs use the Command key. Similarly, the Enter key on the PC keyboard performs the same function as the Mac's Return key.

button or, on the Menu bar choose **File** and select **Open** to open one of your own files. I'll use one of my own for illustration.

There are three main areas of Photoshop Elements you will use to improve your images:

- **Palette well.** An area which by default is in the top-right corner of Photoshop Elements where you can dock palettes when not in use. If it is not visible choose **Window, Shortcuts** from the Menu bar. The Palette well is shown near the right in the next figure.

- **Toolbox.** This holds tools for creating and editing images. If it is not visible choose **Window, Tools** from the Menu bar.

- **Menu bar.** Contains menus for enhancing and improving photos, particularly in the Image, Enhance, Layer, and Filter sections. The Menu bar should always be visible. It is a series of words near the program window starting with File, Edit, Image, etc. The Menu bar is the row of words shown in the next figure.

To learn more about these three areas choose **Help,** select **Photoshop Elements Help,** and click **Looking at the Work Area** (or push F1 instead of the first two steps). This will explain these three parts of Photoshop Elements Work Area. Clicking the link on how to use each part in the right frame of the help window will tell more about how to use each part and give a screenshot showing where the area is located.

The Menu bar and Palette well that appears at the top of the screen on the right side by default to dock any unopened palettes.

![Adobe Photoshop Elements menu bar showing File Edit Image Enhance Layer Select Filter View Window Help and toolbar below]

Say Cheese

When you open an image in Photoshop Elements, it typically retains the file format that the camera saved it in. In some situations it may, however, open the file in Photoshop .pdd format. PDD is Photoshop and Photoshop Elements's own native or proprietary format (most image editing programs will have their own proprietary formats, which are lossless and preserve editing features such as layers). It is very good practice when opening an image file to first open **File,** choose **Save As** from the Menu bar, and save a copy in PDD format before editing the image in Photoshop Elements. The original file remains untouched, and any changes you apply from here on out do not affect the original.

- ◆ After you apply a few effects to the image, you should save the file—but be sure you don't save it with the same name and file type as your original file, or you will copy over it.

- ◆ If you plan to work on your file during another Photoshop Elements session, leave it in the PDD format (because the PDD format might or might not be readable by other programs).

- ◆ If you plan to store or open the image file in another program, save the file in a nonproprietary format, such as TIFF. (If you want to archive the image, you can choose a high-value JPEG 2000, which is lossless, or compress the file in WinZip or StuffIt.)

- ◆ Note that instead of using the Save command to save your image in a different file format, Photoshop Elements requires you to either use File, Save As or Save for Web from the Menu bar. A dialog box then appears that enables you to name the file and save it in a number of common formats.

Shaping Your Image

You can, within reason, increase the size of your images. If you resize too much, the image will start to degrade. In most cases, you can increase the size of your image 150 to 200 percent and still retain good detail.

But why would you want to enlarge your image? Suppose you took a picture and just couldn't get close enough. Or you took a photo and you cropped the image down to make a nice composition. You can then take the image and increase the size so you can see the detail. Another good reason to increase the size of your images might be to use all those 8×10 frames your friends keep bringing over to the house (hint, hint!).

There are a few ways to resize your images, which we'll discuss as follows. The important thing to remember, and this is a constant through Photoshop Elements, is that there are many ways to obtain the same results. You can resize your image and change the proportions of the image (Free Resize) or resize the image and keep the proportions frozen (Resize). Choose your options and have fun. If you save your images before you start a resize operation, you can have fun and experiment without worry.

Free Resize

The Free Resize feature allows you to resize an image and change its proportions at the same time.

To use the Free Resize feature, do the following:

1. Open the **Image** menu, choose **Transform,** and select **Free Transform.**

2. You may be prompted to make your background a layer at this time because most transformations apply to layers, click **OK** and proceed. Because your photo has only one layer at present this presents no problem.

3. Small corner markers, or handles, appear in the corners and at the midpoint of the sides of your image. Use the midpoint handle to change the image proportions.

4. When you move your cursor over these handles, the cursor changes into a double arrow. Drag the cursor, and the image handles follow.

5. Click the checkmark in the Options bar; the image's size and proportions are altered. If you want to dump the changes in the trash and retain your original size, click the hashed circle instead. Note that you can use the undo feature after resizing to revert as well.

This you'll like. If you want to make your image larger than what you can see on the screen, you are in luck. I often get frustrated when working on a small monitor and want to make the image bigger but run out of monitor real estate. It is tough to drag the resize handle when you bump up against the edges of the monitor. Here is a good solution: Reduce the size of your image on the screen by zooming out the image. Zooming out is something like taking a step back from your work to get a better overall view. It doesn't change the actual size of your image file. Click the **Zoom Tool** icon in the Toolbox (or press "Z"), hold the **Alt** key down and left click the image. Note that the mouse pointer changes to a magnifying glass and that the "+" changes to a "-" when ALT is pressed. Clicking the image without the Alt key depressed will reverse the process. Alternatively to using this method, you can use the **View, Zoom Out** selection on the Menu bar or it's keyboard shortcut—hold down **Control** and press the "-" key. To reverse the process use **Control** and the "+" key (or "=" key, as it is not necessary to involve the shift key in this move).

CAUTION

Flash

Anytime you make a change to an image in Photoshop Elements (or just about any other pixel-based, image-processing program), you are remapping the pixels in the image. That is, you are changing the position (or color, or whatever) of the pixels. Each time the pixels are remapped, your software is interpolating—the fancy word for guessing—where the pixels should go and what their values should be. Repeatedly remapping the pixels in an image can make the image look terrible!

One way to avoid ending up with terrible images is to always work on a copy of the original image instead of the original itself. That way, if things fall apart, you can always cut your losses and start over with a new copy. Secondly, learn to use the **Undo** button (or its keyboard shortcut, **Ctrl+Z** on a PC or **Command+Z** on a Mac). Using this shortcut enables you to undo your most recent changes to the image. Finally, if you like the changes you've made to your image, save the image before you make a mistake! That way, you won't have to start all over if you mess up or do something you don't like. Many professionals save progressive copies as they work every few steps adding a number the end of the file name, such as myfile1.pdd, myfile2.pdd, etc., so they can revert one

Photo Size

As you can see in the following figure, there is an even more exact way to resize a photo. With the Image Size feature, you can resize an image to exactly the size you want. The Image Size feature is in the **Image** menu under the **Resize** item. You will get a submenu in which you will be presented with your options.

Notice that, when the **Proportions** check box in the **Constrain** area is checked, you can resize your image while retaining its proportions (notice also that the Width and Height entries are tied together as represented by the bracket connecting them). If you check the **File Size** check box in the **Constrain** area, the **Resolution** field is also tied in—meaning that when you change the dimensions of the image, the resolution (dpi) increases or decreases accordingly (the file size doesn't change).

Use the Image Size dialog box to get precise image dimensions.

Canvas Size

If you need to add more area to your image without increasing the picture itself, use the Canvas Size feature. To use this feature, open the **Image** menu, select **Resize,** and choose **Canvas Size.** You will see a dialog box such as the one shown here. The square in the center represents your image as it exists now; type in new dimensions to increase the area consumed by your image. By default your image will be centered on the newly expanded canvas, but if you need to add area only to one side or just to the top or bottom of your image, this is the place to do it. Place your cursor on one of the arrows surrounding the white square (which represents the existing image) in the middle of the **Anchor** area and click on an arrow to one side or the other. When you add canvas area after adjusting the **Anchor** grid, the new canvas is added to the side, top, or bottom, depending on your choice(s).

The Canvas Size dialog box lets you add image area around your photo.

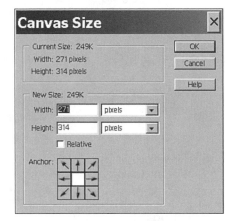

The Canvas Size dialog box can also be used to reduce the canvas area of an image. If you need to make your image a precise size, type those dimensions into the dimension fields. The image is equally trimmed on all sides. If you want to trim your image on one side only, you can move the square in the **Anchor** area accordingly. Type your dimensions in the fields as before, and click **OK.** You are warned that the canvas size is smaller than your image; if you're sure you want to proceed, click **Proceed** and the resize takes place.

Orientation

If you take an image with your camera in the vertical position, your image opens on its side. To rotate your image, go to the Image menu, choose **Rotate,** and select any one of the several options. Note that the second set of options that contain the extra word *layer* only work when a layer is selected.

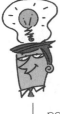

Say Cheese _____

Like its more advanced sibling, Photoshop, Elements can work with layers to achieve more complex image effects. To imagine how this works picture a trio of overhead transparencies that each have a painted image on them. Now stack them. If you were to re-orient one of the "layers" you would only rotate it and not the other layers. With our example, imagine turning the middle sheet on its side without moving the other pages.

You can also flip an image along its axis by choosing **Flip Horizontal** or **Flip Vertical.** This concept has always confused me, so let me try to explain: Imagine an axis drawn though the image from right to left and top to bottom. When you flip an image horizontally, the image flips at the midpoint of the horizontal axis; flipping vertically works the same way except that it flips at the midpoint of the vertical axis. The best way to see what will happen is to open an image and experiment.

If you need to tweak your image just a bit to straighten it up, or you want to rotate it other than 90°, choose under **Image** (on the Menu bar), select **Rotate,** and click **Free Rotate Layer.** If you have not worked on this image before, you will be asked if you want to make it a layer. Go ahead and do so. Handles appear in the corners of the image. Using your cursor to drag and drop these handles, you can freely rotate the image any way you want. By the way, if you click your cursor inside the image and grab one of the handles on the edge of the image, you can move the image as if you were using the Free Resize tool and the rotate tool. This comes in handy if you need to resize *and* rotate an image.

You may have also noticed the **Straighten** and **Straighten and Crop** options under Image, Rotate on the Menu bar. The Straighten function is generally used for images brought into your computer by a scanner that are a few degrees off and it "fixes" images by guessing. If you attempt to apply it to a regular image, it will just make it look weirdly off kilter.

Crop

Many times, your image might size out to be just a bit wider than you would like. For example, it might be 5×7½; and that might be a bit tough to shoehorn into a 5×7 picture frame. You also might find that just on the edge of your image is some unwanted element, like a part of someone's head or a wall. Cropping the photo is a great way to solve these problems.

To reshape or crop your image, do the following:

1. Choose **Window,** select **Tools,** and click the Marquee tool, which is the top left tool in the Toolbox. Alternately, you may press "**M**" on your keyboard. There are several different Marquee selection tools. Choose the **rectangle.**

2. Left click your image and drag a box around the area that you want the image to be cropped down to. Anything outside of the marquee selection box will be deleted.

3. Choose **Image,** select the **Crop** command, and voilà!, your image is trimmed.

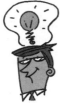

Say Cheese

There are many options for the Marquee Tool. When you press "M" or select the Marquee tool by clicking it the tool Options bar appears. You can select either the elliptical or rectangle shape for your selection by clicking on the correct shape toward the left of the Options bar. There are four choices on the Options bar to the right of that and you should select the left most of those. If you do not set Feather to zero pixels, you will get a selection bigger than your selected marquee area. Last you want the style to be normal. You can achieve all of these settings by clicking the very left most button on the Options bar and choosing Reset Tool.

Correction of Photos

Sometimes photos will not appear normal because of the angle at which they were taken. There are several tools contained in Photoshop Elements to fix these perceptual deficiencies including the Perspective and Distort features.

Perspective

The Perspective feature is a great tool to fix up images that have ungainly or incorrect perspectives. For example, if you photograph a tall building, the top of the building will look a lot smaller than the bottom. Also, the sides of the building will slope in toward the top. This is called *keystoning*. The Perspective feature can help you fix or control this effect.

The Perspective feature is found in the Size menu because it is a form of resizing. You are actually resizing the top of the image while the base stays "anchored." You will notice that, if you were to pull the left-side perspective handle, the right-side handle will mirror the action (and vice versa). Check out the following demo to get a good idea of how this operation works.

To use Photoshop Elements's Perspective feature, find a picture of a tall building or a square object to assist in better understanding of how this procedure works):

1. Open your tall/square image in Photoshop Elements. If you are using a tall building picture taken from ground level you should notice that the top appears narrow compared to the bottom because of the keystoning effect. If the image is too large to view in it's entirety, zoom out using Control and the "-" key.

2. Expand the canvas by choosing **Image** on the Menu bar, selecting, **Resize,** and clicking **Canvas Size** to allow extra working room (you will be stretching the top of the image).

3. Open the **Image** menu, choose **Transform,** and select **Perspective.** Handles appear in the corners of the image.

4. Grab the handle in the upper-right corner and pull it toward the right (see the following figure). You can pull the handles onto the unused portion of the Photoshop Elements desktop if you go beyond the canvas.

5. Release your mouse button. After a moment, the image's perspective is altered.

6. Undo your change; try pulling the handles again, but this time pull to the right and up. (You might have to go through this a few times until you find the correction effect you like.)

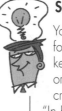

Say Cheese _____

You might want to create a folder on your hard disk to keep all of your demo images or works in progress. I usually create a folder and name it "In Progress" for this purpose.

7. When you get it the way you want it crop the image using the Rectangle Marquee tool found in the Toolbox as explained under cropping earlier in this chapter.

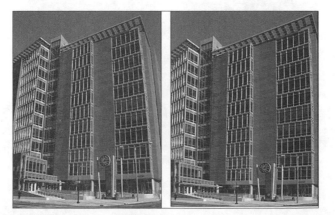

The Perspective feature can really change your perspective as shown in the before (left) and after (right) here!

Distort

Using Photoshop Elements's Distort feature is a great way to correct an image that might not have been photographed "in square." If your camera was not perpendicular to a building or a product package, for example, one side of the building or box would slope toward the top more than the other. This can make an image look a bit strange. You can also use this technique to correct the perspective more to one side of the image than to the other side. Additionally, you can fill in with a color tone the white space that is created when you distort your image, or you can clone in some of the sky from the original image. (Usually, you end up cropping a portion of the newly distorted image and pasting it into another image; more about all that later on.)

Again, this feature is found in the Image menu under Transform. Think of it as resizing one side of the image more than the other.

To use Photoshop Elements's Distort feature, do the following:

1. With any image open in Photoshop Elements, choose **Image,** select **Transform,** and click **Distort.**

2. You will see the now-familiar handles. Grab the handle in the upper-left corner and pull it halfway down and toward the center of the image.

3. Grab the handle in the lower-left corner, and pull it halfway up and toward the center of the image.

4. Let the image process, and voilà! It should look something like the following figure and it is distorted.

The Distortion feature lets you get carried away.

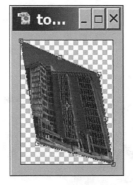

From Darkness to Light

Many times, your images might not come out exactly as you intended. They may come out a bit too dark or flat-looking (lacking contrast). The following features are the perfect tools to help fix up your images and make them sparkle.

Quick Fix

Using the Quick Fix feature is a quick-and-easy way to correct the contrast and brightness of your image. To use this feature, do the following:

1. Open a picture which lacks contrast, maybe a rainy day photo or something with a bleak look.

2. Open the **Enhance** menu and choose **Quick Fix** from the Menu bar.

3. Select any one of the items in the first list, leave the **Auto** item selected in the second list, and click **Apply.** Quick Fix tries to make the image look its best based on the colors and values already present.

   If the results are unsatisfactory, click the **Reset Image** button and move through the options again. This time try adjusting the values manually while watching the Before and After images to see how the changes are shaping up.

4. If you like your changes, click **OK** and the modifications are saved to the image (you can still use the Undo function to go back). Otherwise, click **Cancel.**

Wasn't that easy? Open up a few more images and try this a few more times to get the hang of it. If you're in a real hurry, you can use the Auto Levels, Auto Contrast, and Auto Color Correction tools located just under the Quick Fix item. These have no options and their changes appear immediately, but they can work well on occasion. Give them a try. Going back is only a matter of an Undo.

Brightness/Contrast

If you want your images to be brighter or darker, you can use Photoshop Elements's Brightness/Contrast option:

1. Open the **Enhance** menu and choose **Adjust Brightness/Contrast >**
   Brightness/Contrast dialog box as shown in the following figure.

2. Be sure the **Preview** check box is checked; that way, you'll be able to view your changes onscreen as you make them.

Say Cheese _____

Many times, the dialog box or palette you need to use displays on the screen on top of your image, covering up a section of the image you want to see. To move it, click the dialog box's title bar, hold down the mouse button, and drag the dialog box anywhere on the screen you want.

3. Drag the **Brightness** slider to the right until the field to the right of the slider reads **+30.** (Alternatively, you can type 30 in the number field to avoid using the slider.) The image brightens up nicely.

4. Drag the **Contrast** slider to the right to increase the contrast; the image becomes a little more "zippy" (again, you can type in the number field to avoid using the slider).

5. When you're satisfied with the image, click **OK.**

Brightness and contrast are the first tools to use to fix up your image quality.

Brightness/Contrast ✕

Brightness: 0   OK

Cancel

Contrast: 0   Help

☑ Preview

The Least You Need to Know

◆ One major benefit of digital photography is that it gives you control over your images. You can easily resize them or correct errors in perspective.

◆ If you want to add canvas around a picture or crop unnecessary portions of an image you can easily do so.

◆ You no longer have to suffer with drugstore prints that are too dark or the wrong color; you can adjust brightness and contrast.

◆ Always work on a copy of your image rather than the original.

The Wonderful World of Color

In This Chapter

◆ Use image color controls

◆ Learn about color modes

◆ Discover bit depth

◆ Control image sharpness, blur, and noise

Of all the changes and edits that can be made to a digital photo, the most important and most obvious are color corrections. These corrections make the image come alive. Nothing can be more off putting than incorrect or out of balance color. Take your time and edit your images carefully. With a little bit of practice you will be able to make your corrections quickly and with an expert's eye.

Viva Color!

Color controls can help you make your image really come to life. You can make minor corrections or huge shifts. Always remember not to get too greedy with color. What may look fantastically vivid and lush on your monitor will look like mud on your printer. Your monitor is going to display color in a way that your printer can't reproduce, and vice versa. Professional graphic artists use specialized equipment that costs thousands of dollars to get their special monitors to match with their super expensive printers. You can also calibrate your monitor. Read **Setting Up Photoshop Elements, Calibrating your Monitor** under Photoshop Elements **Help.** Still, the best thing you can do is follow your "inner eye" and experiment! Use inexpensive paper to test your selections on, and when colors and shadows look good, then you can use the photo paper.

Color Balance

There might be times when the color of your image is off a bit. For example, something might be reflecting color into your photograph (a brightly colored wall will add a *color cast* into your shot). If you refer back to the color temperature chart in Chapter 10, you can see that the lighting conditions also affect the true color of the image. Luckily, you're in control! You can easily adjust the color balance of your image:

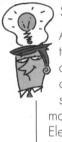

Say Cheese

After you have read Chapter 16, come back to this demonstration. Isolate just part of an image, and repeat the steps. You will begin to see how many of the tools in Photoshop Elements can be used together.

Say Cheese

You can do Color Cast Correction for an entire image, a layer or just part of a layer by selecting it. This is a very powerful feature, but it takes some practice. Be sure when picking a gray to pick a neutral, essentially half way between black and white if possible.

1. Open an image you have that has a color cast to it.

2. On the **Menu bar** choose **Enhance,** select **Adjust Color,** and click **Color Cast** to view a dialog box such as the one shown in the following figure.

3. Be sure the **Preview** check box is checked.

4. As instructed by the dialog box, click any area in the photograph that was supposed to be white, black, or gray. Go ahead and click around the image to see what colors it will change to. You can always click Reset to get back to the original.

5. When you're satisfied with the image, click **OK** and save.

The Color Cast Correction Dialog is pretty foolproof. Just do as it says.

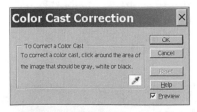

Hue/Saturation and Lightness

Hue (sometimes referred to as color) refers to *where* a color appears on those color triangles I showed you in Chapter 2. Saturation, on the other hand, refers to *how much* of a hue or color is present, or how intense a color is. Both the hue and saturation of an image can be manipulated, as can the lightness of an image:

1. With a photograph image open on your Photoshop Elements work surface, open the **Enhance** menu and select the **Adjust Color** item from the Menu bar. Choose **Hue/Saturation** to open the Hue/Saturation dialog box.

You can adjust hue (which represents a move around the color wheel), saturation (which represents a move across the radius of the color wheel toward the opposite side) or lightness with the Hue/Saturation dialog box.

2. If anything is selected, deselect it with **Select, Deselect** on the Menu bar or **Ctrl+D/Command+D** and be sure the **Preview** check box is checked in the dialog box.

3. With the Edit drop down box in the **Hue/Saturation** dialog set to **Master,** move the **Hue** slider either to the left or the right. Notice how the hue (color) of the image changes? If you move the slider a bit to the right, you change the hue of the image from blue toward pink. Check out how the other parts of the image change hue, also—you'll be able to avoid altering the hue of your entire image after you finish reading Chapter 16, so don't fret.

4. Fiddle with the **Saturation** slider (if you really want to have some fun, slide it all the way to the right). If an image has been captured with diffused (soft) light, "upping" the saturation can liven it up.

> ### Behind the Shutter
>
> Changing one color affects its opposite color (see the color chart in Chapter 2 to refresh your memory about color opposites). Adding more blue to an image is the same thing as taking yellow out of the image. Similarly, taking magenta out of an image is the same as adding more green.

5. Play around with the **Lightness** slider; notice that doing so produces an effect similar to adding white to the entire image (or black, if you move the slider to the left). Note that adding lightness adversely affects the contrast of your image, which is probably why I honestly can't remember using the **Lightness** feature more than once or twice in my entire career. Nonetheless, check the control out and put it in the bottom of your bag of tricks.

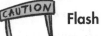

> **Flash**
>
> Color shifts must be done carefully. Don't overcorrect your image. Unless you isolate areas in your image by selecting them (covered in the next chapter), your color correction globally affects your image. Although having wonderfully green leaves is great, do you really want to add green to all the other colors?

6. If you like the result, save your image. If you don't like it, hold down the control key and a reset button magically appears in the Hue/Saturation dialog box in place of the Cancel button. This allows you to restart without having to close the dialog box.

Anybody looks goofy if you use too much color! Good color saturation makes your images come to life—but don't go crazy!

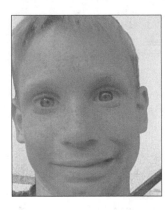

Adjusting color in this fashion actually changes the pixels in the image. Of course you saved a working copy so you could always back up to the original, but you would also loose all other changes you might have made. A better method is to add an adjustment layer and adjust the hue/saturation/lightness on the adjustment layer. By doing this you can later discard just this layer and retain other adjustments, additions and changes to your image. Adjustment layers are special layers because they affect every layer below them. To use an adjustment layer:

1. With an image open and the Layer palette open from the Palette well select the topmost layer you wish to adjust.

2. Click the New Fill or Adjustment Layer button (which looks like a circle with the top left half darker than the bottom right half) on the Layer palette and choose the Hue/Saturation adjustment type (which is probably the sixth choice from the top of the menu that appears).

3. Now you will be back at the Hue/Saturation dialog box where you can make changes to the appearance of your image. Note however that the changes you make are done by a special layer that has been inserted in the Layer stack.

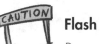

Use the Adjustment Layer icon (see the pointer in the figure) to reveal a special menu. You can then make adjustments to hue/ saturation/lightness by means of a layer that can be removed later if you wish to undo the modification without affect- ing other enhancements to your image.

Variations

The Variations feature is a great tool. It is a quick way to apply a variety of color cor- rections and hue/saturation mixes to an image. Instead of working through each dialog and going back and forth to get the desired result, you can test your adjustments here and only commit to them when you like the outcome. Here's what you do:

1. With the image that you want to correct on your desktop, open the **Enhance** menu on the Menu bar, select **Adjust Color,** and choose **Color Variations** to open a screen with multiple small views of the image, as shown in the next fig- ure. The adjustments are separated by type. You can change them by clicking on the radio buttons marked Midtones, Shadows, Highlights, and Saturation.

2. Click the variation you like best; Photoshop Elements moves the image you chose to the center spot, and gener- ates even more variations based on the image you chose (the images in this round have finer changes and smaller variations in relation to one another). Continue choosing variations until you either go crazy or find one you like.

Flash

Be careful not to over- saturate an image. When an image is oversaturated, it might lose detail. And although a very saturated image might look great onscreen, it may look terrible on paper.

3. Reset the image as needed to work through various changes. Each click adds to the overall modification, so be frugal with your clicks. If you make one extra click, you can use the Undo button instead of having to start from scratch.

4. When you find the variation that you want to use, click **OK.** Your image will appear as your selection.

The Variations feature is useful if you have little time to correct an image, but you have to know when to stop!

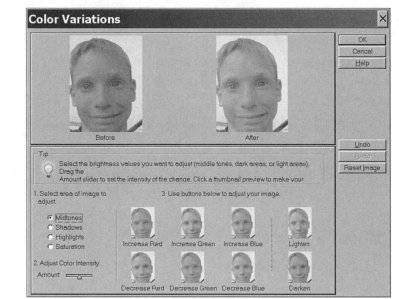

Negative

Open the **Image** menu on the Menu bar, select **Adjustments,** and choose **Invert** to make your image look like a photo negative. I use this control a lot in my commercial work to add interest, especially in faded backgrounds. You might consider this tool a gadget!

Other Color Worlds

Color can be described in many ways; one way to characterize color is to call it a *mode* (not *à la mode*). The most common color mode is the RGB (red, green, blue), though Photoshop Elements offers Grayscale, Bitmap, and Indexed color as well. Other commercial imaging programs, such as Photoshop, can handle color in various other modes—such as CMYK, LAB, and HSB, which allow the color to be manipulated or printed in different ways.

RGB

RGB is the most commonly found color world, or *color space*. We use this model because these are the colors our eyes and brain see and process. When you look around, these are the *spectra* of light commonly found—for example, you typically find blue skies, green leaves, and red berries. If there is no light—such as at night—you see no color; it is only when you add light, such as at dawn, that color becomes visible. This color model uses a process called *additive color*. (There is no color unless it is added.) Your computer monitor works using this process—it starts out with a dark screen until light, provided by glowing phosphors, gives the screen color.

Behind the Shutter

This way of describing color is linear, or one-dimensional. When you add brightness or **tone** to a hue, however, you bring your color into a dimensional space! For example, imagine the color red placed on the base of this space—call this the X-axis. If you add white, or light, to red, it becomes pink; the pink, or brightness, can be described as being on the Y-axis (this axis can be thought of as vertical, if you want). If you move or blend colors and brightness, you will be moving along a lateral, or Z-axis.

This is not intended to be a technical explanation of color theory, but rather to show you the dimensionality of color. Many color models use spheres, pyramids, or cubes to describe the color space. (And you thought you would never use all that high school algebra!)

Under this model, colors in a spectrum change from one hue to another (you are probably familiar with color gradually shifting from red to orange to yellow to green, and so on around the color spectrum). Different combinations of red, green, and blue produce different colors. For example, you can combine red and blue, without green, to get purple. When red, green, and blue light combine at their fullest, white light is produced.

Bitmap Mode

In this color scheme, colors are either on or off, hence black or white. While it is supported in Photoshop Elements, it will seldom be used because grayscale produces much smoother transitions from black to white and thus better images.

CMYK

If you start out with a nice bright piece of white paper, it is as if you are starting with totally *on* or fully reflecting light. You cannot add any more light or color to a piece of paper that is white. You can, however, cover up, or *subtract* from, the paper to produce color. This process is called *subtractive color*, and is used by the CMYK color model. With the CMYK model, which is used in color printing, cyan, magenta, yellow, and black are used in separate layers to produce color on a press. Many desktop printers use this same method of color reproduction.

You will notice this if you refer to the color model in Chapter 2. It's of a Three-Color World (RGB) in which cyan, magenta, and yellow are opposite red, green, and blue, respectively. You also saw these colors interact in the color adjustment controls. Although cyan, magenta, and yellow *are* primary colors, they do not produce black when added together (remember, *black* is the absence of all color). It is only when black (*K*) is added to the CMY model that you can reproduce black and darken other colors.

When you print an RGB image, your image is *separated* into CMYK on-the-fly. Depending on your setup, this might be done by the image-processing software or by the printer itself.

In Plain Black & White _____

The **gamut** of a color world refers to how many colors the color world or device representing that world can reproduce. The RGB color world has a broad color gamut; if, however, you were to reproduce the image on your screen using a CMYK device, you would probably be disappointed by how many colors cannot be reproduced. The color gamut of the CMYK model and CMYK devices is much smaller than for an RGB device. I will get into this in more detail when we talk about printing in Part 5.

LAB

LAB color is a descriptive model based on a consistent set of references. In other words, the LAB color space takes the color-reproducing device (monitor or printer) out of the color equation. If the color can be described independently of the reproduction device, the consistency of the color can be preserved. It is explained in detail in Chapter 22 when we discuss calibration of monitors and printers.

HSB

The HSB model describes color based on hue (the wavelength, or color), saturation (how much of the color is present), and brightness (how much light is present). You may use the HSB model in the Hue/Saturation dialog box and in the Color Picker dialog box, but the images themselves are not in HSB in Photoshop Elements.

Grayscale

The grayscale color mode uses 256 shades of gray, from black to white, to represent color. You can also think of it as representing a percentage of black ink coverage in printed media. No black ink coverage is white and complete ink coverage is black—and the rest is in the middle. You should be familiar with this color mode, because it represents all black-and-white reproduced images. Your imaging software determines which colors are represented by which shade of gray.

Indexed Color

With indexed color the image is reduced to 256 colors. If a color is not on this index, then the program must estimate to the closest color. It also sometimes creates an intermediate color by placing two or more indexed colors in a pattern of alternating pixels. This fools your eye into seeing a color between the two because your eye works to blend the neighboring pixels together. Blending several colors that appear to the eye as another color is called dithering. Indexed color is usually not used when an image is in production because among other problems it doesn't allow you to work with layers, but it is a great mode to use for line art like simple logos or buttons that contain only a few colors. When you save an image in png-8 or gif format, it is reduced to indexed color mode at the time of saving.

To reduce the amount of color in an image, which often translates to a drop in file size, colors can be reindexed or remapped. This comes in handy when you want to place an image on a website, where the size of an image is crucial to its speed of transmission. If you are interested in Indexing color and other advanced functions of digital imaging, you might be interested in *The Complete Idiot's Guide to Adobe Photoshop 6*. Photoshop Elements is more of an introduction version of Photoshop itself. What you learn in Elements translates almost perfectly to Photoshop.

What Is Bit Depth?

Remember that your camera or scanner, both of which are RGB devices, can capture color information on all three layers. If your camera is capable of 8-bit color per channel, it can reproduce 24 bits of color for each pixel (8 bits of information from each of three layers of RGB color). In the following table you see that your camera can describe more than 16,000,000 colors. That's rich!

Bit Depth and the Number of Available Colors

Bit Depth	Binary	Number of Colors
1	2^1	2
2	2^2	4
3	2^3	8
4	2^4	16
5	2^5	32
6	2^6	64
7	2^7	128
8	2^8	256
16	2^{16}	32,768 (enough?)
24	2^{24}	16,777,216 (so they say)
32	2^{32}	Billions and billions!

Behind the Shutter

Your computer presents information in binary digits or bits. Binary code presents data in ones and zeros, or off and on. Color can also be presented as binary information, with black an off bit and white an on bit. The bit depth I just described is one bit deep (you are dealing with only one bit, either off or on); in binary, this is represented as two to the first power.

Let's expand your color world and use two bits. You can describe each bit as being either off or on, representing four colors; that makes your bit depth two deep, or two to the second power. Each time you increase your bit depth (which increases exponentially), you double the number of available colors. Take a look at the following table to get an idea how increased bit depth enables you to reproduce color.

You might see a camera or scanner described as being able to capture color in 12-, 14-, or even 16-bit color. This is wonderful, except you have one small problem: Your printing device can reproduce color only in 8-bits-per-channel color. So what good are all those extra bits? What do you do with all the leftovers—sweep them under the rug, or feed them to the dog?

Because you have all this additional capacity for color information, you can capture and carry a lot more image detail. Instead of having an image that has no information in it in an 8-bit color image, you carry a lot more information in the same area if it is captured in 12- or 16-bit color. To simplify the explanation, you can choose which of those extra bits you want to use when you reduce your image to 8-bit—this is done when you adjust for brightness and contrast. If you were able to view an 8-bit and 12-bit image side by side on your monitor, you would notice much more detail and color resolution in the 12-bit image. You would also be able to make much finer changes in the color, contrast, and brightness, as you'll learn to do next.

Flash _____

Try to avoid oversharpening your image—otherwise, it will look forced or over-worked. It is better to leave an image a tad undersharpened than to take it too far. Of course, because all the sharpening filters affect the contrast of an image, you might do well to keep this in mind when adjusting your contrast as well (note: avoid applying any sharpening filters before making contrast adjustments).

A Sharper Image

You can vastly improve an image by sharpening it. Many times, a tweak to the image's sharpness helps overcome any inadequacies in a camera's lens or chip, or any incorrect focusing.

Take a look at an image that is out of focus, and compare it to one that is in focus. The in-focus image has more contrast. This is the key to the Sharpening tool. When the sharpening filter is used, it creates the effect of increased contrast by creating a border between dark and light areas of the image. On the dark side of the border (I can't resist a *Star Wars* pun here), the pixels are darkened slightly, creating an edge. On the lighter side of the same border, the pixels are lightened a bit. This also creates an edge. The visual effect of this double edge is the illusion of contrast or sharpness; your eye is fooled into thinking the image is sharp.

Say Cheese _____

Sharpening is always affected by the size of an image. If you plan to increase the size of your image, do so before applying any sharpening filters. Sharpening is always the last thing I do.

Sharpen

To sharpen an image, open the **Effects** menu on the Menu bar, choose **Sharpen,** and select **Sharpen** again. You have no control over this filter; no dialog box appears. It does its thing, and it's all over. Note: You might want to undo and reapply the filter a few times so that you can see just how much sharpening has been done (it won't be much).

Sharpen More

I bet you can't figure out what this filter does! This filter (open the **Effects** menu, choose **Sharpen,** and select **Sharpen More**) increases the contrast of the edges at the borders (again, you have no control over the degree of the sharpening effect; simply apply it and see what happens). This yields a sharper effect than just plain old Sharpen. (You guessed right!) Depending on your image, applying **Sharpen** twice might give the same effect as **Sharpen More.** If you're curious, try it out.

Sharpen Edges

Sharpen Edges (open the **Effects** on the Menu bar, choose **Sharpen,** and select **Sharpen Edges**) looks at the border areas and applies the Sharpen filter only in areas that have a good deal of contrast. This filter is a bit more selective than the previous two, but you still do not have any control over the degree of the effect.

Unsharp Mask

You might think this is another one of my silly jokes, but I promise you that the Unsharp Mask (USM) filter is for real—and is very useful. USM acts like a combination of Sharpen, Sharpen More, and Sharpen Edges. This is the only sharpening filter over which you have any control, and the control you have is *very* powerful.

To use this filter open an image you wish to sharpen and do the following:

1. Open the **Effects** menu from the Menu bar, choose **Sharpen,** and select **Unsharp Mask.** You should see a dialog box such as the one shown in this figure.

In Plain Black & White

We professional types call the visible edges between the contrast areas **crunchies;** they look almost like the pixels have been piled up along the edges. I confess—I use USM almost all the time to sharpen my images. It offers the most control, and leaves little to no crunchies in the image.

2. Be sure the **Preview** check box is checked if you want to see the affect on your image as you go. Alternatively, you can toggle between the before and after by clicking and holding on the image in the dialog box which shows you before and releasing which shows you after.

3. The **Amount** field determines how much contrast there is at the borders between the dark and light areas. The higher the value in the **Amount** field, the more contrast. This creates the major part of the sharpening effect.

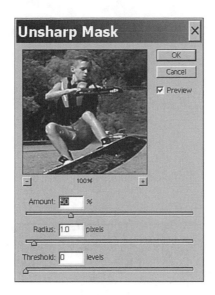

Unsharp mask gives you very sharp control.

4. The **Radius** field determines the number of pixels (or how far or wide from the border) to which the contrast is applied. This affects the width of the edge. A low (less than 1) radius lessens the effect of the **Amount** field.

5. The **Threshold** field describes how much contrast must be present in the areas between the borders before the sharpening will be applied. If a zero (0) value is present (or no difference in contrast), the sharpening always takes effect. If a value of 5 is found, there must be five *levels* of contrast present before the sharpening can occur. Think of the levels as a ratio of contrast between the pixels, such as a contrast of 1:2 or 1:5.

6. The small preview box near the top of the dialog box shows you what the filter will look like on the image if applied. Notice that you can zoom into the image to get a better look at what you are doing by clicking the plus and minus buttons below the preview. Again click and hold to see the before state.

7. When you are satisfied with the effect, click **OK.** If you are unsatisfied either cancel, or if you want to try again hold the alt key down and the reset button will appear so you can give it another go from the default settings for this filter.

In the following table, I've given you some starting points for the settings to use with the USM filter. Remember, these are starting points, and this is not a "one-size-fits-all" filter. Different types of images with different contrast ranges and subject matters require varied USM settings. Experiment and check out your results.

Suggested Starting Values for the Unsharp Mask Filter

Amount (Percent)	Radius (Pixels)	Threshold (Levels)
50	.7	0
75	.8 to 1	0
100	1 to 1.1	0
125	1.1 to 1.2	0
150	1.2	0
175	1.3	0
200	1.5	1
200+	It doesn't matter—you're oversharpening! Try applying 125 twice.	

It is difficult to say which filter to use on your image; all will work. USM works very well, but it takes some time, and a few rounds of experimenting to figure out the settings. Usually, a shot or two of plain old **Sharpen** works fine, but if not you now have the USM solution in your bag of digital tricks.

It's All a Blur

Blur filters are frequently used for correcting selected areas of an image. They can be used to correct stair-stepping at the edges of an image or to dissipate noise.

Behind the Shutter

A larger file can stand much more USM than a small file before any ill effects are visible.

Blur

To apply the Blur filter, open the **Effects** menu and choose **Blur,** then choose **Blur** again. Just like the Sharpen filter, the Blur filter offers no control over how much the image is blurred. When you apply it, the image appears to soften slightly.

Blur More

To apply the Blur More filter, open the **Effects** menu and choose **Blur,** then choose **Blur More.** Not surprisingly, applying this filter renders a stronger effect than simply applying the Blur filter. Note: I would apply **Blur More** before I would apply the **Blur** filter twice.

Soften with Smart Blur

The **Smart Blur** filter is my blur filter of choice, because it is controllable. To apply this filter to an open image, do the following:

1. Open the **Effects** menu on the Menu bar, choose **Blur,** and select **Soften** to view the dialog box shown in the next figure. Note that this dialog box is laid out similarly to the **Unsharp Mask** dialog box.

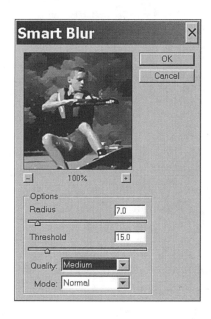

The Smart Blur dialog box utilizes a slider control or a fill-in box, and offers a preview. This gives you good control over the blur function.

2. You can again toggle between the before and after state by clicking on the image window in the Smart Blur dialog box.

3. As with any dialog box with a preview window, you can click your mouse any-where on the image on your desktop to display that area in the dialog box Preview window. (Again, click the zoom buttons below the window to view more or less of the image area.) If you prefer, use the hand in the dialog box preview window to drag to the part you wish to view.

4. Use the Radius slider to specify how much softening will occur. A lower number will soften/blur more.

5. Use the Threshold control to generate a smoother blur. A higher number will smooth more.

6. The Quality and Mode controls give different options. Quality is unexplained in the Photoshop Elements documentation, but we would guess it relates to how much information is used when determining the blur. Mode, on the other hand, gives a different effect to transition areas. Normal works on the whole image, Edge Only adds black edges to areas of transitioning contrast and Overlay Edge adds white to these areas.

7. When you are satisfied with the effect, click **OK.** Again you can hold the alt button and revert to the default settings for this dialog if you are not satisfied and you can toggle the before/after previews by clicking and holding your cursor in the dialog box preview screen.

Despeckle

Many times, your camera introduces *noise* (unwanted color flecks or static), into your images, usually in the dark or solid color areas. The Despeckle filter helps eliminate some of the noise—it won't get it all, but it will clean up a good portion of it. If you have an image with a solid color that appears "dirty," this is the way to clean it. A good example is the sky sometimes will show as very speckled after JPEG compression has been applied. Try fixing it with this filter. To use this filter, do the following:

1. Open any image you have with noise. If you don't have one, take an image with a solid color and apply significant compression when saving as a jpeg. Now we have some noise!

2. Open the **Effects** menu from the Menu bar, choose **Noise,** and select **Despeckle.**

3. The Despeckle filter offers you no control; it does its thing, and that's that.

If you need more control try the Dust and Scratch filter covered in Chapter 18.

The Least You Need to Know

- You can correct the color balance of your photos to make them look more pleasing to the eye or realistic.

- You can add or subtract the amount of color to saturate or de-saturate your image.

- There are many ways to improve your images with the creative use of color manipulation.

- You can sharpen or blur your images in order to improve them.

Chapter 16

Eeney, Meeny, Miney, Mo: Selections

In This Chapter

♦ Using Marquee selections to improve your images

♦ Using Marquee selections to isolate image areas

♦ Using the Lasso selection tools

♦ Using the Magic Wand to make selections

Without selection tools, image editing would be very difficult. The selection tools, which work hand in hand with other tools, effects, and filters, are the key to your ability to copy or remove pixels in your image; they allow you to protect unselected areas from retouching or color correction. When you master the selection tools, you will begin to truly appreciate how much control you have over your images.

Getting Started

Before I go too far into describing how you make selections and why, let's find the tools themselves. As with many Photoshop Elements operations, there is more than one way to get to the selection tools. The quickest way is to select the tool from the floating Toolbox and it is always open by default (if you don't see the Toolbox depicted in the following figure, choose Window, and select Toolbox from the Menu bar to open it). The Toolbox has icons that you click to select the tool you want to use. It also has foreground and background color selectors. You'll be using the Toolbox almost constantly.

The Toolbox contains your tools including Marquee, Lasso, Magic Wand, and Brush selection tools.

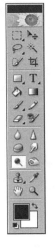

Say Cheese

Floating windows (like palettes and the Toolbox) are a great way to save time and keystrokes; they do, however, take up a small bit of your screen's real estate. You can drag the windows around your workspace by left clicking and holding on the window's title bar, and dragging it anywhere on your screen you like. The beauty of floating windows is that you can keep them close to the area where you are working; that way when you need a tool, you don't need to move your mouse too far to get it.

If you are having trouble seeing the image and all of your open windows like the Toolbox and palettes, check to see if your monitor can be run at a higher resolution.

Why Use Selections?

There are plenty of reasons to use selection tools:

♦ Using a selection tool in your image enables you to move pixels. You can cut and paste a selection, moving it from place to place within an image or from one image into another. You can also *drag* a selection from one place in a photo to another. Say, for example, that you've selected a cloud. You can move the cloud to another location in your image, or you can copy and paste the cloud, creating an entire storm if you want.

◆ After a selection is made on an area in a photo, it is isolated so that operations affect the selected area(s) only. This comes in handy if you need to apply a filter or a color correction to a specific area in a photo.

◆ A selection can also be used as a targeting device, allowing you to place an image that has been copied exactly where you want it. All you do is draw a selection in the place you want the new copy to land. When you drop the new copy into your image, it lands in your selection.

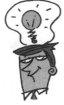

Say Cheese

If you double click on the title bar of any open palette or the Toolbox it rolls up like a window shade with only the title bar and a small part of the window visible. If you want an even better look at what you are working on, press the Tab key. This toggles the open palettes and Toolbar visible and invisible. Once you get used to the keyboard shortcuts to each tool, you may even be able to work on images without the Toolbar visible at all!

Imagine this scenario: You just took the most wonderful portrait of your entire extended family. Folks and relatives from all over the country gathered for this occasion. The sun was shining, and all was right in the world. To celebrate this happy occasion and to show off your new toys, you run inside to your computer and print out an image for everyone in the crowd. But there is one small problem: Your nephew, Pete the Pest, has his eyes closed!

No problem. Simply photograph Peter again, keeping him at about the same distance and under the same type of light as in the original photograph. Then run back inside and download the photo of Pete's smiling face, open it, and select only his face. Then open the family portrait and select Pete's face (the one with his eyes closed). Now all you need to do is paste the new photo of Pete into the selection on the portrait. Because you selected the area on the portrait, Pete's face lands in the right place. You have to do some resizing and rotating of the pasted section, but you can do that with no problem.

Say Cheese

If you want to leave your floating palette or the Toolbox in place for your next Photoshop Elements session, simply leave them open when you shut down the program. The next time you start Photoshop Elements, the floating windows appear in the same locations, ready for use.

Selection Tools

Lets take some time to look at the specific selection tools that Photoshop Elements makes available to you. Although you can follow along by just reading, I suggest you cozy up to your computer and open up an image (if you thought we meant cozy up literally it is time for a little break!). Be sure the floating Toolbox is on your screen, if necessary choose Window, and select Tools from the Menu bar. You access one of the selection tools by clicking the icons on this toolbar. There is also a letter key shortcut for each tool if you prefer. Are you comfortable? Let's begin.

Behind the Shutter

Many times, you can buy third-party filters, additional Effects (called Actions by the Photoshop crowd), or more powerful tools. Many companies, such as Extensis (www. extensis.com) sell add-on software that help make selections much easier.

Most of the time, you can download trial or demo versions from a company's website. This is great, because you can check out the software to see whether it does all that it says it will. Also, you can check to see whether it works on your platform and with your software. Best of all, you can check to see whether you like the software in the first place.

Select All, None, and Invert

Here are four very powerful selection tools located under **Select** on the Menu bar and in their keyboard shortcut forms:

◆ **All.** This selects the entire image. An animated dashed line appears around the entire image. We professional types call these the dancing ants, and they indicate that an area has been selected. Use **Ctrl/Command+A** on the keyboard for the same effect.

◆ **Deselect.** If you want to drop any selection after it has been made or used, use **Deselect.** (The keyboard shortcut command is **Ctrl+D** on a PC or **Command+D** on a Mac—think "D" for "drop," as in "dropping" a selection.)

◆ **Reselect.** If you dropped something that you didn't want to, select this item, or use **Shift+Ctrl/Command+D** to get it back. You can also use the Undo button on the Shortcut menu or Control/Command+Z as this does the same thing.

◆ **Inverse.** Use this command (or press **Shift+Ctrl+I** or **Shift+Command+I**) to select the opposite of what was originally selected. For example, if you are working on an image of a flower, and you want everything but the flower in the foreground to be slightly blurry, select the flower, invert the selection, and apply the Blur filter.

Flash _____

There are two different button types in the Toolbar. Type one gives you just one tool when you click it. Type two, which has a small black triangle in the lower left corner of the button, have multiple tools hidden under them. There are three ways to open the correct tool:

1. Click the tool and then select the desired tool from the choices on the Option bar.
2. Left click and hold until a sub-menu appears.
3. Right click the button icon and the sub-menu will immediately appear. Both the Marquee tools and the Lasso Tools are multiple tool icons.

Marquee Selection Tools

Marquee selection tools are the easiest and simplest of all the selection tools. They are so named because the border resulting from the selection of an object resembles an old movie theatre's marquee with the flashing lights. The tools are very helpful when selecting a large area to move, rotate, or resize the image. The marquee selection tools are the Rectangle Tool and the Elliptical Tool.

Rectangle Selection Tool

To use the Rectangle tool, click on any corner of the area you want to select, and then drag down diagonally to the opposite corner. When you release the mouse button, your selection is complete, like the one shown in the following figure.

You can "constrain" the shape of the rectangle selection tool to a square by holding the Shift key while dragging. In fact, this constraint works in quite a few places. Try using it to select a perfectly square object! If you prefer, you can use the Style dropdown box and select Fixed Aspect Ratio, which also results in a square selection. There is also a choice for Fixed Size, which is helpful if you are trying to capture exact size portions of an image, say for making web buttons or icons.

After the selection is made you can click in the marquee box and drag to relocate it, but it will remain the same size.

When you just want part of an image to be affected you select it with the Marquee tool.

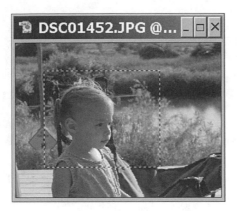

DSC01452.JPG @...

Demo: Removing Color from Portions of Your Image

Have you ever seen an advertisement or a photograph that seems to be black and white but has color in selected areas? I'll show you how it is done:

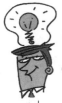

Say Cheese _____

If you decide that an operation isn't going to work, but you've already started it, you can easily stop it by clicking the **Cancel** button in the palette. If no Cancel button is available to you, press and hold **Escape** (Windows)/**Command+period** (Mac) to stop the operation. This can save you a lot of waiting time, especially on time-consuming operations.

1. Open any image, and then click the **Marquee** tool from the Toolbox. If you want the color to blend out to the colorless part try setting a Feather number between 5 and 25 in the Option bar text box.

2. Using your mouse, **Shift+click** and hold+drag to select a square area (about an inch or so) in the middle of your image.

3. From the Menu bar choose Select then **Inverse** to select the area outside the box you just drew.

4. Open the **Enhance** menu on the Menu bar, choose **Adjust Color,** and select **Remove Color** (or just use **Shift+Ctrl/Command+U**).

Like the following figure, the image, except for the protected area, becomes black and white; the area you protected when you drew the original square selection remains colorful!

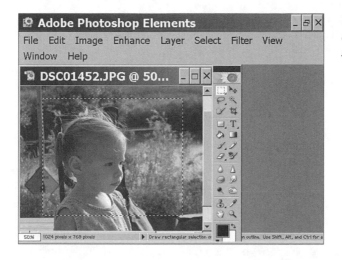

You can highlight a portion of your photo by de-colorizing surrounding content.

The Elliptical Marquee Tool

Guess what? The Elliptical Marquee tool works just like the Rectangle Marquee tool, except it draws circles or ovals. You can alter the shape of the oval, making it oblong or squat, by altering the direction you drag the cursor. To draw a perfect circle, hold down the Shift key as you drag to make a selection. When using the Elliptical Marquee tool, be sure anti-alias is checked or you will get some jagged results.

Say Cheese

You might have noticed that all the fixed selection tools draw across the screen in the direction of the cursor drag. If you hold down the **Alt** key (**Option** for the Mac), the selection grows outward from the center (the center being where your mouse was pointing when you clicked it to begin dragging).

Lasso Selection Tools

Lasso selection tools allow you to draw a selection in freehand. There is no fixed shape to the tool. These tools are precise, enabling you to follow along a line or a shape easily. The freehand selection tools are the Lasso tool, Polygon Lasso tool, and the Magnetic Lasso tool.

Lasso Tool

You can use the Lasso tool to trace an object of an unusual shape. To use it, click, hold and drag your cursor around the object you want to trace. Note: For a selection to work, it must be "closed," meaning that you must drag all the way around the object until you reach the starting point. If you don't, the cursor "snaps" itself closed to connect the point where you released the mouse button to your starting point. The

Lasso tool is for freehand drawing where you control the path. Often zooming in before starting is helpful.

> **Say Cheese**
>
> Suppose you're tracing an image that contains both squiggly lines and straight ones. Drawing a perfectly straight line freehand is pretty hard; usually, your hand tremors ever so slightly, making the line that's supposed to be straight look squiggly.
>
> Fortunately, Photoshop Elements provides a way for you to trace perfectly straight lines, even while using the Trace tool. To do so, press and hold the mouse button, and then press and hold the Alt (Option on a Mac) key on your keyboard. Release the mouse button (keep pressing Alt or Option), and move your cursor to the other end of the straight line. When the line is as long as you need it to be, click to anchor it. You can repeat so long as you hold down Alt/Option, adding segment after segment. When you finally release the Alt (Option) button, you are again able to draw "squiggly" lines.

Lasso Polygon Tool

The Lasso Polygon tool is another freehand selection tool, but unlike the Lasso tool, which enables you to draw both squiggly and also straight lines, the Lasso Polygon tool draws only point-to-point straight segments. Try using an image that has a clearly defined solid object in it to get a good handle on how this tool works:

1. After selecting **Lasso Polygon** from the Toolbox, click to start your selection, move to your next position and click again. Each click adds a segment to your line.

2. Keep clicking until you have nearly selected the entire object.

3. Double-click to close the selection and it might look something like the following figure.

The Lasso Polygon tool lets you select straight-line segments.

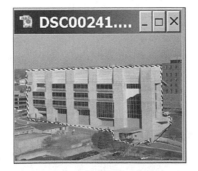

Selecting by Color

It is always easiest to let the computer do as much of the work for you as possible. Selecting by color is one way of letting your computer's "horsepower" do some of the work for you. Instead of drawing a complicated selection around a beautiful red rose, why not let the computer do it for you? By selecting the red color, your rose can easily be isolated from its green, leafy background. So easy and so simple!

The Magnetic Lasso

If you were following closely under Lasso Tools, you may have noticed we skipped one, the Magnetic Lasso Tool. If you have part of the image with a consistently defined edge, use this tool to follow the edge to make a selection. It works well even if the part being selected contains several different colors as long as the edge is clearly defined. If the part to be selected is one solid color, then save the effort of dragging around it by using the next tool instead.

The Color Magic Wand

The Magic Wand enables you to make selections based on similar colors or tones. This comes in handy when you want to choose large areas of color, such as when you want to select the entire lawn or sky in a photograph. The downside of using this tool is that it can take a while for you to clean up all of the "blinkers" that were not included. This happens when a different color range is located inside of an object you want to select. You can Shift+click on these gremlins to add them to the active selection. I often use the elliptical or other selection tool to get the blinkers.

If you want similar colors regardless of where they appear in an image un-check the Contiguous box in the Option bar, otherwise the Magic Wand won't select similar colors if there is a barrier of contrasting color. Note also that it will jump layers to get similar color if you select the Use All Layers option.

 Flash _____

If you set the tolerance too low, such as at 1, then the tool selects only those pixels that are exactly the same color as the one selected by the wand (lower tolerances can come in handy if you want to pick a specific color and change it, however). If you choose an excessively high tolerance, such as 255 (remember from Chapter 14 that there are only 256 colors available in an image), then all the pixels in your image will be selected.

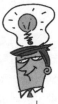

Say Cheese _____

If you accidentally add a large portion of your image to the selection you can use the **Undo** command.

The Magic Wand's default Tolerance is set to 32. You can adjust this by typing a new value into the Tolerance box on the **Options** toolbar. Try using an image that has a single distinctly visible object to get a good handle on how this tool works. Essentially, just click inside of the object you want selected.

The Magic Wand in action finds the yellow sunflower. To get the best result for this particular picture I used 100 for the tolerance setting and unchecked contiguous. There are a number of blinkers in the center I would clean up with another tool.

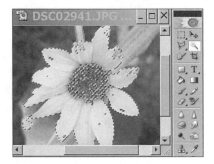

In Plain Black & White _____

At some point, you will be left with some small **blinkers,** or blinking selections, in your image. (You'll know what they are when you see them!) You could try selecting these portions of the image with the wand (thus ruining your eyes), but the easier way to finish is to change tools and utilize the Selection Brush tool for smaller areas, and brush over the blinkers to select them, or the Lasso tool or Elliptical Marquee tool.

A Selection Saved Is a Selection Earned: Saving Selections

After all the work you have just done to make the most perfect selection, wouldn't it be nice if you could save it to use again? Even better, wouldn't it be nice to save a selection in progress—like if you hadn't finished working on a selection and you needed to close the file and do something else—like eat dinner? Saving selections also helps when you work on the same file over and over again.

Photoshop Elements allows you to save your selections, a very powerful action. Here's how:

1. After you've finished making the selection that you want to save, open the **Select** menu from the Menu bar and choose **Save Selection**.

2. The New Selection item will already be selected in the Save Selection dialog, your only job is to name the selection. When you are done, click **OK.** Voilà! You now have a saved selection ready for re-use.

3. To use your newly saved selection again, open the **Select** menu and choose **Load Selection.** Select your saved selection from the Selection pull-down menu, and click **OK.** Your selection will be restored!

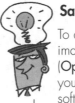

Say Cheese

To duplicate a portion of an image, press and hold the **Alt** (**Option** for the Mac) key as you drag the selection. The software automatically makes a duplicate of the image, meaning that you don't end up with a giant piece of white background.

Addition and Subtraction, All Without a Calculator!

What if you want to add to, subtract from, or otherwise combine a couple selections. As previously indicated, you can hold the shift key while making another selection to add to it or hold the alt key while selecting to subtract from the selection. If you want to save your fingers the walking, check out the four options pictured in the next figure that are located on the Option bar for most of the selection tools: New selection, Add to selection, Subtract from selection, and Intersect with selection.

The four options for selecting appear on the Option bar.

♦ New selection will remove any prior selection and replace it with the current selection.

♦ Add to selection will keep any existing selection and combine it with the new selection, just like holding the shift key did.

♦ Subtract from selection will take away the new selection from the existing selection, the same as holding the alt key.

♦ Intersect with selection will select only those portions of two selected parts of the image that overlap, tossing out the rest.

Flash

There are four very powerful methods of adjusting selections hidden under Select, Modify on the Menu bar. If you want to expand or contract by a set number of pixels, select only the border of what is selected, or smooth (think anti-alias) a selection, hit this menu item!

The Least You Need to Know

- ◆ Selections are an important part of preparing to enhance your images.

- ◆ Using selections, you can duplicate and move elements, and protect certain elements while you color-correct others.

- ◆ You can select large areas of your image using fixed selection tools or select very fine detail and shapes using freehand selection tools.

- ◆ You can select areas using the Color Wand Tool to select a particular color or range of colors.

- ◆ You can save your selections for re-use in the same or other images.

- ◆ You can add to, delete from, modify, choose intersecting, expand, and contract selections.

Chapter 17

Color Me Beautiful: Adding Fills and Color

In This Chapter

- ◆ Learn how to fill your selections
- ◆ A selection can be filled with color or texture
- ◆ Draw on your images using the Brush, Shape, Eraser, and Pencil tools

There are many ways to enhance your images. Here we will cover filling areas with color or pattern. You can lay down these in a strong, bold way, blend one color to another, or subtly just add a tint.

For those of you who always wanted to paint and draw, you are in luck. Photoshop Elements has tools that allow you to draw or brush color onto your photos. You can draw over a few faded pixels to beef them up or draw a smile on a face to add comic relief.

Photoshop Elements offers a few different ways to add color to your image:

- ◆ Using fills, you can easily fill large areas of your images with colors or patterns. You can also use fill gradients that gradually move from dark to light, or even from one color to another.
- ◆ Using paint tools, you can draw on your image.

Fills

With Photoshop Elements, you have two basic categories of fills at your disposal:

- Selection fills fill the selected portion of your image with a solid color or pattern.

- Gradient fills work similarly to selection fills, because they also fill in a selection. However, this type of fill fills the selection with two colors, fading one into the other.

Selection Fills

To apply a selection fill, begin by selecting the portion of the image that you want to fill (or select the part you don't and use **Select > Inverse** on the Menu bar). Then open the **Edit** menu and choose **Fill** to view the **Fill** dialog box. As shown in the following figure, this dialog box is broken into two main parts:

- Contents

- Blending

A selection is drawn in an image (here the flower from Chapter 16 after the blinkies are cleared). The Selection Fill dialog box allows many options to be applied to the selection.

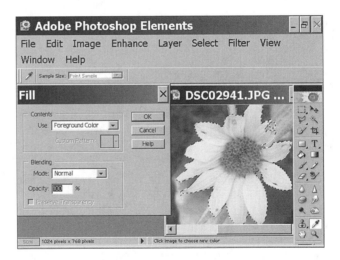

Contents

The Contents section offers two options:

- Select the **Pattern** option from the Use menu in the Fill dialog to fill your selection with the pattern you select from the Custom Pattern menu that will appear. Use the small round arrow button on the right side of the open Patterns menu to select the type of patterns to be shown, including Artist Surfaces, Nature Patterns, etc. Click **OK**.

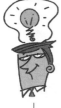

Say Cheese _____

The options menu in the Custom Pattern menu is chock full of features, many of which you may never use. One feature you may want to pay attention to, though, is the Presets Manager. With this tool you can add more patterns by clicking the **Load** button. Patterns come in the form of a file with the ".PAT" extension. Just search for PAT and Photoshop using your favorite web search engine and start looking. There are hundreds of sites out there with patterns, some free and others not.

◆ Select the **Foreground Color** or **Background Color** options to fill the selected area in your image with color. This can be a little confusing when you cannot select a color in the **Fill** dialog. You need to select a color by using the swatches at the bottom of the **Toolbox** *before* you use this Fill feature.

The easier way to make a color fill for a selection is to use the Paint Bucket tool. It's quite easy. Make your selection, select your color from the Tools palette, select the Paint Bucket tool, and click inside of your selection. You'll have to experiment with what works best, but use the **Mode** and **Opacity** options to change how your modifications look.

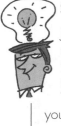

Say Cheese _____

Just a reminder for those of you who like to experiment, set your Undo States to something much higher than 20 and you'll save yourself some grief. To do that, go to **Edit** on the Menu bar, select **Preferences,** and then **General.** Change the default 20 to something more realistic, like the maximum of 100! Of course, there is a caveat. The more states you save, the more RAM and Scratch Disk space you'll need, so if you are on the lower end of the Minimum Requirements scale, leave it at 20 or 30.

Blending

Use the **Blending** area of the Selection Fill dialog box to specify *how* the color or pattern you picked will be applied to the image:

◆ Use the **Opacity** field to specify how transparent the applied fill will appear. Choosing 100 percent means that the fill will be completely opaque. If you want the fill to resemble a tint rather than a robust color, try setting this field to 50 percent.

◆ Use the **Blend** drop-down list to specify how the fill will be applied. You have the following options: Normal, Darken, Lighten, Overlay, Difference, and Color.

- ◆ Select **Normal** to fill the selection so that it completely covers the base or layer below. Check Chapter 20 to learn more about layers.

- ◆ Select **Color** to fill the selection so that the area below the selection keeps all its shadows and highlights. This is a good way to lay a color tone over an image while retaining the original image detail.

- ◆ Select **Lighten** to apply the fill color only to pixels that are lighter than the selected color. This would darken all the affected pixels. All pixels that are darker than the selected color will be left alone.

- ◆ Select **Darken** to apply the fill color only to pixels darker than the selected color. This would effectively lighten all the pixels that are chosen.

- ◆ Both the **Overlay** and **Difference** options are really esoteric functions that we graphics professionals like to make more complicated than they really are. Suffice it to say that they both involve multiplying or comparing color information— they can, however, produce cool results. The best thing to do with these modes is to experiment.

Gradient Fill

Applying a gradient fill is similar to applying a selection fill; begin by selecting the portion of the image that you want to fill. Once you have selected your target area, click on the Gradient Fill tool in the Toolbox, it is the fifth one down on the right that looks like a rectangle of varying shades of color.

Use the Gradient Fill tool to fill your selection with a gradient color and other related effects.

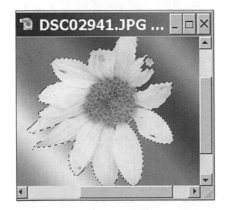

You will notice pretty quickly that this tool has plenty of bells and whistles.

Demo: Using a Filter to Change the Weather

With the use of selection tools and fills, you can borrow the blue sky from one image and place it over the gray sky in another. People will think you always go on vacation during the best weather!

1. Open any weather related images you have. One of a sunny locale and another of a dreary one will do.

2. Using either the Rectangle Marquee tool, the Magic Wand or a Lasso Polygon selection tool, select the sky area in the background of the dreary picture which will place marching ants around the sky as the next figure shows. Remember to make use of different tools and use the add and subtract options covered in Chapter 16.

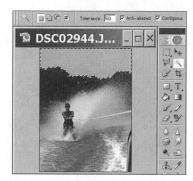

Use the Magic Wand tool to make a selection in the sky area. Remember to uncheck the contiguous box if there are other areas of similar color.

3. Switch to your sunny image.

4. Click on the Foreground color block in the Toolbox to open its Color Picker shown in the following figure.

5. Move the pointer off of the Color Picker and it will change to an Eyedropper tool. You may need to move the Color Picker to see your target colors on the sunny day photo.

6. Place the eyedropper pointer at the very bluest part of the sky in the sunny day image and click. The blue of the sky fills in as your **Foreground** color. Click **OK** to close the dialog.

7. Repeat steps 4, 5, and 6, but this time click on the Background Color block in the Toolbox and select a slightly lighter shade of blue, gray, or white, depending on your preference. Click **OK** to close the color picker.

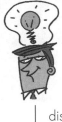

Say Cheese _____

When you catalog your images, it's a good idea to make note of which images have great cloud formations and wonderful skies. This will be the beginnings of a great archive of "bits and pieces" of images for you to use. I routinely use cloud formations I took years ago to fill in new images. It sure beats waiting hours for the right clouds to appear! It can be used directly, or with the Clone Stamp tool discussed in Chapter 18.

8. After you have both your beginning and ending colors chosen, switch back to your dreary image.

The Color Picker dialog is used to grab the natural blue sky color from a photo.

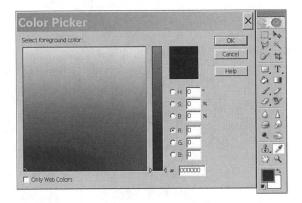

9. The dreary image should still be on your screen, with the sky selected. Your beginning and ending colors are still in the Foreground and Background color blocks on the Tools palette.

10. Choose **Filter,** select **Render,** and click **Clouds** and Photoshop Elements will build a nice blended sky for you like that shown in the next figure.

A beautiful blue sky; only you know the truth!

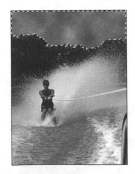

Paint Tools

The painting tools are a lot of fun to use. You can use them to clean up or enhance part of your image or you can use them to draw on your photos. If you are using Photoshop Elements to make business presentations, you can draw arrows or circle parts of your images to draw attention to a specific point.

Behind the Shutter

Programs such as Adobe Photoshop, Adobe Illustrator, and Corel QuickDraw offer even more robust paint tools, and options than does Photoshop Elements. Nonetheless, the painting and drawing tools that are included in Photoshop Elements are quite a close match to what is offered in the full-bore Photoshop and offer plenty of options for even fairly skilled digital image buffs.

Photoshop Elements offers a variety of paint tools for you to use, including the following:

◆ The Brush tools

◆ The Eraser tools

◆ The Shape tools

◆ The Pencil tool

◆ The Airbrush tool

The Brush Tools

This tool is really two tools. The Brush tool acts and behaves just like a paintbrush. It is a very nice way to apply color in a freehand manner. The Impressionist Brush tool can convert any image into a nice Van Gogh. Note that the impressionist look will be slick, but the authenticity might be questioned if you include any modern objects in the image like a car or a microwave oven.

To use the Brush tools, choose the **Brush** tool from the Toolbox. It is the sixth one down on the left. Options for these tools appear on the Options toolbar, shown here, enabling you to specify the brush's size, color, and mode and opacity options. It might be a good idea when working with this or any other tool to click on the left-most icon on the Options bar to reset the tool to the default settings.

The floating palette allows you to pick the brush's size, type of edge or shape and color.

Setting the Brush Size

On the left end of the Options bar is a squiggly line that is a representation of the size of the brush and what consistency it will have when applied. You can select from numerous pre-defined styles by clicking on the small arrow to the right of the iconic display. There are different edge styles you can choose from. The options have predefined sizes, but you can set brush size in pixels in the Size box to any number or by using the slider that drops down below the Size box if you click on the down arrow on the right end of it. The characteristics of the brush will be preserved when you resize it.

Behind the Shutter

In programs such as Illustrator or Photoshop, the brush cursor takes on different "characters," such as a paintbrush, pencil, or airbrush. By default, the cursor for Photoshop Elements's Brush tool is simply round. However, you can use the Cursor Preferences dialog box (open the **Edit** menu, choose **Preferences,** and select **Display & Cursors**) to specify how you want your cursor to appear onscreen. This dialog box is divided into three sections; the section on the far left is for the painting tools—such as the Brush tool.

Choose the **Standard** option if you want your cursor to look like the tool's icon. For example, if you are using the Brush tool, the cursor looks like a little brush—making it easy for you to remember which tool you are using. If you choose the **Precise** option, your cursor resembles a small crosshair—making it easy for you to finely control the tool you're using. Finally, you can select **Brush Size** to make it so that your cursor reflects the size you've selected for the tool (I usually have this option selected).

Setting the Brush Color

This is an easy one; the brush will paint in the foreground color set in the swatch in the Toolbox. If you want to change the brush color, click on the swatch and use the Color Picker dialog to find just the color you want.

Setting the Brush Mode and Opacity

You can alter the mode and opacity of the color drawn by the Brush tool. Select a mode from the Mode menu. Most of these are somewhat esoteric, so you might want to experiment with them. With some you won't even be able to tell if it did anything at all. Have fun with them.

You can use the Opacity menu to define the percentage of opacity that will be applied when you use the brush. You can effectively use this to apply a light mist around a friend or family members head, making them appear lost in a fog of thought, or myriad other effects that can modify the emotion of a picture.

Say Cheese _____

You can also control the opacity of the brush tool by controlling the opacity of the layer on which you're drawing. See Chapter 20 for more information on layers.

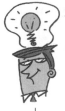

Say Cheese _____

If you have a selection activated but hidden from yourself—for example, you might be zoomed in on a different section of your image—trying to use the Brush tool will be frustrating (remember, you can't draw outside a selected area). Select the Zoom tool and click on the Fit On Screen button on the Options bar to find the selected area, or drop the selection (press **Ctrl+D/Command+D**) just to be sure.

Drawing with the Brush Tool

Click and hold the mouse button, and drag the Brush tool across your image. Squiggle it. Do the loop-de-loop. Dab. Have fun. Remember, you can also use a selection to limit where you draw. To get more complex and interesting results, create a new layer before trying out an effect. This also allows you to later chuck that layer entirely when you are done playing around.

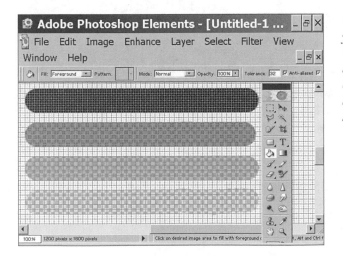

You can control the opacity of your brush strokes. I used **View, Grid** _from the Menu bar to give me drawing reference. This shows lines brushed at 100, 75, 50, and 25 percent opacity._

The Eraser Tools

The Eraser tools erase the image from the photo. If you are on the "background layer" of an image, the standard Eraser tool erases to black and white checkerboard underneath the image (see the following image). If you are on an upper layer, it erases the pixels on that layer, allowing pixels on submerged layers to show through.

The Background Eraser tool is a neat gadget. It works best on images with strongly contrasting elements. For example, a white table, chair, and umbrella set on a dark stone patio overlooking a smooth surfaced cobalt blue sea would be an excellent candidate (not to mention a fantastic vacation spot). The tool works by sampling, or looking at, what is directly underneath the "+" in the middle of the pointer circle and then removes that color in the brush area, as shown in the upper left corner of the next figure. The idea is to drag it around the image while it removes elements that match what it finds.

In our example image, you might want to remove the dark stone patio floor and replace it with a carpet texture fill. You would then click on the stone area and drag the brush around, being careful not to drag across the white areas. The result is a complete removal of the stone flooring and a nice transparent place to insert your carpeting.

The Magic Eraser tool works in a similar fashion, but with less control. You simply click on a color and it removes that color from the entire image. This works best with solid colors or only slight gradients. Complex surfaces will just take forever as you click on each individual pixel so its best to avoid those or just use the Background Eraser. With these tools, though, you could fix that picture of Uncle Fester so that he looks like he's floating in space or walking on the moon!

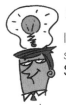

Say Cheese

If you need to draw a perfectly straight line, press and hold the **Shift** key while you draw.

The Eraser tool behaves exactly like the brush tool—almost. Like the Brush tool, you can specify the size of the eraser; unlike the Brush tool, no color selection need be made. You can use the numeric keys on the keyboard to set the opacity just as you did with the brush tool. To open the Eraser palette, open the **Tools** menu and choose **Eraser.**

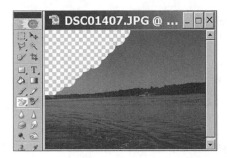

The Background Eraser tool exposes the transparent base layer of the photo.

The Shape Tools

The Shapes tool is one of the best buttons on the Toolbar. It holds a plethora of tools:

◆ **Rectangle Tool.** For drawing either rectangles or squares.

◆ **Rounded Rectangle Tool.** This thing is neat, you can draw a four sided shape, but the corners are rounded on it which breaks up the squarish world that often follows digital images around.

◆ **The Ellipse Tool.** For drawing ovals and circles.

◆ **Polygon Tool.** For drawing shapes with a preset number of sides. The greater the number, the more likely you are to think the shape is a circle. You can also set special Polygon Options (see the little down arrow just to the right of the tool icons on the option bar as shown in the figure), including a star.

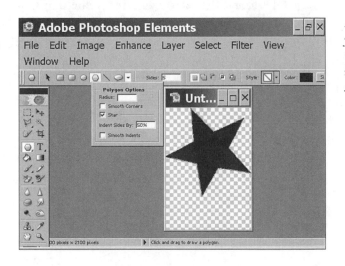

By clicking the small arrow you get a drop down Polygon Option dialog, which can really unlock some great shapes for you!

- ◆ **Line Tool.** Well … what can we say, you can draw a line as a shape or use the Brush or Pencil tools. One advantage of the shape tool is the resulting line is a vector image.

- ◆ **Custom Shape Tool.** This is where you will find a whole host of preset geometric shapes, arrows, and other neat elements to spice up your images. Don't be fooled by the word custom—Adobe defines the shapes, you don't!

- ◆ **Shape Selection Tool.** This is used to create a bounding box around the shapes you create so that you can resize, move, rotate and generally just do as you please.

There are many options that go with the shapes tools. Very similar to the additive and subtractive options for the selection tools discussed in Chapter 16, there are options to allow you to draw a new shape layer, add a shape to your existing layer, subtract a shape from the existing image, render a shape comprised of the intersection of two shapes, or just the reverse of that, render a shape comprise only of that portion of two shapes which doesn't overlap.

> **Behind the Shutter**
>
> Shapes in Photoshop Elements are rendered in a special form called vector images. We discuss vectors in some detail in the Text tool section of Chapter 19, but what makes this a huge advantage is that you can resize, warp, rotate, and mess with shape layers without any loss of quality.

One of the best features of the shapes Option bar is the Style setting. Be sure to click the down arrow on the right of the Style option menu, notice the small circle arrow that appears in that dialog box, click that and play for hours with the various options found there. You will find some that make you forget to look up and know if it's time for bed!

The Pencil Tool

Located on the toolbar, it looks and acts almost like the Brush tool. However, it will have a harder edge than the Brush tool. Now this is misleading because you can pick a soft edged pencil, but don't be fooled, if you pick the same width and style of brush (now that is a confusing term—but they call the style of pencil a brush!) for the Pencil tool and for the Brush tool, the result will vary just a little in terms of the softness of the edges.

The Airbrush Tool

Hidden but present, the Airbrush tool allows you to spray or speckle your paint on the image canvas. It is actually an option to the right of the Brush tool Option bar. You select it by pressing on the icon. I don't need to tell you the magic of the airbrush if you have been to a beach town where they have T-shirt artists. Some very impressive effects are possible with practice using this tool.

The Least You Need to Know

- You can fill a selection with color.

- You can use Gradient Fills to change images wholesale or in a selection.

- You can draw on your image with the brush, pencil, and airbrush tools or create shapes using the various shape tools.

- You can do more than just erase with the erase tool.

- All drawing tools have numerous controls.

The Clone Tool, Pattern Stamp Tool, and Dust and Scratch Filter: The Ultimate Retouching Tools

In This Chapter

◆ Using the Clone Stamp tool

◆ Retouching out unwanted elements

◆ Cloning from one photo into another

◆ Using the Pattern Stamp tool

◆ Using the Dust and Scratch filter

One of the most useful tools in the Photoshop Elements arsenal is the Clone Stamp tool. This fairy-tale tool allows you to copy over "bad" pixels with "good" pixels, enabling you to remove scratches, dust, and other annoying maladies on your photos and even take out (actually cover up) distracting elements such as a building from a remote seashore photo or phone lines from a scenery shot. This tool is so important and so beneficial to your photos that it deserves its own chapter. Its programmer (mother?) would be so proud!

Getting Started

Photoshop Elements's Clone Stamp Tool is a descendant of Photoshop's Rubber Stamp tool, which is why the Clone Stamp tool's cursor looks like a rubber stamp. It is located second from the bottom left corner in the Toolbox and can be selected by clicking on the icon (in the alternative hit the "S" key on your keyboard when in an image is open). When you click the Clone Stamp Tool, the Options bar will change to reveal there is another tool on the same icon in the Toolbox called the Pattern Stamp tool. Each is a powerful tool in the correct context and you can toggle back and forth between the two by using the icons near the left of the Options bar, or by right clicking the icon in the Toolbox and selecting the one you want. For now we will concentrate on the Clone Stamp tool, and later in the chapter we will cover the Pattern Stamp tool.

When you open the Clone Stamp Tool you will see that you can set the size of the tool. I often work with the tool at about 50 to 100 pixels, but the type of cloning you are performing will often dictate the pixel size you should use. Because of this it is helpful to know the size of the tool. You can see the outline of the tool in the default cursor setting and look at the Options bar to see the size. There are two other options for your cursor when using this (and any other additive tools like the Paintbrush or Pencil tools you learned about in Chapter 17):

1. Open the Preferences menu (**Edit, Preferences, Display & Cursors**).

2. Under the painting tools, the Brush Size button should be selected by default. You may like to try either of the other two choices to see what you prefer. After selecting one, close the dialog box by clicking **OK**.

For this particular tool I prefer the Brush Size selection so I can see the entire area to be affected.

Demo: Removing Distracting Portions of an Image Using the Clone Tool

Open any image that you really don't like because of numerous "baddies," and I'm going to show you how to eliminate the problem. Examples of "baddies" might be a building in the background of your image, telephone lines running through your building, your mean uncle in the family picnic picture, or other distracting things in a photograph.

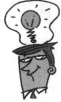

Say Cheese

As you go along, especially after you have accomplished a difficult clone, save your image again using a progressive name like filename1.pdd—you'll be glad you did. If things go sour, just use the **Revert** function in the **File** menu. Remember you only have a limited number of undo functions and each click of the clone tool is a step. The default is 20 levels of undo, but when using something like the Clone Stamp Tool, which uses many repetitions, you may wish to increase the number up to the maximum of 100 undo levels. Use **Ctrl+K/Command+K** and increase the History States.

Do the following to use the Clone Stamp tool:

1. Click the **Clone Stamp** icon on the Tools palette or press "S." If this opens the Pattern Stamp tool, click the left tool icon on the Option bar.

2. The Clone Stamp options appear on the Options bar shown in the following figure, enabling you to choose an applicator—or brush—size, hardness of edge, opacity, etc.

3. Perform any image correction you feel is necessary to make the image look as good as possible in a pre–Clone Stamp state, such as adjusting perspective (see Chapter 14) or balancing color.

The Clone Stamp options allow you to pick a tool's size and its edge effect and opacity, among other things. There are basically three types of Brush under the Default Brushes (click on the drop down menu box between the Clone Stamp icon and the Size box on the Option bar to see the brushes), soft edged, hard edged, and special effects.

4. Zoom into the image so that the baddies you would like to eliminate and some surrounding good parts of the image fill your screen. You don't have to get all baddies in at the same time.

5. Open the brush selection dialog by clicking the small down arrow on the Option bar and selecting the 35-pixel soft brush on the Default Brushes menu (it should be about the thirteenth one down). You get the paint for the Clone tool's brush by "sucking" the pixels that you want to clone from your image. Drag the colored area with the crosshair in its center (I call this the *clone source*) to the pixels you want to clone—in your case pick some good pixels. Your good pixels might be perhaps some bushes or grass for example if you are trying to cover a building surrounded by bushes or a lawn (like the following figure demonstrates), the sky if you are covering telephone wires, etc. Make sure that the Aligned option is checked and the Use All Layers option is not on the far right side of the Option bar.

Behind the Shutter

Like the painting tools you learned about in Chapter 17, the Clone Stamp tool also uses a brush. The Clone Options bar features a brush menu that allows you to select the shape of the brush's tip. Some brush tips are hard edged. Others have fuzzy tips, which leave soft, feathered edges (these are the best brushes to use, because they help blend the clone into the photo). There are also some that are very unusual which would be used more for effects than for picture correction, such as the Flowing Stars brush. The text box to the right of the Brush selection drop down menu produces a slider with which you can select an exact brush size, all the way from 1 pixel to 2,500 pixels in diameter. That's a mighty big brush tip! If you prefer you can type the desired pixel number into this box.

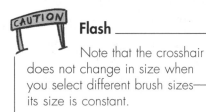

Flash

Note that the crosshair does not change in size when you select different brush sizes—its size is constant.

6. With the cross hair clone source over some good pixels hold the Alt key and left click, but do not release the Alt key. You've just loaded a clone into the stamp, a copy of the good pixels centered on the crosshair and in the width specified for the brush.

7. To "stamp" out the baddie drag the cursor with the Alt key still depressed to place the cursor over the baddie and then release the Alt key. Now click if it is a small defect and the cloned pixels from the source cover the spot you clicked. You can repeatedly click as you move around the baddie, or you can also click once and drag if you have a large good pixel area.

8. Save your image when you are finished.

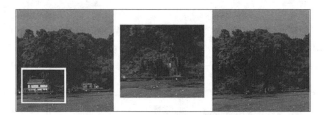

This is a cut out from a larger lakeshore image. Notice that there are three areas of baddies in the left, the building on the left side (highlighted), the gazebo in the middle and an area in the trees on the upper left, which is overexposed. The center image is the highlighted portion blown-up showing the building as partially stamped out. The right image is the final Stamp corrected image.

Behind the Shutter

As you clone, you will notice a small crosshair that follows along with your Clone tool. This crosshair indicates the spot from which the Clone tool is picking up pixels, and stays in the same location in relation to the Clone tool that the original clone source was. If you find that you don't like the pixels being used as a source, change sources by using the alt key again while clicking on the new source; the relation between the traveling crosshair and the brush will change.

Also note that if you release the mouse button and start dragging again, the brush starts copying from the source point again. To make a perfect duplicate of an area, don't release the mouse button until you are finished making the copy.

Cloning takes a little bit of practice and a steady hand, I think it's the ultimate test of hand/eye/mouse coordination. This is a really good place to try and learn to use a pen tablet. The tablets use the pressure you use to draw with to control the amount of "brush application," In other words, the harder you press with the tablet pen, the more ink or in this case opacity will be applied by the onscreen tool.

I sometimes get lost when trying to remember what is selected and what's not. Try zooming out the image size. Look at the borders of the image, if you see the selections there, you generally have flipped or selected the opposite of what you intended. Don't worry, you'll get the hang of it, and when you do, you will have fun!

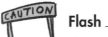 **Flash**

If you try to perform any operation outside an active selection, nothing happens! Also, if you don't have Use All Layers checked, you won't get the result you expect.

 **Say Cheese**

When cloning, change the clone source to avoid too much duplication. Gradient areas are the worst to clone in. Try not to drag the cursor along if it is going to create a noticeable line. Try using different-size brushes. Clone sources from above and below the area you're cloning over. Dab at the spot you want to clone over. Lower the Opacity setting and clone the same baddie more than once. If your clone target area has grain in it, try to duplicate it. Try to match the source and target areas the best you can. Use the Zoom tool to get really close and align pixel by pixel. In other words, mix it up and take your time—a poorly done clone is easy to spot—but with practice cloning can really clean up your digital images.

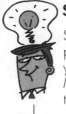

Say Cheese _____

Sometimes you might need to work on both sides of a selection (suppose, for example, you also wanted to make changes to the tree without affecting the sky). If so, you don't need to redraw the selection. Instead, invert it by going to **Select** on the Menu bar and selecting **Inverse** (Shift+Ctrl+I). You can then draw or paint against the selection from the "other side."

Cloning Between Two Photos

Just as you can clone from one area of a photo to another, you can clone between two entirely different photos as well:

Say Cheese _____

When you finish a clone, zoom out and take a look at it. Walk away from your monitor and come back to it. See whether the clone stands out from the image. If it does, fix it or start over. Particularly if you are doing some significant cloning, saving intermediate copies under progressively numbered names so you can revert part way back if necessary.

1. Open the image you want to clone to (I'll call this "Image A").

2. Activate the Clone Stamp tool.

3. Open the second image, which contains the clone source (I'll call this "Image B").

4. Activate the Clone Stamp Tool here, also.

5. Move the clone source crosshairs over the area you want to clone from in Image B.

6. Return to Image A by clicking the image or the top title bar. Your Clone Stamp Tool should now be laying down pixels from Image B to the clone target in Image A.

I have found it helpful to make a layer in Image A and clone from Image B to the layer. I can then resize or reposition the layer. For example in the following figure, I get rid of old Uncle Joe by reestablishing that area of the photo where the boats should be from a second snapshot taken moments later. I could not clone without duplicating the boats from elsewhere or the clone would be obvious. I use the Clone Stamp tool to lift the boats from the middle image and transfer them to the left image rendering the Joe-less image on the right.

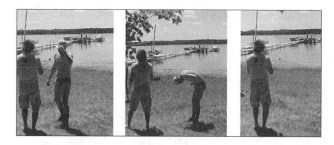

You can use the clone tool to stamp out Uncle Joe or other unwanted parts of an image. I happened to have two pictures, one where Uncle Joe is masking the boats with his body (pretty literally), and one where he is not masking the boats.

Cloning Patterns with the Pattern Clone Tool

Sometimes you may want to fill in an area of an image with some texture. You can use the Pattern Clone tool to paint with texture. When you select this tool by clicking the stamp shaped icon in the Toolbox and then selecting the right stamp icon on the Option bar you will see a new option, Pattern. Select a Pattern and then you can paint on your image. In the following figure, I used the Marquee tool to select the little girls. Then I used Select, Inverse on the Menu bar to actually highlight the area around the girls. I painted texture into this area using the Pattern Clone tool and to give it a nice effect, I then used Filter, Sketch, Chalk & Charcoal from the Menu bar to give it an interesting look. Last I again used Select, Inverse to highlight the girls again and applied the Recessed Frame effect from the Effects palette in the Palette well. I think this creates a unique image that makes the girls jump right out at you. Try it on a photo you like.

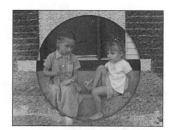

Using the Pattern Stamp tool you can generate some nice enhancements to your photos.

Fixing Minor Blemishes with the Dust and Scratches Filter

If you have some minor blemishes on a photo, leave your big gun the Clone Stamp tool in your Toolbox and turn instead to the Dust and Scratch Filter. Like using acne cream on a teenagers face, a little bit of this tool applied consistently can go a long way to solving the problem. Open your image (this works great for your old black and whites you scan into your computer) and zoom in on the area you wish to repair. This tool often works best when you select just the area where the blemish exists as depicted in the next figure. Follow these steps:

1. On the open image make a selection of the problem area using the Marquee tool, a Lasso tool, the Magic Wand, or the Selection Brush tool contained in the top part of the Toolbox.

2. Choose **Filter,** select **Noise,** and click **Dust and Scratch** to apply this filter. A dialog box will appear that lets you adjust the Radius and Threshold of your correction.

3. If you are correcting a large part of the image, move your cursor to different areas to be affected and click, which will change the portion of the image shown in the Dust and Scratch dialog box. You can also use the minus and plus icons in the dialog box to zoom in and out. You may also wish to check the preview box to see the changes reflected in the actual image. This may slow down the process for larger selections.

Say Cheese

Our experience says that it is best to select smaller parts of a photo for this type of correction and then repeat the process for another area needing correction. The reason is that what may be the perfect blend of Radius and Threshold adjustment for one blemish may actually create a new blemish elsewhere if the selection is too big.

4. Try different settings for the Radius and Threshold settings either by pulling the slider bars with your cursor clicked or by typing numbers directly into the text boxes. With trial and error you will get pretty good at estimating how much of each is required.

5. When you are satisfied with a correction, save a copy of the image and then if necessary, repeat after selecting another part of the image.

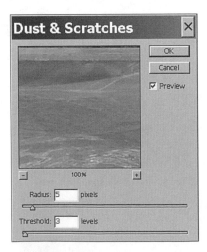

The Least You Need to Know

- ◆ You can use the Clone Stamp tool to cover up or move pixels in your image.
- ◆ You can clone with different opacities.
- ◆ You can clone from one image to another.
- ◆ Remember you can mix up the cloning tools and brush sizes to make a more believable clone.
- ◆ Use the Pattern Stamp tool to paint with texture onto an image.
- ◆ For minor blemishes use the Dust and Scratch filter.

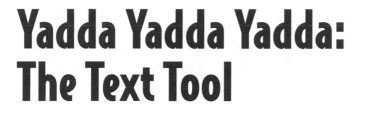

Chapter

19

Yadda Yadda Yadda: The Text Tool

In This Chapter

- ◆ Including text in your images
- ◆ Secret type tricks
- ◆ Adding drop shadows
- ◆ Giving your type a new glow
- ◆ A neat trick with opacity

You might want to include type or text in an image to produce a greeting card or calendar. It is also nice if you are making a logo or web button, want to explain or caption your photo, or want to add a word bubble to the great picture of your aunt scratching her behind at last week's family reunion. Fortunately, Photoshop Elements includes a Text tool, which you can use to add text to your images.

Adding Text

You can add text to an image in several ways, but no matter which way you use, begin by opening the image itself (if you want to practice on a solid white background, create a new image by pressing **Ctrl+N/Command+N**). Then, activate the Text Tool by clicking the **Text** tool in the Toolbox (the one that has a "T" on it) or by pressing "T" on the keyboard. An Options bar will open like the one in the following figure.

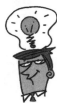

Say Cheese

Learning the keyboard shortcuts for the tool in the Toolbox is well worth the effort! It allows you to easily toggle between tools while working in an area of your image without requiring your cursor to flutter around your screen.

There are four tools available on the Text tool button. You can toggle between them using the icons on the Option bar shown in the figure, or by right clicking the "T" icon on the Toolbar and selecting the one you want to use. The choices are as follows:

- Horizontal Type tool
- Vertical Type tool
- Horizontal Type Mask tool
- Vertical Type Mask tool

Use the Text Tool Option bar that contains four different Text tools and lays out the different option settings available when adding text to an image.

| T | T | T | T | Medium | Courier (T1) | 14 pt | a₍a₎ | T T T T | |

The horizontal or vertical variation is self-explanatory: Do you want your text to run across the page or down it, as though you had hit the carriage return after each letter?

The difference between the Type tools and the Type Mask tools is a little harder to discern. The Type tools place text directly on the image, much like you were typing it there. By contrast the Type Mask tools actually select type shaped portions of the image. You can then apply effects and filters to the selected type shaped portion of the image, or you can copy the mask selected type shaped portion of the image and use it elsewhere. Now that was a mouthful, so while we chew read on, and then we will show you how to use the Type Mask tool later in the chapter.

To add text to your image, do the following:

1. Choose the **Horizontal Type** tool on the Option bar and then select a type style such as regular, bold, or italic (note that the options available will vary

depending on the font you select because not every font has italics, for example), then choose a font and a point size from the three drop-down menu boxes on the Option bar.

2. Just to the right of the font size selection box is an icon with two "a's" in it. This is the anti-alias toggle and your best friend in digital imagining of text. You will almost always want to use anti-aliasing, so make sure it is white, meaning selected. To see the difference it makes choose a very big font and toggle it on and off. With it off you will see jaggies around any diagonal or rounded portions of the letters. With it on, Photoshop Elements gently blends your text into the background in a way that fools your eye into seeing smooth edges on the letters.

3. Choose the paragraph alignment you wish to use from the Option bar. Your choices are left aligned, centered, or right aligned. This really only matters if you plan to enter multiple lines of text.

4. Pick a color for the text you will be adding by clicking on the color box on the Option bar. Use the Color Picker dialog box to select your choice; it works the same way as with the painting tools (see Chapter 17). If you are making the image for the web only, you may want to check the Only Web Colors choice in the lower left corner.

5. Move your cursor over your image and notice it now displays a fancy "I" shaped cursor with a box around it (if you switch to the Vertical Type tool the fancy "I" shaped cursor rotates ninety degrees to indicate your tool choice). Click anywhere inside the image (or a selection, if one is active) and a bar cursor will appear with a height equal to the type size you selected. You can type in your text and it will appear on the image.

6. Select all or a portion of the text (you can use Ctrl+A or triple click on the text itself or double click on the "T" thumbnail in the Layer palette). Any text selected will be affected by the changes you make in the Text Options bar. Use the **Font** drop-down list to find a different font (type style) you like.

7. Click the **checkmark** button to the right of the Option bar, because even though most adjustments to formatting are shown instantly they are not committed to the image until you confirm at this step. At this point, it's a good idea to open up the Layers palette, which is probably docked in the Palette well. Notice that the text you added is in its own layer. Generally each time you click on the checkmark the currently added text is committed to an automatically created layer. This is evident in the next figure that shows two text layers. Check out Chapter 20 to find out more about layers.

8. After adding text, save a copy of your image using a progressive file name. You will want to save it in a Photoshop Elements format like PDD unless you are absolutely positive you will never want to edit it again to preserve layers and information about the text.

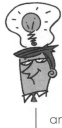

Say Cheese

Some true type fonts contain duplicate sets of letters, for example one is normal face, another is italics and another is bold. If the font you choose offers those choices, they will appear in the drop down box. What if your chosen font lacks italics? Never fear, Photoshop Elements is here: When you begin editing the Options bar will display four icons to the right of the anti-alias icon that are faux bold, italics, underline and strike-through. Even if your font lacks one of these choices, Photoshop Elements will render your font the way you wanted it!

The text is contained on its own layer, allowing it to be modified and positioned independently of the rest of the image and other layers.

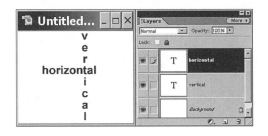

Notice that the text you highlight while in Type Tool editing mode is not in a bounding box (read about selections in Chapter 16). You can place a bounding box around it by clicking on the Move tool in the upper right of the Toolbox (or by typing "V" on the keyboard *after* committing your text to the layer with the checkmark. Once the bounding box appears you can resize, move, distort, and rotate the type by applying the same filters and tools that you would to other image elements. You also can use the Change Text Orientation button to the far right on the option bar if you want to go from vertical to horizontal or vice versa (in fact, I usually create my text in horizontal fashion, and then convert it for convenience).

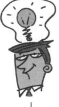

Say Cheese

Don't forget the Layer Styles palette in the Palette well as a way of applying some cool effects without touching the rest of the image. You click the Layer palette tab or, better yet, click and drag it out of the well, click the layer you want to affect, and then go to work with the Effects or Filters palette. If you have more than one palette open at the same time, you can dock them to each other. With one palette already open, drag the other on top of it to get them in the same palette window.

Demo: Applying a Drop Shadow

Drop shadows are literally a shadow of an object, in this case text. They help define and add depth to the type and also make the type appear to float above the image. You will see drop shadows used a lot by graphic designers to enhance the type quality, but like Brylcreem (for the old greasers out there) "a little dab will do ya!"

To add drop shadow to text in an image:

1. Open up any image or create a new one with **File, New.** Add any text you want with the Text Tool found in the Toolbox. Of course set the color, font, size, and other similar options as explained a minute ago.

2. Select all the text with either a Ctrl+A, by triple clicking on the text, or just open the Layers palette from the Palette well and click on the text layer you want to drop shadow. Your text layer is shown in the Layer palette with a large capital "T" in the thumbnail window and the text that you entered will be shown to the right of the thumbnail.

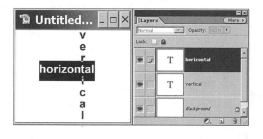

If you triple click the text in any layer of your image, it will be highlighted and the layer will be selected in the layer menu. Notice that there is no "f" icon in the highlighted section of the Layers palette. In a minute there will be!

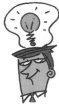

Say Cheese

Here's a really cool trick. Select all of the text on a layer and click the Warped Text button (the "T" with the curved line under it near the right end of the Option bar) and the Warped Text dialog will appear. Fiddle around with the various gizmos and gadgets in here to make your text do some very interesting things. When you open the Warp Text dialog it shows "Style: None" by default, which means if you click okay without changing the Style, you will apply no style. Who wants to be without style? Use the drop down to change the style as the next figure shows and the dialog box comes to life with scads of options.

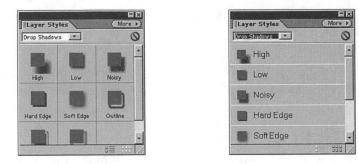

The Layer Styles palette dialog box (which will look like one or the other of these figures) enables you to select Drop Shadows from the drop down menu and then pick from some predefined styles of drop shadows and related styles like Neon or Outline. You can toggle back and forth between these views of the Layer Styles using the toggle buttons in the lower-right corner of the palette window or by using the More button in the upper right and selecting either List View (shown right) or Thumbnail View (shown left). The More button is only available if you drag a palette off the Palette well.

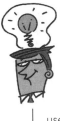

Say Cheese

One of the best features of Photoshop Elements is that any Layer Style added to your image is wed to the content. If you change the text in a layer, the drop shadow changes to match—Peter Pan would have liked this feature! One of the worst features of Photoshop Elements is that the drop shadow is gray, you don't have the ability to modify it. You will have to later simplify the layer, which unweds it and then use one of the color modification techniques if you want a different color drop shadow.

3. Click the **Layers Effects** tab in the Palette well and drag it onto your work surface. Alternatively, you may select **Window, Layer Styles** from the Menu bar. Select Drop Shadows from the pull down menu just under the Layer Styles tab in the palette.

4. Examine the drop shadows that are provided and select any one you prefer. Clicking it will apply it to all of the selected text similar to the next figure.

5. Now you have a drop shadow; let's fine-tune it a bit to make it look good. Double click the "f" icon (see the following figure) in the layer with the **Shadow,** which will bring up the Style Settings dialog.

6. Make adjustments until you like how it looks and save your changes in PDD format. Again we encourage the use of progressively numbered files.

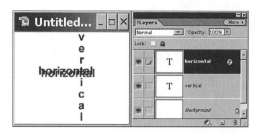

Once you add a Layer style such as Drop Shadow to a layer, an "f" icon appears in the Layers palette to the right of the layer name or text contained on the layer (in this case, to the right of the word "horizontal"). Double click the "f" to get available options for that Layer style.

The options available for drop shadow are the lighting angle (use global angle will tie all drop shadow or similar effects to the same light source), shadow distance, and preview. Smaller numbers usually work best (say 2 to 7 pixels) for drop shadows.

Changing the Opacity of Your Type in Photoshop Elements

Officially, there is no way to change the opacity of your type, but I'll show you a way to cheat (to be politically correct, we'll again call it a workaround). Actually, I already have! If you followed the preceding demonstration, by changing the file into a Photoshop format, you will note that each text entry committed with the check icon on the Option bar then appears in the layer stack as a normal layer. Well, guess what, that layer can have its opacity or blending mode changed. The Blending Mode options affect how the pixels of the current layer interact and mix with the layers below it. Conversely the Opacity setting determines how transparent the layer is and this allows you to see what is below it more clearly if the opacity has a lower number. Either will give a different look to your text.

On an image with a few layers, including one or more text layers, give this a try. Open the Layer palette from the Palette well and notice the drop down Blending Mode menu and Opacity text box just below the Layers tab. Try changing the blending mode to soft light and see the change. Experiment with some other modes to see what you like. Now go ahead and decrease the opacity number and watch your type become transparent. Again, this procedure relies on layers, so you might want to come back to this after you read Chapter 20.

Demo: Making Your Type Glow

In this demo, you'll learn how to make a glow appear around your type. To begin, open the file you just worked on, or repeat steps 1 to 6 in the previous demo to generate a new image with type, then do the following:

1. Open the **Layers** palette from the Palette well.

2. Duplicate the shadow layer by dragging it over the **Page** icon at the bottom right corner of the Layer palette.

3. Rename this new layer by double-clicking it in the layer stack and typing *glow* in the dialog box that opens.

4. Deactivate the original drop-shadow layer by clicking the **Eye** icon—we'll keep this around for safekeeping, but leave it hidden from view.

5. Click the **Glow** layer in the Layer palette if necessary to select it.

6. Open the Layer Styles palette from the Palette well. There are really three ways to place this palette on your workspace:

   ◆ You can click and drag it open independent of any other open palette.

   ◆ You can click and drag it over a title bar of another open palette and continue to pull it downward until you see a line appear over the open palette (about where the More button is), which docks this palette in the same palette window under the open palette.

   ◆ You can repeat the step above but continue dragging downward even further until you see a faint dotted outline around the entire open palette window and release, which will place both palettes one on top of the other in a tabbed format.

7. Click the small slashed circle icon in the upper-left corner of the Layer Styles palette to remove the existing drop shadow from the glow layer and then choose Outer Glows and choose Simple by double clicking it (or you can drag it to the layer on the Layer palette if it is visible). Like drop shadow, you don't have much choice of color, you get white for most of the options under the Layer Style palette.

8. Save the image if you like the result. I actually like the look even better when I re-activate the healthy layer as it gives the text a very nice three-dimensional look as you can see in the following image.

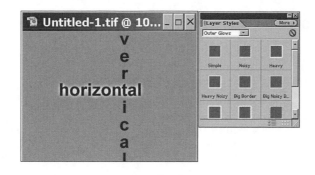

You can get some very nice results with the Layer Styles palette Outer Glow choices. Notice how the two active palettes are joined in a tabbed format in one window.

There are some other ways to get outer edge effects on your text layers. In fact there are a whole host of effects on the Layer palette which work only for text, including Outline and Brushed Metal for example. They aren't too hard to find as they all say "ABC" clear as day if they are special text effects. Unlike the Layer Styles, you can control the color of the Outlines when using the Effects palette, which works off of the current foreground color set at the bottom of the Toolbox.

Vectors to the Rescue

Photoshop Elements renders text in a vector graphic format. Now unless it is after your bedtime and you want a reason to stay up late, you may be saying, "So?" Well, it is a great favor Adobe did for you when they decided to make text render in this format because what it does is make a geometric formula to describe the text. You can therefore resize a text layer, rotate it, and otherwise mess around with it and the program will redo the math and render the text error free for you. Some programs render text in a raster format where color is mapped to bits and if you make significant modifications it will degrade the quality of your text image.

There are certain functions you may perform with text that will require that the text be converted from vector to raster format. If so, the Photoshop Elements will prompt you and ask if it may simplify the layer, meaning make the conversion in format for the layer. If you expect you will have to resize or make other significant modifications to the text layer, you should rethink your order of attack to complete those modifications before simplification occurs.

The Least You Need to Know

- Text can be put onto a photograph.

- Text will create a new layer.

- Text can be manipulated to change its size, position, and color.

- With a little bit of workaround you can adjust the opacity of text.

- Drop shadow, outer glow, and other effects can really dress up text.

- Text is rendered in a vector format but may need to be converted to a raster format.

Chapter 20

Layer Cake: Adding Elements

In This Chapter

◆ Separate elements and reality

◆ Add hierarchy to reality

◆ Adding and deleting layers

◆ Want to see through a wall? Add transparency

The biggest advance in digital imaging happened when Adobe brought out Photoshop 3.0 which enabled the use of layers. Many other companies soon followed Adobe's lead. Layers make imaging fun, spontaneous, and artistic. Before the advent of layers, every image brought into a Photoshop document had to be pasted onto the background layer. Every time you brought an element into an image, you had to save and rename the image to avoid overwriting earlier versions. If you didn't and made a mistake, you had to start all over.

What's a Layer?

Think of a *layer* as a plate of glass with an image on it. For example, one layer might have text, another might have the original photograph, and another might have a selection from a second photograph. (Usually, it is best to keep each image element on its own layer so that the element can be moved and manipulated without affecting the rest of the composition.) Each plate can be opaque, semitransparent, or fully transparent.

These layers are stacked one on top of the next to create one entire image, and each layer can be reshuffled in the stack to alter the image's composition. Layers can also be turned on or off, making its contents visible or invisible.

Lemme See One

With an image open in Photoshop Elements, open the Layers palette docked in the Palette well. By default, every image in Photoshop Elements starts with the background layer like the one shown in the next figure. When image pixels are erased from the background layer, a checkerboard pattern shows through indicating that you can see through the layer—which is called transparency. The background layer itself cannot be erased, but it can be duplicated or converted into a regular layer.

The Layer palette shows the background layer.

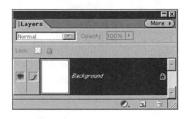

Using Layers: The Basics

The easiest way to learn about layers is to experience them yourself. To begin, let's create a new image:

1. Create a new image by pressing **Ctrl+N/Command+N.**

2. Because the image will be for onscreen viewing only, keep the resolution at 72 pixels/inch (commonly called 72dpi), size it at 5×4 inches (or 360×288 pixels), the mode to RGB and Contents either White or Transparent, using the options available on the New dialog box.

3. Select the entire image with **Ctrl+A** or choose **All** from the **Select** menu on the Menu bar.

4. Notice that the initial layer has been labeled the background layer, but it is actually Layer 0, as you will see in a minute. In the Layers palette, select the background layer and open the **Effects** palette docked in the Palette well. Then

select **Sandpaper** under the heading **All** in the drop down box and click the **Apply** button in the upper-right corner of the **Effects palette.** Now, if you look at the Layers palette, you will see that a new layer, "Layer 1," has been added to the image which contains a Sandpaper texture. Some Photoshop Elements steps automatically add a layer to your image like this one did.

Adding Layers

If you want to bring new elements into your image and keep them separate from your original image, you will need to put them on their own layer when Photoshop Elements doesn't do it automatically. To add new layers manually, do the following:

1. With the image you just created open on the desktop, click the new layer creation icon in the lower-right corner of the Layers palette. We will be using this image a little later on in the chapter for a continued demonstration. Alternatively, you can use the Menu bar Layer, New Layer or Shift+Ctrl/Command+N.

2. Look at the Layers palette and observe that a new layer appears, already named Layer 2 (Layer 1 was created earlier and now contains a Sandpaper texture). You will notice that Photoshop Elements automatically shows Layer 0 as the background layer, but it is not actually numbered. You can name your layers to help you keep track of them and I want to give you a little practice naming layers.

3. Repeat steps 1 and 2 to create Layer 2.

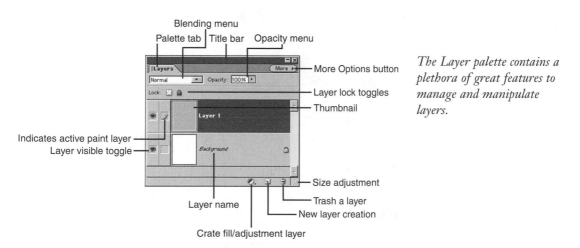

The Layer palette contains a plethora of great features to manage and manipulate layers.

Flash _____

If you are trying to paint or delete on a layer and nothing is happening, be sure that you have activated that layer. If you have indeed forgotten to activate your target layer, check the other layers to be sure you didn't end up painting over or deleting something on them! (I can't tell you how many times I've done this.)

4. Double click on the Background layer which is on the bottom in the Layers palette and the Layers Option box will open where you can type in the new name of the layer (it says "Background" in the layer, but when you open the dialog, it will say Layer 0).

5. Double click on the words "Layer 1" in the Sandpaper layer and you will see that a text box forms around the words and you can then type in the word *Sandpaper* to rename that layer. This option is not available for the Background layer until after you rename it.

6. Save your image in PDD or another Photoshop Elements format to preserve your layers for later editing.

Activating a Layer

No operation—a color change, fill, or movement—can be done to a layer until that layer has been *activated*. Conversely, when a layer has been activated, operations on it will not affect any other layers. Activating a layer is simple. Click the layer in the Layer palette to highlight it; that's all there is to it.

Layer 2 is activated, as indicated by the highlight box.

Showing and Hiding Layers

On the left side of each layer in the Layers palette is a small Eye icon. When the Eye appears, by clicking on the space on the left, next to the layer, the contents of the layer are visible. Clicking on the Eye icon "closes" the layer so it becomes invisible.

Notice in the following figure that the green circle is no longer visible in the image; not surprisingly, that layer does not have an Eye icon next to it in the Layers palette. Note: A layer can be active and yet invisible.

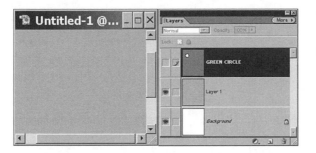

The Circle layer titled "Green Circle" has visibility turned off.

Deleting Layers

This can't get much simpler. If you want to delete a layer, grab it in the Layers palette and drag it onto the Trash Can icon at the bottom of the palette. If you goof up and drag the wrong layer—or change your mind—you can undo the action (remember, however, that you may undo only a limited number of actions, only 20 by default unless you have increased your undo preference using Edit, Preferences, General, modify History States from the Menu bar). If you are not quite sure you want to delete a layer, try hiding it instead (see the preceding section to learn how).

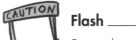 **Flash**

Remember the text layer cannot be activated unless the file is in a Photoshop file format (PDD or PSD). To save in Photoshop Elements format use File, Save As from the Menu bar and set Format to Photoshop.

Understanding Layer Hierarchy

The only thing that is better than having layers is the ability to shuffle the layers up and down the Layer pile or stack. A layer on top of the stack will always cover whatever layers are below it. But you can take this top layer and move it lower down the stack, closer to the background. This allows us to change how the layers, and the elements on the layers, relate to one another. You cannot move a background layer without first converting it to a normal layer.

Before we delve into layer hierarchies, let's draw on the layers of the image we created in the section titled "Using Layers: The Basics":

1. If you did it right, there will be a background layer and a sandpaper layer. Any extra layers can be deleted from the layer stack by highlighting them, right clicking and selecting delete, or by dragging them to the trash icon. Make sure the sandpaper layer has the Eye icon visible.

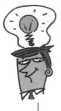

Say Cheese

More than one layer can be made invisible at the same time, but at least one layer in the image must always be visible or you won't see anything in the image. Duh!

2. Using the **Rectangle** tool from the **Toolbox,** draw a fairly large red rectangle. If you don't remember how to draw shapes back up and review Chapter 17. You will notice that doing this creates a new layer in the Layer palette stack.

3. Hide the background and sandpaper layers by toggling the eye icon in the Layers palette to the left side of each layer.

4. Activate the red rectangle layer by clicking it in the layer stack in the Layer palette, and be sure its Eye icon is visible.

5. Draw large green oval using the Elliptical Shape Tool from the Toolbox.

6. Hide the red rectangle layer by toggling the eye icon off for that layer in the layer stack.

7. Activate the green oval layer by highlighting it in the layer stack in the Layer palette, and be sure its Eye icon is visible.

8. Use the **Polygon Shape** tool to draw a blue triangle and again make sure it is visible by toggling the eye icon.

9. Save the file in PDD or PSD format. You've come too far to lose it now! It should look like the following figure.

Only two layers are visible. Notice how layers cover one another, with the shape in the layer on the top of the stack in the Layer palette covering any visible layer below where they overlap.

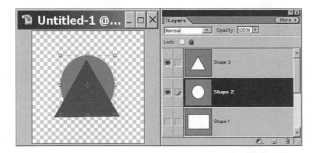

To demonstrate the hierarchy of the layers, note the following:

1. The green sun is setting behind the blue mountain, but the sandpaper and red rectangle layers are not visible. Even though they are not visible, if you saved in Photoshop format, they are still in the image and can be restored to visibility.

2. Toggle the eye icon for the sandpaper and red rectangle layers and note that you now have a sun setting against a red sky near a blue mountain in a desert—this is a creativity exercise for heavens sake.

3. Let's shuffle the deck a bit. With your cursor, which should look like a little hand, grab the green oval layer in the Layers palette and click and hold while you pull it down below the red rectangle. The blue triangle will be the top layer, covering the layers below it, but the red rectangle now also covers the green oval where they overlap. This is a great way to hide an element behind another element, as shown in the next figure.

4. Try adjusting the opacity of the red rectangle layer by highlighting it in the layer stack and using the opacity slider. It should fade toward pink as it becomes partially transparent, and your green oval will probably reappear, but in a brownish or olive shade because you are now seeing it through the red.

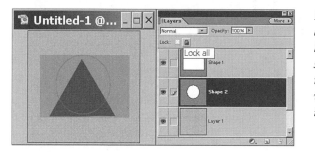

Because the green oval in my case was completely over-lapped by the other two shapes it disappears. Note the circle in the image, which shows where the circle is even though not visible.

Working with Layers

After you've got the basics of using layers down, you can get into the nitty-gritty of really making them work for you.

Rotating, Distorting, and Resizing Layers

While you have a layer activated, select the **Move** tool from the upper right corner of the Toolbox. As soon as the layer is selected, the selection handles appear. As before, you can resize, distort, and rotate the layer. Remember, all the objects on the layer are going to be affected. If you want to rotate just one part of the layer, you must first select that area using the Rectangle or Selection Brush tool.

Moving Layers

To move a layer within an image, do the following:

1. Click to activate any layer in the Layers palette.

2. Select the Move tool from the Toolbox. Your cursor should change into a solid black triangle.

3. Place the cursor over the image itself, and then press and hold the mouse button down.

4. Move your mouse to move the layer.

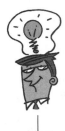

Say Cheese _____

If you don't feel like using the Layers palette to activate the layer you want to move, click directly on the object in your image that you want to move and select the Move tool. Once you move your selection, you will see the layer titled floating selection. (Note that if you inadvertently pick the wrong spot, you might activate the wrong layer.)

Say Cheese _____

When you make a selection, it floats between the layers, which means that you can apply that selection to any layer. However, it is effective on the active layer only.

Behind the Shutter

Well, do you think that the numbering of layers from zero is a bug in the program? Very confusing, but very typical! Many computer languages number from zero up, and programmers wrote this program. It made sense to them, no doubt.

To move a layer from one image to another, do the following:

1. With one image open, open up any other image using either the File > Open or Window > Browse method from the Menu bar.

2. Position the images so that both are visible on-screen (if you need to make the images smaller, go ahead, using View, Zoom Out from the Menu bar).

3. Click the title bar of image two you just opened and highlight any layer with content in that image. Then with the **Move** tool click and drag a layer to your originally open image.

4. As you drag the selected layer onto the first image with the move tool the first image will automatically become focused as the active window. Release it there.

5. Take a look at the Layers palette; the new element appears as a new layer. In some circumstances it may be shown as a floating layer. If so, proceed with step 6.

6. To make this a new layer, drag the floating layer to the icon at the bottom of the Layers palette that resembles a piece of paper.

7. The new Layer is automatically named the next number in the existing numerical order.

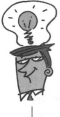

Say Cheese

Often, when you copy a layer or selection from one image into another image, the pasted-in layer or area is too large or too small. After all, when you took the two different pictures, you probably weren't standing the same distance from each subject. To resize the pasted-in area or layer, select it using a Selection tool or the Layer palette and resize as needed.

Erasing Layers

The Eraser tool allows you to erase pixels from one layer, and have pixels from the layer below show through. This can be quicker than making a selection and then deleting an area. To use the Eraser tool, open the **Eraser** tool from the Toolbox. Choose a brush size from the Erasers Options bar, and then drag the Eraser tool over an active layer (use a large fuzzy brush and carefully erase around the edge of your image to achieve a nice blended effect).

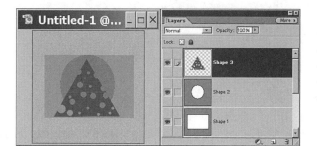

The Eraser tool allows you to erase pixels on one layer and have pixels from the layer(s) below show through. Turns out this was a picture of Swiss cheese, not a mountain.

Transitioning from One Layer to Another

When you place one layer on top of another—especially if the top layer has been selected and copied or cut from one location to another—you sometimes end up with what I call a *cookie cutter* effect, where the edges look abnormally sharp. Follow these steps, and I'll show you what I mean!

1. Be sure the Layers palette is open on your screen from the Palette well.

2. Open any image that has a few independent objects that have flat color.

3. Zoom in on a flat colored object.

4. Choose the **Magic Wand** tool from the Toolbox.

5. Choose the object. You might need to use the Selection Brush tool to trim your selection if you grab some of the color around the object.

6. Open the **Edit** menu and choose **Copy** (or press **Ctrl+C/Command+C,** the same keys used in almost all programs, word processing and spreadsheets alike, to perform copy-and-paste operations), which copies the object to the Clipboard.

7. Open another image, this time with darker colors.

8. Paste the object into the new image (open the **Edit** menu and choose **Paste** or press **Ctrl+V/Command+V**). The object appears in the center.

9. Zoom into the object. You will notice that the edges look very sharp—what I call a cookie-cutter appearance like that shown in the following figure of a flower placed atop a head.

To correct this cookie-cutter appearance try Feathering.

The flower is pasted onto the girl's hair creating a new layer. It has a hard edge on it.

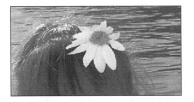

Feathering

Many imaging software programs allow you to feather a selection, which makes the elements on one layer "flow" nicely to the layer below. Using the previous example, you can soften the edges of the flower and make it blend a little better into the image by doing the following:

1. Be sure the pasted object's layer is active and the object is selected, and then open the **Select** menu on the Menu bar and choose **Feather.**

2. The Feather dialog box opens as shown in the next figure. The default number of pixels used to feather is "20."

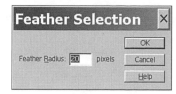

Use the Feather dialog box to blend your images together.

3. Use the Feather Radius field to set the amount of feathering (that is, how much of the object's edge will be deleted to soften the image). The number you enter varies depending on the size of the floating image and your image resolution. You'll have to experiment with it until you get the hang of it, but for now, try 5 or 10.

4. Click **OK.**

5. Cut and then paste your object back into the image.

Say Cheese

Remember, you can undo the feather and play around until you get the effect you like. Experiment with all the options to get the hang of how feathering works. Mastering this part of cutting and pasting really makes your images come together and look untouched (of course, we know better).

When you have finished working on your image and you are delighted with it, you can flatten it before you save it. This reduces the file's size. Click the More menu in the upper-right corner of the Layers palette and choose **Flatten Image** from the menu that appears. All the layers merge together; save your image, and you're done!

Soft Edges Make Pleasing Pictures

For a nice effect on images try the following:

1. Pick a selection tool, usually the Elliptical or Rectangle Marquee tool from the Toolbox.

2. Set feathering to a number between 5 and 25, a higher number makes for a softer edge.

3. Select the main part of your photo and choose **Image, Crop** from the Menu bar. This trims the photo to just larger than the selection.

4. Finally choose **Select, Inverse** on the Menu bar and press the **Delete** key on the keyboard.

You should get a nice, soft edged picture that fades out to the background color specified in the color swatch on the Toolbar like the one in the next figure. Use of the Elliptical tool for this purpose makes an image you would commonly call a cameo.

You can get away from same ole, same ole square pictures with the soft edge technique.

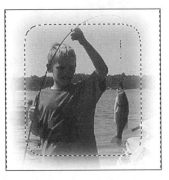

The Least You Need to Know

- ◆ Elements can rest on their own layers.
- ◆ Layers can be rearranged in their hierarchy.
- ◆ An element on a layer will cover the element on a layer below it.
- ◆ A layer can have opacity.
- ◆ Selections can be feathered.

Filters and Effects: Funky and Fun

In This Chapter

- Learn about the many varieties of filters
- Apply filters to your image for the effects you want
- Apply multiple filters that can give you some unique results
- Effects can make quick work of photo transformations

Filters can be used to improve or add visual effects to your photos. Sharpening filters make your images look crisp and clear. Blur filters help you create effects such as depth of field and can help blend areas of your image together. Artistic filters can add texture, color, brush strokes, and a whole range of visual effects to your images. A whole range of filters are available to help you make your imaging experience fun and enjoyable.

Daddy, What's a Filter?

Filters are magical! Well, okay—to be honest, filters are simply mathematical formulas (called *algorithms*) that, when applied to an image, perform a specific task. That task can be as simple as finding every green pixel and changing it to red, or as complex as finding every pixel that has a neighboring pixel darker than it and darkening it. Some filters are easy to apply to an image and *actuate* very quickly, whereas others cause your computer to grind away for many minutes.

> ### Behind the Shutter
>
> The most amazing—and most used—filters are the sharpening filters, which we covered way back in Chapter 14. These filters, and in fact much of digital photography, owe their existence to scientific and military research. The ability to single out a specific star amongst a cluster of constellations or to determine the crop yield of a Nebraska farm from space is all due to digital photography and the filtering, or sharpening, of digital information.

Whoa, There!

Filters can be a lot of fun to play with; making and applying special effects to your images can keep you busy for hours on end. You can create new "looks" for your images, and change their mood and intent. But before I let loose and describe all the wonders of filters, I must warn you that filters can be harmful to your images if used in excess or applied too strongly.

> ### In Plain Black & White
>
> I might or might not have been the first to coin the phrase **filter surfing** (trying out every filter until you find one that you like), but it describes the serious problem of covering up a low quality image with filters that offer no noticeable improvement.

Use filters sparingly. Let them add a sparkle or a subtle hint to your photos. Don't apply a filter just because you can. If you find that you need to apply filter after filter to make your image look better, you probably don't have a good image to start with. Leave your image alone, retake the image if you can, or go on to another image. When I teach digital photography or electronic imaging, I don't let my students anywhere near filters until they demonstrate creative composition and basic photographic skills. Filters should be used to enhance an already sound image, they won't turn digital junk into image trinkets.

Obtaining Filters

Photoshop Elements includes a host of filters. If you are using another program that came bundled with your camera it may also offer filters.

Most imaging programs, including Photoshop Elements, allow you to add additional filters. In fact, Photoshop Elements is represented as accepting and supporting any Photoshop plug-in designed for RGB images. Many companies offer specialized filters, or plug-ins, for your imaging software. For a pretty good list see www.thepluginsite. com/resources/, which separates them by free and commercial types. (Filters are often called plug-ins because of the way they are added onto the original program code. Most programs have a folder called Plug-ins, where the filters are stored.) Some of these filters can be had for free, whereas others might cost $150 or more. It is very common that popular filters offered by third parties are incorporated directly into the software in later versions.

Most third-party filter companies have websites where you can get information and descriptions about their filters, so you might also try your favorite search engine. Many also offer a demo version of their product for you to download. In most cases, demo filters are limited in their functionality or durability—but you can be sure that there will be more than enough to whet your appetite. Note: Before you buy a filter, try that filter's demo version so you can be sure that it will be able to run on your platform and with your specific version of software. It would be a shame to find out that the $100 filter you just purchased won't work with your software unless you upgrade or spend money on hardware or operating system upgrades.

Say Cheese

Filters are great, but don't overlook the Effects and Layer Styles palettes in the Palette well. Each can produce some really great looking enhancements that would take several different filters to achieve.

Let's Go

We could explore every filter ever known to man, but that would take a lot of time— and it would also take all the fun out of it for you. Instead, we will look at one or two filters in a few of the filter families or groups. A good way to familiarize yourself with the various filters is to open an image and open the Filters palette from the Palette well. There you will find many filters. Go ahead and try out any filter that catches your fancy, and enjoy yourself!

When working with filters, keep the following in mind:

◆ Most filters in Photoshop Elements can be found in the **Filters** menu.

◆ Filters can be applied to entire images, but you can also isolate an area of an image, applying your filter only to the selected area.

◆ If you don't like the result of a filter, immediately undo it by pressing **Ctrl+Z/Command+Z.**

◆ If you play with the settings of a filter and then want to revert back to the defaults for the filter, hold the alt key down and click on the reset button that appears.

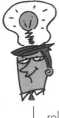

Say Cheese _____

You can zoom in or out of the preview box by clicking the + or - button below the box. If you put your cursor on the image inside the preview box, you can drag the preview to view a different section of your image. This comes in handy when you want to check an effect on a specific part of your image. Left clicking in the preview window will toggle you back to the pre-filtered image so you can compare and releasing will toggle back to the preview of the post-filter result.

The filters are grouped in the Filter palette by type. Plug-in filters you add are generally placed at the bottom of the list. Only specially designed plug-ins will display a preview thumbnail in the Filter palette. Without further adieu, the categories as listed in the following figure are: Artistic, Blur, Brush Strokes, Distort, Noise, Pixelate, Render, Sharpen, Sketch, Stylize, Texture, Video, and Other.

You can access the Filters under the Filter palette from the Palette well or by using the Filter choice on the Menu bar as shown here. Under each category of filter there are filter choices. Notice that whatever filter you last used appears at the top of the menu (Ctrl+F or Command+F) but it will apply with the same settings used last time.

Last Filter Ctrl+F		
Artistic ▶	Colored Pencil...	
Blur ▶	Cutout...	
Brush Strokes ▶	Dry Brush...	
Distort ▶	Film Grain...	
Noise ▶	Fresco...	
Pixelate ▶	Neon Glow...	
Render ▶	Paint Daubs...	
Sharpen ▶	Palette Knife...	
Sketch ▶	Plastic Wrap...	
Stylize ▶	Poster Edges...	
Texture ▶	Rough Pastels...	
Video ▶	Smudge Stick...	
Other ▶	Sponge...	
Digimarc ▶	Underpainting...	
	Watercolor...	

In Plain Black & White _____

"Digimarc" appears at the bottom of list under Filter on the Menu bar. The word is short for "Digital Watermark" and it represents a technology used for embedding code in images that permits them to be traceable to enforce copyrights. When you unpack Photoshop Elements it comes with a reader to see if the image you are working on is protected by a digimarc, but you can buy a plug-in from www.digimarc.com to embed your own marks in your images.

Artistic Filters

Artistic filters are generally filters that add effect over the top of images, such as adding colored pencil strokes or glowing colors. Photoshop Elements provides tons of different artistic filters; here, we'll take a look at the Colored Pencil filter.

1. Open an image that you think would look nice as a pencil drawing, some contrast and color usually makes for a good choice.

2. Open the **Filter** menu from the Menu bar or drag the Filter palette out of the Palette well, choose **Artistic,** and select **Colored Pencil.**

3. The Colored Pencil dialog box opens as shown in the following figure; click and drag the three different sliders to vary the filter effect. The preview area enables you to see how the filter effect will look before you apply it to the entire image.

4. Click **OK** when you like what you see in the preview box.

5. Open the **File** menu, choose **Save As,** and rename the image to preserve the original.

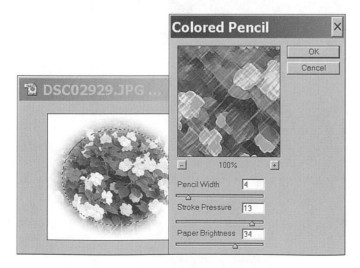

Many filters use dialog boxes with preview areas to help you visualize the filter's effect before you apply it.

Blurs

Usually, blur filters are used to improve image quality. However, in some cases, such as with the Motion blurs or Circular blurs, very nice effects can be rendered:

1. Open an image whose foreground object could use a little acceleration.

2. Open the Layers palette from the Palette well or by using Window, Layer on the Menu bar.

3. Duplicate the background layer by clicking and holding while pulling the background layer thumbnail down over the "page" icon at the bottom of the Layers palette.

4. Click in the duplicate layer in the stack in the Layers palette to activate it.

5. While you can apply this filter to the whole image, it is often best if you select some portion of the image (see instructions below) that you want to keep unaffected and then open the **Filter** menu or Filter palette, choose **Blur,** and select **Motion Blur** to apply the filter to the balance of the active layer.

6. Adjust the settings however you like, and click **OK.** It is usually best if you can keep the motion in the direction of travel for moving objects like we did with the runner in the figure below, but if you are simply seeking depth of field, direction of motion blur is discretionary.

You can leave a portion of your image unaffected by a filter. Try only selecting a portion of your image and applying the filter. Everything outside of the selection area remains unmodified. You can make something look like it is really moving. In this case I used the magnetic lasso several times to select the subject and turned an overly busy background into a canvas to show speed.

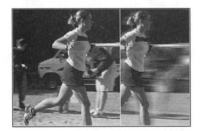

To capture only your subject you need to select the correct selection tools, keeping these points in mind:

1. For a square, rectangle, oval, or circular object try the Marquee tools from the Toolbox.

2. For a solid color object use the Magic Wand tool from the Toolbox.

3. For a person, car, plane, train, tree, etc. use the Magnetic Lasso tool from the Toolbox, clicking where you need to hold a hard point, and trusting the magic for the rest. You can also try the Lasso or Polygonal Lasso tool. Remember you can add and delete from the selection by using the middle two of the four icons that show on the Option bar between the tool selection icons and the Feather option. Be careful, note in the figure above that I was sloppy and lost a chunk of the subject's forehead and right thumb.

4. After selection, invert the selection with **Select, Inverse** on the Menu bar.

5. Apply the blur filter and get amazing results.

Smudge Tool

Similar to blurring, the Smudge tool, which looks like a pointing finger located on the Toolbar, enables you to smudge and smear areas of your image like I did in the following figure. The Smudge tool grabs either the pixels under the brush (regular mode) when you first click, or uses the foreground color in the Toolbox color swatch (in finger paint mode—when the checkbox in the Option bar is selected) and drags the color through the image after the cursor. (You can reclick to grab more color and go over an area a few times to enhance the effect.) The Options bar enables you to pick the smudge's size and fuzziness; no color selection need be made unless you have finger painting selected. I have the best luck with this tool when I create a duplicate copy of a layer to smudge and then turn down the duplicate layer's opacity after smudging in the Layer palette.

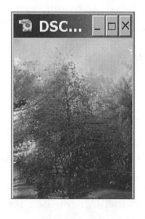

Using the Smudge tool gives images an artsy windblown effect.

Texture Filters

Okay, before we move on from filters, let's dig in to one more category, Textures. Texture filters can be a lot of fun and can be used to create many wonderful backgrounds or interesting effects. Don't be afraid to experiment. The Texture filters that come in Photoshop Elements are: Craquelure, Grain, Mosaic Tiles, Patchwork, Stained Glass, and Texturizer.

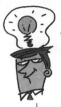

Say Cheese _____

You don't have to use the filters I have chosen for this demo; use any ones you want. By all means, experiment!

1. Open an image using **File, Open** or **Window, Browse** from the Menu bar.

2. Either open the Filter palette from the Palette well or use **Filter, Texture** from the Menu bar.

3. For the next figure, I tried two different Texture filters, the Mosaic Tile and Patchwork filters.

The Texture filters can give many different looks to one image. The one on the right, Mosaic Tile, has a look as if it is printed on a textured surface. The one on the right, Patchwork, looks as if it is created by needlepoint.

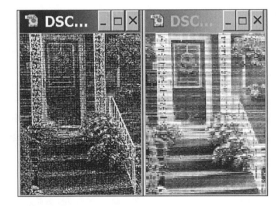

Demo: Applying Multiple Filters

More than one filter can be used on an image. You can build some interesting effects by applying one filter on top of another:

1. Open the **File** menu from the Menu bar, choose **New,** and create a new image that is 4 inches wide, 5 inches tall, and 72dpi.

2. Select the entire image using **Ctrl+A/Command+A** or the **Selection, All** choice on the Menu bar.

3. Set the foreground color using the toolbar color swatch to a primary color and then go up to the **Edit** menu on the Menu bar, select **Fill,** and fill the entire image with the solid color.

4. Open the **Filters** menu from the Menu bar or in the Filter palette, choose **Noise,** and select **Add Noise.**

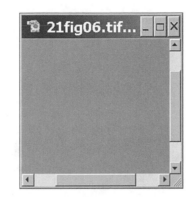

Start with a solid color background.

5. In the **Add Noise** filter dialog box, click the **Gaussian Blur** option button, and type 155 in the **Amount** field.

6. Click **OK.** Either shag carpet or a nice background!

7. Using the Rectangle selection tool, select about two-thirds of the center of the image.

8. Open the **Filters** menu on the Menu bar, choose **Blur,** and select **Motion Blur.**

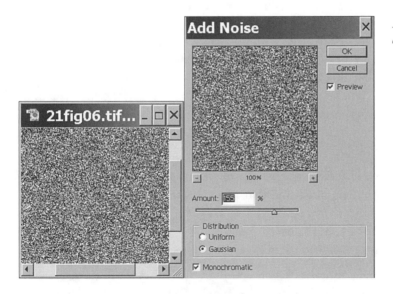

Noise filter applied to solid color background.

9. Adjust the settings however you like in the Motion Blur dialog, and click **OK** to get something like the above figure.

10. Again using the Rectangle selection tool, select an area inside the blur area.

11. Open the **Effects** menu, choose **Distort,** and select **Ripple** to apply the Ripple filter to the image. Your results, which are subtle, should look like the following image.

After applying a motion blur to the selection go for a ripple.

Create Your Own Filter

If you don't find quite what you want for a filter, or find yourself doing things manually over and over, consider making a custom filter. On the Menu bar choose **Filter, Other, Custom.** You are confronted with a Custom dialog box, which at best is obtuse as to what it does. In quick form, there is a column and row matrix containing 25 text boxes. The center box represents a pixel in the image that is being evaluated by the filter. The filter will step through the entire image using the matrix and mathematically adjust the brightness of pixels. The surrounding boxes adjust brightness relative to the evaluated pixel. There is a range for the brightness multiplier of –999 to +999. Less significant numbers are usually in order.

Adobe suggests that you try to keep the sum of all numbers at or near one to avoid a completely black or white result. I find that most sets that I like have a scale number that equals the sum of the array set. As you increase the sum in the array boxes, you get a lighter image and as you decrease it you should get … you guessed right, darker. You don't have to include a multiplier in every box. Those left blank will be unaffected.

This is big time trial and error, but when you figure it out, you can do some very cool things. When you get one you like, you can save it and reload it later. An example matrix of values I found on the Internet suggests this to give a slight blur:

0	1	2	1	0
1	−1	−2	−1	1
2	−2	4	−2	2
1	−1	−2	−1	1
1	1	2	1	0

Play with the Scale number and you will get a smoother blur as you increase the number. You can also play with the offset, which will tend to lighten/darken the image. Both are mathematical formulas being applied. They say, "for scale, enter the value by which to divide the sum of the brightness values of the pixels included in the calculation." Now there is plain English, not! Suffice it to say that there are whole books on this stuff, but the beauty is you can fiddle and learn as you go like I did in the following image. I used 8 for Scale and 0 for Offset. Save it and you will see it is saved as an .ACF file. I created a special folder to keep these in.

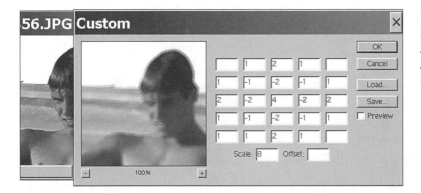

Use the custom filter dialog to adjust your images. This shows the before (left) and after (right) because the preview box has been unchecked.

If you look on the Internet you will find recipes for these types of custom filter settings to achieve looks you want. Let's try one more, for smoothing:

0	1	2	1	0
1	3	4	3	1
2	4	9	4	2
1	3	4	3	1
0	1	2	1	0

The sum of these numbers is 53, enter that into the Scale box and leave Offset at 0. This is actually an approximation of a gaussian blur. See what it does, and save it if you like it.

Effects Make Quick Work of Photo Transformations

Photoshop Elements has a whole 'nother bag of tricks up it's sleeve called Effects. Many effects are just filters with specified settings, or even a combination of filters. Others are new tricks you haven't seen before, but whatever they may be, they bring power to your image processing. There are really three types of Effects:

> **Flash**
>
> For some of the Effects if you are working on a vector image (such as shapes, type, or layers containing one or the other) you will first need to simplify, meaning convert to raster, before the Effect will take hold. You will be asked if you want to, but understand once you convert, you cannot convert back.

- ◆ Selection
- ◆ Layer
- ◆ Type

Selection Effects work on any selection you have made in your image, which can of course include the selection of the entire image. Layer Effects work only on the active layer or layers. Finally Type Effects work on text.

Let's Have an Effect!

One of my favorite things to do is take a decent image and put a border around it. The Effects palette offers many good framing choices for those who prefer not to make their own. To open the Effect palette drag it from the Palette well. Click the drop down menu and choose Frames. I particularly like foreground color and brushed aluminum. However, take a look at them all.

Let's try one more. The Fluorescent Chalk filter can make some interesting photo effects like the next image displays. Note that the Effects work without any options at all. They just do their thing and you either like what you get, or leave it.

You can make some interesting photos, such as this one created with the Fluorescent Chalk Effect filter from the Filter palette.

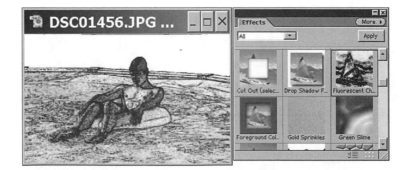

The Least You Need to Know

◆ A filter is a mathematical algorithm that is applied to the image.

◆ Besides the filter that comes with your software, third-party filters can be purchased, or you can even make your own using the Custom Filter dialog.

◆ You can select areas of your image to filter and also protect areas from being filtered.

◆ You can use multiple filters together on the same image.

◆ You can use effects to whip up some great image enhancements.

What You See Is What You Get: Calibration

In This Chapter

- ◆ Taking the frustration out of color calibration

- ◆ Calibrating your monitor, not your eyes

- ◆ Calibrating your printer, stop wasting paper

- ◆ When all else fails take an educated guess

- ◆ Tagging images for color management

The next time you are in an appliance store, take a good look at all the televisions lined up next to one another. You will notice that every screen in the store looks different! Some are dark, some are light, one is too green, and another is too contrasting. But which one has the right color? Which one do you prefer? Is the one you prefer the right one?

You have run smack into one of the most aggravating problems of digital photography: color management. How do you know that what you see on your monitor is correct? If the image looks good on your screen, will it look good on someone else's? Will it be too dark, or too green? Will the contrast look right?

Color management doesn't end at the monitor; printers can also wreak havoc. Every printer reproduces an image differently. You can go to a computer store and print the same image on three different brands of printers, and get three totally different results. In fact, you can take three printers of the same model and get three different-looking prints. This problem with color varying from one device to another is called device dependant color. If left untouched, each monitor will do as it pleases and printers will follow. Soon we will have color anarchy! But have no fear. Color can be successfully and easily managed so it becomes device independent. With a little bit of testing and careful planning, you can get consistent and predictable results every time regardless of what monitor or printer you are using.

How the Pros Do It

To get a good idea of how color management can be achieved, I am going to talk you through a system that professional photographers and printers use; I will then explain how you can use it without too much trouble. This system not only provides consistent color, but also allows for different devices (monitors and printers) to be swapped in and out and have the color results remain the same. We're going to get a little technical here for a while, so don't worry if you get confused. Just sit back and relax, and it will all make sense in the end.

CIE

Suppose you took all the colors that the human eye can perceive and globbed them all together in a three-dimensional space, such as a cube, sphere, or even a pyramid.

To describe where a color exists in that space, you can use a system based on three axes: Luminance (or lightness), A (green-red), and B (blue-yellow). In this manner, you can accurately describe where a specific color is in the color space. For example, suppose that the color "Fire Engine Red" exists at 44-L, 25-Y, and 100-Z. (I made these numbers up; don't go looking for them!) As long as the color world we made up stays consistent from person to person, the coordinates used to describe the location for the color "Fire Engine Red" will be the same for each person. Because this point in three-dimensional color world exists, we can accurately describe it and it is device independent.

Well, in 1931, the folks in the Commission Internationale de l'Eclairage (CIE) made up a color world like we just did, and in 1976, that model for color was updated; they call the model *CIE LAB color system*. It theoretically displays every color perceived by the human eye and allows us to specifically describe each color. As long as everybody uses the CIE LAB space and its numerical description for finding colors, everybody will be looking at the exact same color when given its description. That is, when we are told to look at 65-L, 62-A, 64-B (orange), we will all be looking at the same color. This consistent approach to describing color is the key to color management, in that you can use this color model as a constant, or control, to compare other colors and color devices.

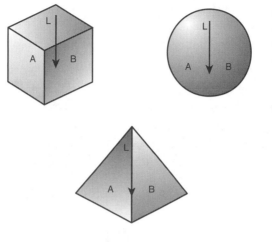

A simple diagram shows the three color axes used to describe the L*A*B* color space.

Behind the Shutter

All through this book, I have been talking about RGB color spaces. So, why all of a sudden am I hawking CIE LAB? Here's the deal: RGB color spaces describe how much color is present because it is an additive method. The RGB color space describes how much red, green, and blue light is present—in the case of a monitor, how many pixels are illuminated and at what intensity. We have not talked much about the CMYK color system, which is used in printing, but it describes how much cyan, magenta, yellow, or black ink is on the paper, so it is additive.

The problem is that different monitors use more or fewer phosphors to produce the same color. On monitor A, you might need 235R, 28G, 28B to produce Fire Engine Red. On monitor B, 235R, 25G, 31B will produce the exact same color. In a like manner, for CMYK, different quantities of ink are used by individual printers to reproduce the same color.

Because the RGB and CMYK color worlds measure how much phosphor or ink is needed to reproduce a color, both systems are considered device dependent. Depending on the device, a color's description changes according to what is needed to reproduce the color. Because the CIE LAB space describes where a color is in its color world and not how much ink or phosphors are needed to render the color, the color space is considered device independent. No matter what device is used, Fire Engine Red will look the same—although different devices will use differing amounts of inks or phosphors to reproduce it.

So now what? The answer is simple—we calibrate your monitor and printer to the device independent CIE Lab color system and your monitor and printer will then render colors to perfection. Think of it as cross-indexing. This chapter tells you how to do it.

ICC Profiles

Using the CIE LAB color space, you know how to describe every color we want, including Fire Engine Red. Now that you have a target to aim at, you need a method to tell you how far you are from that target. The International Color Consortium (ICC), which is made up of a group of eight industry leaders such as Kodak, Adobe, Apple Computing, and Agfa, developed a method to do just that. Once we know how far off we are, we can make a correction and index it so that our color is perfectly rendered.

The ICC system is simple. With it, you can calibrate every device that handles color. To begin, you display series of colors for which you know CIE LAB coordinates on your monitor or printer (I'm using a monitor for this example). After a color is displayed (say, for example, that you're displaying color L-100 A-80 B-60), you could use a monitor calibrator, shown here, to measure it. The calibrator reads the color displayed by the monitor, and describes it in CIE LAB space. So suppose the L-100 A-80 B-60 color you sent to your monitor measures up on your screen as L-98 A-80 B-60. What do you do, panic? Nope, you're a professional. You take note that your monitor is –2 from your CIE LAB space. This notation is called an *ICC profile*.

Of course you probably don't have a monitor calibrator handy, so what next? The answer lies in pre-defined ICC profiles that manufacturers now develop for each device, or by creating a custom profile using your eyes. By using the standard profile for your device (you may need to get it from your manufacturer if it is not in the documentation), you can make the correct adjustments with almost as much precision as the pro downtown who bought a fancy schmancy calibrator; you will come pretty close using just your eye.

Monitor calibrator measuring monitor color to develop an ICC profile.

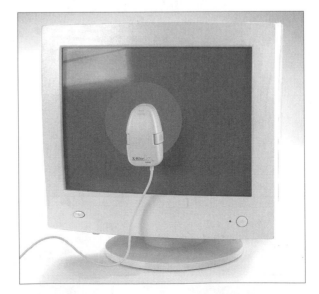

Calibrating Monitors and Printers

If you really want to spend the serious money you can buy a professional grade monitor with a calibration package and monitor calibrator included. You may also purchase calibrators and software separately. These devices and software might range in price from $100 to $1,000. Unless you are very serious about your color, or a professional photographer, a low- to midrange calibrator will do. The best place I have found to purchase a calibrator is through a catalog or on the web. Take a look at www.color.com (Color Solutions) to learn more about color-management software and calibrators.

Fortunately, with standard profiles now widely available and monitor calibration software included with Photoshop Elements for Windows and standard on a Macintosh, the average person can do just fine without any of that!

Calibrating a Monitor with Macintosh/Windows

A rose is a rose is a rose, but let's be sure a red rose is red and a yellow rose is yellow. Lets get to work. Macs have a Color Sync control panel, which coordinates, keeps track of, and implements all the profiles you have. (A similar tool is found on Windows systems.) The ColorSync control panel reads the profile you have for your monitor. "Ah hah," it says, "according to its ICC profile, this monitor is –2. I'm going to add 2 to everything that the computer sends to the monitor. That way, the color #100 will look like it is supposed to." Pretty smart little control panel!

Every calibration system is going to go about the calibration task a bit differently, but here is the basic procedure:

1. Warm up your monitor by using it for about a half-hour.

2. Start your calibration software. For a Mac use your Color Sync control panel, for a Windows machine look in your Program Files/Common Files/Adobe/ Calibration folder on your hard drive. It may also have been placed in your control panel. Click **Adobe Gamma** shown highlighted in the following figure.

3. Choose **wizard** and hit the next button, but if you select control panel by mistake there is a chance at any time to go to the wizard for instructions.

4. Follow through the wizard screens, which will ask you to choose a profile for a starting point. If you are unsure of your ICC profile use the one that appears, but otherwise click the **Load** button and find your profile.

5. Click **Next** and you will be presented with brightness and contrast settings as shown in the following figure. Do as it asks and click **Next**.

Start the Adobe Gamma utility, which comes packed with Photoshop Elements, to begin calibration on a Windows system.

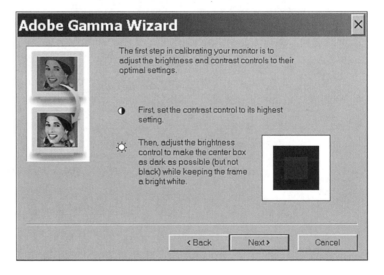

Use the wizard to find a setting that makes the center square nearly black while keeping the outside ring white.

6. Pick your phosphor settings if known (you should be able to find this in your monitor documentation or get it from the manufacturer, but if not, use custom) and click **Next.**

7. Uncheck "View Single Gamma Only" and you will get the red, green and blue channels. Use the sliders to make the center boxes match as nearly as possible the surrounding ring of striped color as shown in the following figure. When you have it set, click **Next.**

Make the three color channels match the outer rings with the sliders in this step. For the gamma you can use a number between 1.0 and 3.0, but you are probably best to use Windows default.

8. Measure the Hardware White Point (with the lights out) by selecting the most neutral gray square, and read the instructions carefully as you progress through this step.

9. You will also be asked at this point if you prefer to work at a different white point than the calibrated point. It is best to say no in most cases. Click **Next** to get to the last step!

10. You now can toggle back and forth before the adjusted and pre-adjusted settings using the toggle buttons as shown in the following figure. If the adjustment looks good, click **Finish.** Otherwise you can click Back to redo a step or click Cancel to leave all well enough alone.

Behind the Shutter

It is important to note that the ColorSync control panel does not change the original file. It changes only how it is reproduced on the screen or the printer. When the file is sent to someone else's printer or monitor, and that person has calibrated to ICC profiles for his or her devices, the file will reproduce just the way it did on your system.

After you calibrate, don't rest on your laurels. Monitors slip further with age, so periodically recalibrate. As you begin to understand calibration more clearly, you can use the Control Panel Method.

You get a chance to see the changes before confirming them. Toggle back and forth between the current and proposed calibrated state before accepting it.

Experienced calibrators can skip the wizard and work their own magic.

Calibrating a Printer with Macintosh/Windows

Some printers now come with calibration tests included with the bundled software. It usually involves diagnostics where you print a test page and then pick a set of color swatches that match with established colors/patterns.

The pros can do it the fancy way using printer calibration equipment to index to CIE LAB values. You make a printout and measure the printout with a printer calibrator, such as the one shown here. The calibrator, with a little help from some software, develops an ICC profile for the printer. For example, my printer reproduces the color #100 as #110, which means it has an ICC profile of +10. So when my system sends color to be printed, it subtracts 10 from the color as it is shipped to the printer.

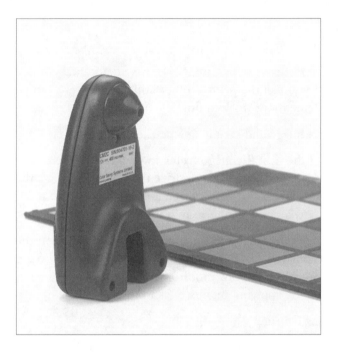

A printer calibrator is used to read any reflective medium, such as paper

Fortunately for the rest of us it is no longer that tough! Photoshop Elements now includes color management. Follow these steps:

1. Choose **File, Print Preview** from the Menu bar.

2. Select **Show More Options** below the image preview by checking the box.

3. Choose **Color Management** from the pop-up menu and make a selection as is appropriate for the type of printer you have.

4. Finally select a rendering intent, usually Perceptual for photographs.

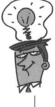

Say Cheese

You can embed an ICC Profile (Windows) or Color Profile (Mac) in an image using **File, Save As** from the Menu bar by checking the correct box. This will force the correct color as your printer is calibrated.

Manual Labor: Printer Calibration Made Hard

If you can't use a recent Photoshop program or beyond or ICC profiles, you're going to have to calibrate by hand:

1. Calibrate your monitor as explained previously.

2. Cut and paste the Monitor calibration file into the image you opened; name the file Original Image.

3. Print the Original Image file.

4. Compare the print to the onscreen image. If it is an acceptable match, you are done. If, however, you feel the print is bluer and, say, darker than your onscreen image, you have some more work to do.

5. Copy the onscreen image and save it. Name the copy Test #1.

6. Adjust the color of the Test #1 image (refer to Chapter 14) so that it is less blue (more yellow) and lighter. The idea is to drive the onscreen image the opposite color of your print. (If your image is too red and too light, drive the test image toward green and make it darker.) You might have to adjust the contrast, also.

7. Keep track of the amount of color you added or subtracted from the test image, and how dark or light you made it. Jot this information down on a piece of paper—better yet—tape it to your monitor. Call these changes your "calibration set," which you will be applying manually as follows.

8. Print out the Test #1 image.

9. Open the Original Image file; close the Test #1 image or hide it from view. Does your new print look closer to the Original Image? You might have to go through this test a few times until you get a good result (remember to keep track of your color changes).

Applying this system is easy:

1. Adjust and manipulate any image you want to print, so that it looks best on your screen.

2. Save the image.

3. Before you print the image, apply the color, brightness, and contrast calibration adjustments you made previously (refer to your calibration set).

4. Print the image.

5. Your printed image should look like the image you had on the screen before you made your calibration changes.

I realize that this is a contrived and weird way to print out an image, but it works. You might find that your calibration set varies with different images, but it's a good starting point.

Tag Your Images with Color Calibration Information

Remember back to playing tag as a child? Maybe you haven't grown up yet and just played last week. If you are good at tag you usually choose in advance the target of your strike. You then chase that target with purpose until you can tag it. Image color management is much like this. If you know in advance the purpose of your image, web or print, you can embed information in it which makes it more likely to be reproduced device independent if you send it forth into the world for someone else to work on.

With an image open choose Edit, Color Settings from the Menu bar (or the shortcut Shift+Ctrl/Command+K). You then can choose No color management (seems silly, why did we open this dialog window), Limited color management (which optimizes your image for onscreen viewing), or Full color management (which optimizes them for print). The difference is that onscreen uses the additive RGB color model while print uses CMYK subtractive color.

The Least You Need to Know

- ◆ Device independent color can be achieved by using ColorSync or Adobe Gamma, which employ ICC profiles.

- ◆ If you have older printing equipment, you must calibrate your system and apply the color management manually.

- ◆ You can make ICC profiles for your monitor and printer using a color calibration meter if you are that serious, but for most people available software now allows you to get it close enough using your eyes to calibrate.

- ◆ You can tag images with ICC profiles to optimize them for print.

- ◆ You can tag images with limited color management information to optimize them for onscreen display.

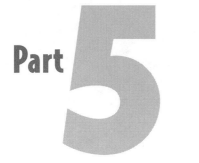

Part 5

Output

Seeing your image glowing on your screen is fun. Printing out your image is even more fun. Producing a beautiful print that is "suitable for framing" is a rewarding experience.

Printing is easy to do. By applying calibration techniques, you can make prints that look just like your monitor screen. What's more, you can repeat your results as many time as you like. Just think—you will never have to buy another greeting card again. Just flip on your printer and make your own!

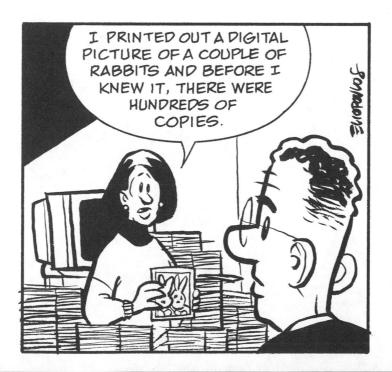

Chapter 23

Print It Out

In This Chapter

- ◆ Printing out your images
- ◆ Making multiple copies
- ◆ Printing directly from the camera
- ◆ Making contact sheets

The only thing more exciting than seeing your image appear on your screen is seeing it emerge from your printer.

In Chapter 5, we reviewed printers and described the benefits of the various technologies; now let's take a look at how to print out your images. Printing is fast, fun, and easy!

Get Connected

Before you spend a lot of time, paper, and ink, you should familiarize yourself with your printer. If your printer is not yet connected to your computer, connect it now—follow your printer's setup instructions and be sure to load all the printer drivers (computer-to-printer instructions) into your operating system. All printers should come with an installation program that will automatically install the printer, or at the very least guide you through the installation process.

It can be very frustrating to try to print out a photo from your imaging software only to have your printer sputter ink and spit out paper shreds. Try testing your printer out on familiar software, such as your word-processing software. That way, you will eliminate any questions about whether you have properly installed your imaging software. Chances are good that if your word-processing software prints correctly, your imaging software will, too.

Resolution: One More Time

I have talked about image resolution many times in the book; this is where it all pays off. If your image doesn't have enough resolution (that is, if your file is not big enough), you are not going to have good results. Your images are going to look *pixelated*, or lack sharpness. Without enough digital information, you won't see much in the way of detail. To put it more simply, garbage in … garbage out!

> **Behind the Shutter**
>
> Back when "real" printing presses were used, resolution (or dpi) was determined by how many dots could be resolved on the negatives from which the printing plates were burned. (Negatives were made and then contact printed, or burned, onto a metal plate. The metal plate was used to transfer ink to the blanket, which, in turn, transferred the ink to the paper.)

Printer Resolution Versus Image Resolution

You measure a printer's resolution by counting how many dots the printer can reproduce on a line one inch long. This is referred to as *dots per inch*, or *dpi*, and has pretty much been the standard of measure for a long time.

> **Behind the Shutter**
>
> Modern computer printers can resolve smaller and smaller dots than ever before. You might see printer manufacturers hawking "Micro Dot," "Tiny Dot," or even "Teeny Weeny Dot" technology. This differing terminology sometimes makes it hard to compare one printer with another. Unfortunately, the only real way to tell which printer makes the best prints is to test them and compare the results. Check out Chapter 5 for more information on how to evaluate and buy a printer if you haven't already done so. (You weren't skipping ahead, were you?)

Put simply, ppi, or pixels per inch (image resolution), does *not* equal dots per inch (printer resolution). Many printers can resolve many dots for each pixel in the image. Your best bet is to read your printer's instruction book to find out the optimal pixel-per-dot ratio. Also note that you may find the info on the box as one of the listed selling points.

After you have found the optimal ppi for your printer, you can determine how large you can make your print. If you reverse the process, you can find out how big your file needs to be to make a specific-size image. For example, say your printer likes to see a 300ppi (remember, that's pixels per *inch*) file. If your file measures 675×1,200 pixels, your output print will measure 2.25×4 inches (675 pixels ÷ 300 pixels per inch = 2.5 inches; 1,200 pixels ÷ 300 pixels per inch = 4 inches). In the same manner, if you want to print out a 6-inch-long image on that same printer, you will need a file that is 1,800 pixels long. In most cases, or when in doubt, assume that your printer likes to see 300ppi file resolution.

If you lower this ratio, you will start asking your printer to print at a less-than-desirable resolution, and your prints will look the same: less than desirable. For example, if you took that same 675×1,200 file and printed it out to be 5 or 6 inches long instead of 4 inches, your files would look less than optimal. You would start to see pixelization and fuzzy images.

In Plain Black & White

When you bring your file to a commercial printer, yet another standard is used to determine file size and resolution. Commercial printers establish the resolution of a printed piece by counting how many lines (of all those dots) per inch can be printed. In trade lingo, this is called **lpi**. Ask your printer (the human one) what lpi he will be using. The standard ratio between dpi and lpi is 2:1, so if the job will be printed at 150lpi, your file should be 300dpi. If this gets really confusing, ask your printer how big your file needs to be for him to print the job at the size you've specified.

Let's Print!

To print your image from within Photoshop Elements, do the following (note that you should read Chapter 22, if you haven't already; you will be glad you did):

1. Open your final, ready-to-print image. (That was easy.)

2. Use your selection tools to select the area of the image that you want to be printed. (If you want to print the entire image, don't select anything.)

3. Open the **File** menu and choose **Page Setup** to open the **Page Setup** dialog box (this dialog box might vary from printer to printer, and might look a little different depending on whether you're using a Mac or a PC).

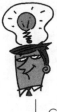

Say Cheese

If you haven't yet flattened the layers of your image, you can hide layers to prevent them from being printed. For more information about hiding layers, refer to Chapter 20.

4. Select which printer you will be printing to, and what paper size you will be using.

5. If you have not yet done so, set your image size and resolution. Do this by entering the appropriate information in the **Photo Size** dialog box (to view this dialog box, open the **Size** menu and choose **Photo Size**).

Set your paper size and image orientation in the Page Setup dialog box. This box will look different depending on which printer and printer driver you are using. Relax, go with the flow!

6. Preview the image to see how it will fit on your page (this is a great way to avoid wasting paper!); open the **File** menu and choose **Print Preview.** The choices you made in previous steps will affect how the page looks (if you need to, readjust your paper size or page orientation), and will become the default settings until you change them again.

The print preview will help you avoid making costly printing mistakes.

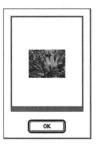

7. Okay, let it rip. Open the **File** menu and choose **Print** (alternatively, press **Ctrl+P/Command+P**) to activate the printing process.

8. The **Print** dialog box pops up on your screen. (This dialog box might differ depending on what type of printer you have; many of the options should be present, but arranged differently.) There are many options to play with here—you can choose paper quality, dpi, color inks, and the number of copies you want to print.

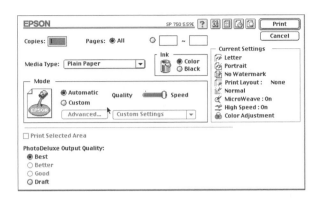

The Print dialog box will let you select the options for your printer.

Printing Multiple Copies on One Page

It is a shame to waste paper, especially the good, high-quality, expensive stuff. If your image is small, why not print up a few on the same page? It will take only a few moments more to do, and you'll have copies to give out to all your friends. After all, everybody wants to see a picture of your kid's first bath (just as much as you wanted to see a picture of their kid's first haircut!).

If you have a copy of Photoshop Elements 2.0 installed, you are in luck. You can print multiple copies on a single sheet by opening the **File** menu, choosing **Print Layouts,** and selecting either the Contact Sheet or Picture Package option. The Contact Sheet option takes a folder of images and prints them into small thumbnails with a number of them on a single page. The Picture Package option allows you to print out one or a number of images in various finished formats, a lot like what you get from a photographer's studio or Sears' Picture Studio.

For those of you using Photoshop, I offer a simple solution:

Say Cheese

The paper size is important. If you are printing on a smaller-than-normal sheet of paper or on an envelope, you need to fill in that information here. Otherwise, you might find your printer losing track of the page count and not feeding paper correctly.

1. With your image open, open the **Layers** palette (**View, Layers**). Make your canvas size the size of the paper that you will be printing on (**size, canvas size**). Label that layer "canvas size." Determine how many of these precious images you can fit on one page by sizing them. Remember to leave a little room on the edges of the page and to include space between the images.

2. Make as many copies of the original layer as you need (if you can fit four images on the page, make four copies). See Chapter 20 if you need help with this.

3. Activate the bottom base original layer (the one we labeled canvas size).

4. Press **Ctrl+A/Command+A** to select the entire layer.

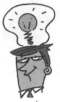

Say Cheese _____

If you haven't printed your image out before, I suggest that you make only one copy to start with. Then, if you like the way it printed, go ahead and make as many as you like.

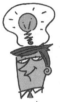

Say Cheese _____

Need help aligning the images? Turn on the rulers along the side of the print by pressing **Ctrl+R/ Command+R.** If you look carefully, you will see a small indicator in the rulers that show your cursor's position; this can aid in the positioning of your copies.

5. Fill the layer with white. This will serve as the base or background color for your page, and will ultimately be the border of your print. (See Chapter 17 if you need help with this.)

6. Activate each copied layer, moving each one into position on the page. Remember to leave space between each print for a border (if you want a ¼-inch border around each print, leave a ½-inch space between the pictures because you will be cutting this border in half when you separate the prints).

7. Save and rename your image (be sure you identify it as a "multiple").

8. Although you can now print the image as is, I suggest that you flatten the layers before you do so. The file size will be smaller, and your image(s) will print out much faster. If you need help flattening the layers, refer to Chapter 20.

9. Print the image, and use scissors, a razor blade, or a paper cutter to separate the prints.

Printing a Contact Sheet Directly from Your Camera

Believe it or not, many—if not most—cameras enable you to print directly from the camera. The camera is hooked up directly to the printer; no computer is needed. I frequently use this feature to get a *contact sheet*, which is a catalog of thumbnail-sized images currently in storage on the camera.

As each camera and each printer will handle it differently, I won't go into the nitty-gritty of how to accomplish this task. Suffice it to say that your camera and your printer must be connected (in most cases, you'll use a cable to connect the port on your camera that you normally use to transfer data to your computer to the port on your printer that is usually used to receive information from your computer). Read your camera's and printer's manuals for more details.

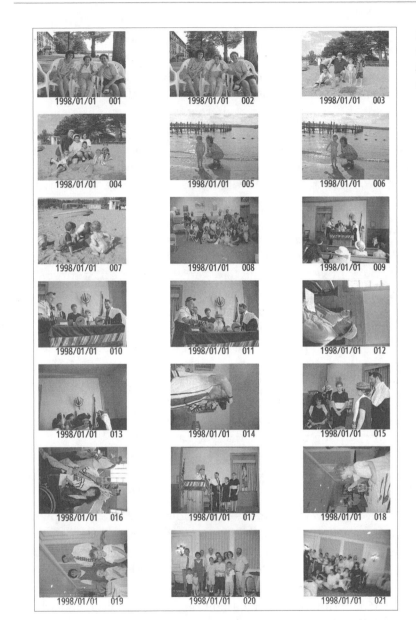

Printing directly from your camera can be a quick way to see all the images you have taken.

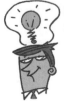

Say Cheese

When aligning your images, you might even want to go one extra step: Add another layer just above the base (white) layer. Using the Line tool, draw a grid on this layer. You can use this grid as a guide for placing your images; just be sure you hide the grid layer before you print. Save a copy of this image with the grid to use as a guide for your next set of multiple prints.

Photo-Quality Papers: Suitable for Framing

Many printer manufacturers sell "photo-quality" paper for their printers (you might have gotten a little sample pack when you bought the printer). As these photo-grade papers are expensive, you might want to try a few alternatives. If you are using an inkjet or laser printer, you can substitute any type of paper that you would normally print on (be sure it will travel through your printer without jamming). For example, you might go to your local office-supply store and pick up some good-quality stationery or laser paper and try it out (you'll find that paper with a glossy surface works the best).

Say Cheese

Some types of paper have a very high acid content, which will cause the paper to yellow or discolor over time. To avoid this problem, ask your paper dealer for archival paper. You will have a good chance of getting this in an art-supply store. You might find the acid content of stationery paper written on the package.

You might also want to go to an art-supply store and try out some artist papers. A thin, good-quality watercolor paper can make a very good and interesting surface for your images. Try using colored paper. Experiment and have fun! My technical editor pointed this out to me and I'd like to share it with all of you. "If you have a laser printer, make sure the paper of your choice is for laser printers or you can ruin parts of your printer! Laser printers use heat and if you use the wrong type of paper (specifically inkjet glossy paper on a laser printer), it will melt onto your rollers. Trust me on this one. This was a very expensive lesson for me. Laser printers have their own line of glossy paper that you can choose."

Third-Party Inks

Third-party printing inks for the dye-sub printers can be found in professional photo stores or in photo magazines. These inks can yield even more beautiful colors than the inks supplied by the manufacturers. For example, some of the black-and-white ink sets yield startlingly beautiful quality—many let you print a four-color black-and-white image using subtly different colors of gray and black for the inks. I've seen prints made from inexpensive (under $600) printers sit beside traditional (analog) black-and-white prints with no discernible differences. With all that power and technology at your fingertips, you can make a superb color or black-and-white print and never get your hands wet! That's why we're digital. Viva control!

The Least You Need to Know

◆ For a quick-and-easy print, use 300dpi as the printing resolution of your images.

◆ You can print multiple copies of your image when you send the first image to the printer. You can also gang up multiple copies of your image on one page.

◆ You can print multiple images or contact sheets in order to get a record of the images you've taken. This will also serve as a good "hard copy" catalog.

◆ Better-quality paper for your printer will give great results. Try to use a glossy stock.

Chapter **24**

Showing Your Pictures to Mom and Other Cool Tricks

In This Chapter

◆ Sending e-mail and attaching photos

◆ Building a website and including text and photos

◆ Putting your pictures on TV for all to see

◆ Converting your digital photographs into desktop wallpaper for your Windows and Macintosh systems

◆ Using AOL's You've Got Pictures and Apple's iPhoto Album service

It might not always be convenient to drag someone over to your computer screen to look at your new beautiful piece of art, and printing an image out on paper and mailing it off to someone seems so slow and antique. After all, we live in the world of high-speed Internet connections and e-mail. We can zip a message or file to someone anywhere in the world within minutes. So why not take advantage of this and send out your photos via the web?

Let's look at two ways of getting your images out in the world:

♦ **Via e-mail.** I might not go into great detail on how to use your specific e-mail program to send images to friends and family—there are so many programs out there that it would be impossible to cover them all. I will, however, show you the basics on how to prepare an image for transfer, and briefly discuss sending attachments via Microsoft Outlook and embedding images in messages in Netscape Communicator.

♦ **Via a website.** Most Internet providers will allow you some space on their server to post a website. Why not take advantage of this great technology?

So read on and let's get ready to go cyber!

Preparing Your Images

The first thing you need to do is to determine what you want the receiver of your image to do with the file you are sending. Do you want her to be able to print the image out, or just admire it on her screen?

Remember, it can take a long time to push a big file down a phone line. You can get someone on the receiving end of your e-mail pretty mad if a huge file jams up her download, especially if she has a slow modem. If you want the user to be able to print out the image, you will need to send her the entire file. If you want her to just be able to view it on her screen, you should reduce the file size to speed up the download time.

Here are some guidelines:

♦ If your image is destined for a monitor only, reduce the resolution of the file to 72ppi. After all, your screen reproduces an image at only 72ppi, so any more information will just be wasted. (Note: If you make your file size 5×7 inches at 72ppi, it will reproduce on the recipient's screen at 5×7 inches.)

♦ If color is not very important and if it's a monitor-only image, you can reduce the file size by changing the bit depth. When viewing an image on the screen, the difference between millions of colors and 256 colors is negligible. (See Chapter 15 for more information.)

♦ Compress your file. All files, whether for printing or screen display, should be compressed before being sent. The best compression format for photographs is JPEG (**File, Save As, JPEG File**). As far as settings go, I find that 5 works fine, but you can experiment to find a setting that works best for you. (Note: The lower the setting, the more detail is lost.)

◆ If you are sending a few images at the same time, you can shed some additional file size by grouping the files together and "zipping" them in a lossless compression program such as StuffIt, PKZip, or WinZip. Many times, you will gain 100KB or so.

◆ Watch your file size. Depending on your modem speed and the receiver's modem, a large file can really clog up the works. Files larger than 300 to 400KB can take forever to transfer. To test how long it will take to send a file, I sometimes start a transfer as a test. Most modem software will give you an estimate of how long it will take to upload a file. If you find that it will take longer than you are willing to have your phone line tied up, cancel the upload, reduce the image's file size, and resend it.

Sending Digital Photos via E-Mail: Attaching and Embedding

Just like any other type of file or document, you send digital photographs via e-mail as *attachments*. If you've ever attached a document to an e-mail message using your e-mail program, then you already know how to send photos! If you attach an image file to an e-mail message, the e-mail recipient must then save the attachment to her hard drive. Then, she can open and print the file using an imaging program.

 Flash

I cannot stress enough that you should use a virus-checking program to check all files that are downloaded to your computer. If possible, set your virus-protection program to automatically check all downloads. If you are the recipient of an attached file, check it before you open it. If you are sending or forwarding files, take the responsibility to check your files before they go out. You never know when some little varmint has gotten into your machine.

Depending on what type of e-mail program you have, you might also be able to embed the image right into the body of an e-mail, which means that when the recipient opens the e-mail message, the image is visible (she need not download it and open it in an imaging program to view it). The downside to this is she might not be able to have access to the entire file. Also, although it can be printed out as part of the e-mail message, it most likely will not contain a lot of resolution.

Demo: Sending Attachments Using Microsoft Outlook Express

Attaching a photograph to a message sent via Microsoft Outlook Express, which is a popular e-mail program, is easy.

1. After you've compressed your image file, open Outlook Express, and click **New** in the top menu toolbar.

2. A new message opens. Type the recipient's e-mail address in the **To** field, and type the subject of the message in the **Subject** field.

3. Type your message. To attach a photograph (or any other type of file) to the message, click the little **Add Attachments** button (the one with the paper clip).

4. Navigate your file directory until you find the file you want to attach.

5. Select the file you want to attach, and click **Add.**

6. When all the files you want to attach have been added, click **Done.**

7. In the lower section of your message, you will see a thumbnail for the photo(s) you have chosen. This indicates that the photo will be delivered to your recipient with your message.

8. Click **Send Now.**

The Add Attachments button

Microsoft Outlook Express can send a photo with e-mail as an attachment.

Attached photo

When the e-mail message arrives at its destination, the recipient will be able to see the image in the body of the message. Pretty cool!

Demo: Embedding Attachments Using Netscape Communicator

Sending an attached file in Netscape 6 is similar to using Outlook Express:

1. After you've compressed your image file, open Netscape 6.

2. Open the **File** menu, select the **New** item, and choose **Message.**

3. A new message opens. Type the recipient's e-mail address in the **To** field, and type the subject of the message in the **Subject** field.

4. Type your message. To embed a photograph in the body of the message, open the **Insert** menu and choose **Image.**

5. Navigate your file directory until you find the file you want to attach.

6. Select the file you want to embed, and click **OK.**

7. Your photo will be inserted into the text body. Click **Send** to send the file.

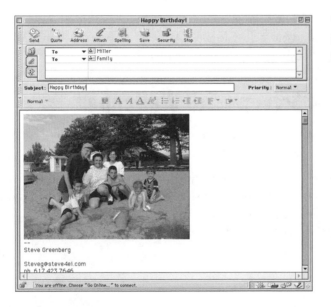

The letter appears at the recipient's computer with the image as part of the text body.

What's Your URL?

Last weekend, I attended a family party. At the end of the party, I gave all my relatives my website address. When I got home, I quickly downloaded all the images from my camera and did a bit of editing. I then built a web page and posted it and the images to my Internet service provider (ISP). Everyone at the party was able to log on to the website and view my images!

What better way to show the world your photographs than posting them on your own website? There are many web page authoring programs available; many offer WYSIWYG (*What You See Is What You Get*) page building. Adobe's Photoshop Elements 2.0, which we used earlier in this book, can do great things with pictures and HTML, and all automatically. Check out Chapters 14 through 21.

Hi, Mom! I'm on TV!

Many newer digital cameras have the capability to send out a video signal, which enables you to view the images stored in the camera's memory on your TV! Actually, the TV is not the only device that you can send a video signal to. The camera can be hooked up to an LCD screen or overhead projection system, which means that you can use your camera for a business presentation. Imagine you just spent the day touring your manufacturing plant and need to show the bosses how they can increase production. All you need to do is hook your camera to a projection system and give your show.

To do this, insert one end of a video cable in your camera's video out port, and the other end to the port on your television, VCR, or projection system. (And some people think torture via slideshow is a thing of the past!)

Sprucing Up Your Screen with Wallpaper

It is very easy to take your favorite photo and use it as a background, or "wallpaper," for your Windows or Macintosh screen.

Before you actually turn your image into wallpaper, you want to adjust its size so that it gives you the best look at all resolutions. To do so, you must first find out the pixel dimensions of the image. If the image you want as wallpaper is smaller than your resolution, it will have to be resized and that will make it look bad.

Say Cheese

I use wallpaper all the time. One thing I've learned is to avoid activating Windows Active Desktop feature. Windows will turn Active Desktop on in order to use a JPG file as wallpaper. Avoid this by converting that JPG to a Windows BMP. Do you need a tool for that? IrfanView for Windows is a fantastic, indispensable freeware tool for conversions and a wide range of other tasks. You can download it at www. irfanview.com. Don't forget the plug-ins!

If you run Windows and don't know what resolution your screen is set to, you can determine this by right clicking on the desktop, selecting the Properties item, and looking up the resolution in the **Settings** tab. If your computer is a Mac, simply look in the Monitor control panel, found in the Control Panels folder.

In general, anything at or above 1,280×1,024 will look good on both Macintosh and Windows computers. If the picture is larger, it will be reduced to fit, making the pixels finer grain and clarifying the picture more. Of course, large images are just that, large. They can take up a lot of space, so be spare or archive them regularly on an external storage drive.

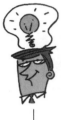

> **Say Cheese**
>
> Mac users need cool tools, too. Sadly, there are no free tools, but there is one that is about the most powerful tool on the planet and it's very inexpensive. That tool is Graphic Converter from LemkeSoft. You can download a trial version from here: lemkesoft.com. As always, please pay your shareware fees. In this case, it's a mere $35 for tools you will always use.

Using AOL's You've Got Pictures

America Online offers subscribers the option to send and develop their film with them, through a deal with Kodak. While this really pertains to those that still use old-style film cameras, they do offer online picture albums that you can share with friends and family. Just log onto AOL and click on the You've Got Pictures button on the Welcome screen (where it says, "You've Got Mail!"). From there you can upload images and save them to various albums of your making. Just think, now you can share pictures of your cats in an organized way!

Sending iPhotos to Get Booked

iPhoto is one the great applications that's come along in a while. Sadly, it's only available for an Apple Macintosh computer running Mac OS X version 10.1.2 that has USB ports. Of course, if you have a recent model Mac then you're in luck, because it's free! Now, in order to use the application you must have a compatible camera. If you don't, another option is to use a supported storage card reader, of which there are several. Instead of connecting your camera, you remove the storage card, place it in the reader, and iPhoto does the rest.

Once you have your images downloaded into iPhoto, it's a dream to examine, fix, and organize them in any way you see fit. iPhoto's simple yet powerful interface really makes it fun to work with even thousands of images. That's not all that iPhoto does, though. Once you've collected a number of images that you'd like to retain for posterity, you can organize them into what Apple refers to as a Book. It's easy to do. Just click on the Book button under the main display, select a Theme, organize your pages and pictures, add material, and then order it.

The results are breathtaking, though only as good as your pictures. Take the time to take really good pictures of treasured people and places and your book will come out beautiful.

Other Cool Things You Can Do with a Digital Camera

In case you didn't know, some digital cameras can double as a web cam. What's a web cam, you ask? Simple, this type of camera connects directly to a port on the back of your computer (USB these days, but some still inhabit the Serial port) and takes pictures of whatever happens to be in front of it. This kind of camera is really nothing more than a video sensor. It's the software on the host computer that takes care of the rest.

What you do with a web cam is entirely up to you. The one site on the web that started the whole idea of a web cam in the first place is the Trojan Room Coffee Machine cam, located in the computer laboratories of the University of Cambridge in England. Every 15 minutes, the software would snap a new picture of the coffee pot that the camera was pointed at. The cam was created so the people upstairs didn't have to walk downstairs just to find that the coffee pot was empty. The original pot is at this address: www.cl.cam.ac.uk/coffee/coffee.html, but it is no longer there. A German company purchased the original coffee machine in an auction on eBay and it can now be seen here at www.spiegel.de/netzwelt/netzkultur/0,1518,174146,00.html.

Click on the link near the top center of the page that is labeled "Cam 1" and a new window will pop up with the picture. If you are located in the United States, you may want to visit the camera early in the morning (afternoon in Germany) or it will be dark.

The second oldest web cam on the internet is Netscape's Fish Cam. Originally started by founding Netscape developer Lou Montulli, it soon became a popular stop on the early World Wide Web. Despite the fact that the Fish Cam came second and therefore was not original it is still considered by most to be the epitome of uselessness. The fish are quite pretty to look at, though. Netscape, though now owned by AOL, still maintains the Fish Cam. You can see it at wp.netscape.com/fishcam/index.html.

Lastly, the most interesting feature of a number of digital cameras available today is the ability to record short bursts of video. You're typically limited to 30 to 60 seconds, but that can catch a lot of material. Some cameras limit your capture to a set length of time. Others allow you to capture as much video as your storage medium will hold, so that 1GB CompactFlash card isn't such a silly idea after all. Once you have your video masterpiece, you'll find out just how large these can be, and you will grow to deeply appreciate just how much DVD discs can hold.

Some Helpful Websites

America Online has more than 30 million subscribers. It stands to reason, then, that some of you reading this have an AOL account. For you there's nothing less than Keyword: Digital Cameras. Hosted by *PC Magazine*, this section of exclusive AOL content covers all manner of buying tips and a neat 27-tip section on printing digital photos so they look good.

The New York Institute of Photography is an honored educational facility that offers students the opportunity to learn how to take compelling pictures. Thankfully, they also offer a lot of free tips and tricks on the website (www.nyip.com). If you happen to live in the area, consider taking a course!

The Least You Need to Know

- ◆ You can send your images attached to your e-mail.
- ◆ You can also embed your images into your e-mail text.
- ◆ A personal website can be made very easily and quickly, where you can post your photo for the world to see!
- ◆ You can use most digital cameras to show your captured images on a television.
- ◆ You can use your digital pictures as a Macintosh background or Windows wallpaper.
- ◆ Both AOL and Apple can help you process your digital photos into real prints.

Speak Like a Geek: Digital Photography Words

acquire   To transfer files from digital equipment such as a camera or scanner. Also used to transfer from one format or program to another.

aperture   The mechanical opening in the lens that lets light in. Refers to the iris or diaphragm.

artifact   Erroneous information in the image. Usually due to faults in compression, low light, or poor-quality cables.

ASA/ISO   Rating given a camera or film denoting its sensitivity to light.

auto focus   A camera or lens that focuses itself.

available light   Light present in a room or environment, such as sunlight or existing room lighting, without the addition of flash or flood lamps.

bit   Geek speak for a binary digit.

bit depth   Refers to the color capacity of a pixel. For every bit, a pixel can carry one color.

bitmap   The description of an image or graphic onscreen bit by bit.

bleed   When an image exceeds the size of a page. If an image needs to cover an entire page, it is bled off the page so no edges show after the page is trimmed by the printer.

bounce light   Light that is reflected off a card or wall.

byte   Eight bits equal one byte.

CCD   Charged couple device. A CCD converts light into electrical current.

CIE   Color model developed by the Commission Internationale de l'Eclairage.

cloning   To copy one part of an image over another part. Also an essential part of a Fellini movie.

CMOS   A Complementary Metal-Oxide Semiconductor that converts light to electrical current. Cheaper to manufacture but not used as much as CCD devices because of noise issues.

CMYK   Cyan, magenta, yellow, and black color world used in printing. A color press uses cyan, magenta, yellow, and black inks.

color balance   The process of compensating for too much of one color in an image. If an image is too blue, or out of color balance, yellow is added to bring the image back in balance or neutral in color.

color model   A method of defining color. RGB, CMYK, and HSB are examples of color models.

color temperature   An indication of the relative redness (warmth) or blueness (cool) of a light source. Color temperature is measured on a Kelvin scale. A household light bulb has a color temperature of 2,800° Kelvin. Daylight has the color temperature of 6,500° Kelvin.

compression   The process of shrinking or squeezing data in an image file.

continuous tone   Continuous and uninterrupted flow of bright to dark tones in an image.

contrast   The ratio of dark tone to light tones. An image with much contrast will lack mid or gray tones.

crop   To remove unwanted portions of an image.

cyan   A bluish/green color.

data   Digital information in a computer.

default setting   A preset setting suggested by the software; a starting point.

depth of field   The measure of what area of a photograph is in focus.

digital   Describes a system or device that stores, computes, or manipulates binary information. Also, a soon-to-be-forgotten computer company purchased by Compaq Computers.

disk   A device that stores digital information. Usually, it is transportable.

download   To transfer from one computer device to another, usually from a larger one to a smaller one. Example: You would download from a website.

dpi   Dots per inch. Refers to the measure of detail on a printer.

drift   The changing from calibration of a device such as a printer or monitor.

driver   Software that communicates between two devices, such as between a printer and a computer.

EPS   Encapsulated PostScript. A type of graphics file usually associated with printing.

export   To change from one file format, usually the native format, into another. Example: exporting a native PhotoDeluxe format to a TIFF format.

exposure   To let light strike film or a digital chip. Also the determination of how much light strikes the film and for how long.

exposure meter   An instrument that measures light to determine which aperture setting and shutter speed to use.

f/stop   The measurement of the diaphragm or iris opening. The smaller the f/stop (higher the number), the greater the depth of field. Example: f/16 will have more depth of field than f/2.8.

file   A collection of information such as an image or document.

file format   The description of the arrangement of information within a file. Many software programs have native file formats, which enable them to read the file. Some file formats are specific to a program.

filter   A colored piece of glass which is attached in front of a lens. Also, an algorithm that is applied to an image to change it. Example: a sharpening filter.

filter surfing   The less-than-suitable practice of covering up a poor image with filter effects that results in no noticeable improvement.

fire wall   A software program or hardware set to protect your computers from outsiders (read: hackers) reading or stealing your data. It will also protect your computer from unwanted viruses.

fish-eye lens   An extremely wide angle lens that yields distortion.

fixed-focus lens   A lens that cannot be variably focused. It is preset to one range of distance, usually 12 feet to infinity.

Flash Pix   A multi-resolution file format. Not as yet widely recognized.

focal length   Distance from the midpoint of the lens to the convergence point on the film plane. The focal length of a lens determines whether it is a telephoto, wide, or normal lens.

gamut   Range of colors that a device can reproduce.

GIF   Graphic Image Format. Originally a file format used by CompuServe and now a standard on the web. A lossless file compression.

Gigabyte   1,000,000,000 bytes.

grayscale   An image containing no color. Grayscale images contain white, gray, and black shades.

GUI   Graphic User Interface. This helps the user control the computer or software by use of graphic images such on screen icons or pull down menus.

half-stop   Half of a full f/stop.

halftone   An image produced on press. The press plates are exposed through a screen of dots to give the image a continuous tone.

HSB   A color model describing hue, saturation, and brightness.

HSL   A color model describing hue, saturation, and lightness.

hue   Color.

index color   Reducing the colors available to fit a smaller fixed gamut. Eight bits or less in depth. Usually used to reduce file size. Many colors used in images delivered on the web are indexed.

jaggies   Stair-stepped pixels usually on diagonal or curved parts of an image. Caused by low resolution.

JPEG   Pronounced *jay-peg*. The Joint Photographic Experts Group developed a de facto standard lossy compression routine.

key light   Main light source.

kilobyte   1,000 bytes.

lossless compression   A file compression routine that does not lose any information.

lossy compression   A file compression routine that does lose information. Unnecessary information is thrown away.

lpi   Lines per inch. A measure of resolution on a printing press.

mask   A layer or selection in a file that is used to protect a portion of the image.

mega-pixel   The measurement of a CCD field that totals more than 1,048,576 pixels.

Megabyte   1,000,000 bytes.

monitor calibrator   A device, which attaches to the monitor screen, which is used to calibrate your monitor.

noise   Unwanted artifacts in an image. Usually, noise appears in the dark areas of an image.

normal lens   A lens that has the same focal length as the human eye. Approximately 50mm in relation to a 35mm camera.

PCMCIA card   A removable memory card.

PICT   File format, standard on Macintosh computers.

pixel   Short for picture element.

pixelation   A special effect that produces small squares or rectangles on an image. Also a result of low resolution.

platform   Computer system.

plug-in   Add-on technology or computer code. Usually associated with a filtering or special-effects program.

ppi   Pixels per inch. Measure of image resolution.

RAM   Random Access Memory. The thinking capacity of a computer. The part of the computer where information is processed.

red eye   A red appearance of your subject's eye caused by the camera flash bouncing off the back of the eye. Red eye can be avoided by moving your flash farther away from the taking lens.

resolution   Detail.

RGB   A color model with red, green, and blue.

ROM   Read Only Memory, where the computer stores its operating instructions.

saturation   Purity or intensity of color.

shade   A gradation of color with reference to its mixture with black.

sharpness   Refers to focus, the ability to display detail.

shutter   Device that opens and closes to allow light to strike film or a chip. Shutter speed determines your ability to capture action.

SLR   Single Lens Reflex. A camera that allows the user to see through the taking lens.

speed   The sensitivity of film or a chip to light.

strobe   Electronic flash.

TIFF   Tagged Image File Format. An image file format that is recognized by Macintosh and Windows platforms.

tone   Value, brightness, or lightness. The amount of light a color reflects.

TWAIN   A standard of communications between digital devices such as cameras and scanners, and computer software. TWAIN drivers allow the import of data from cameras and scanners.

vignetting   Gradual falling of detail and tone of an image at the edges.

virus   An unwanted software program that is invisible to the user that takes control of your computer or programs. A virus can severely damage your computer and data.

wide-angle lens   A lens that has a very wide field of view. It can see a wide area. A typical wide-angle lens is 35mm (35mm camera equivalent).

WYSIWYG   What You See Is What You Get. A term that refers to what is seen onscreen being what and how it will reproduce in print.

zoom lens   A multiple focal length lens. A zoom lens can zoom between 80mm to 250mm, for example.

Putting It All Together: Panoramas

Getting Started

Sometimes a great scene presents itself but your camera just won't let you capture it in one shot. Perhaps you don't have a wide-angle lens, or maybe using a wide-angle lens will cause undesired distortion or loss of detail. If you can take a series of slightly overlapping shots, Photoshop Elements will reassemble them for you later.

Putting Images Together as One

In the color insert of this book, you will find a sunset picture I snapped one night while out on a boat with my family. Because I had only my digital camera with one set lens, wide angle wasn't an option, but my wife said "Get this sunset." Because I just installed my copy of Photoshop Elements, I decided it might be a good panorama situation for experimentation. I took 25 pictures, starting on the left side of the scene and progressively snapped to the right five shots, then up a row and back to the left, then up a row, and back to the right until I had the whole scene. For your enjoyment, I present only 3 of the 25 and reassemble them with Photoshop Elements Create Photomerge feature.

To assemble a panorama, I recommend that you start by opening all images (File, Open) you wish to include. I assemble them on the desktop side by side and generally try to overlap them. I then make any macro adjustments to color if there is great variation. Do not overcorrect at this juncture; just try to get them in the same range of color and contrast. As you can see by the first figure in the color insert (page 5), my middle shot had higher saturation. I therefore used the techniques in Chapters 14 and 15 to more closely match the exposure of these three images by adjusting them individually. This is important because in the next step the pictures will be combined and blended together automatically and I have little or no control over the process.

Flash

Before taking pictures for this purpose, read the entire appendix. It will save you some of the trouble I go through here. Page 5 of the color insert shows two versions of the panorama I made. The top version shows the image immediately after it was combined and the bottom one after I worked on it.

Assemble the Panorama

From the **Menu** bar select **File** and choose **Create Photomerge.** A dialog box like the one in the following figure will then appear. It will contain each image that was already open in Photoshop Elements, but you can add more images if you need to at this time.

The Photomerge dialog box shows the images to be merged and enables you to add or delete images using the Browse button. The Help button will open Adobe's help screen with information about merging photos.

Once you have the correct images, click **OK** to create the merged photo. Depending on the number of pictures, you might have time to go say hello to your family while the program chugs away. It compares similar pictures' common elements and then makes an educated guess how to lay the pictures atop one another to create the resulting image. Depending on the pictures, it may assemble them correctly, but my experience is that at least one picture is usually misplaced.

Say Cheese

If you don't have any documents open, you will get the Photomerge dialog box and will have to manually add images. If you are sure your images are similarly balanced for color, you don't need to take the time to open them individually.

Moving Images to the Proper Location

Miracle of miracles, the assembled image appears in a window that is also called a Photomerge dialog (funny how two windows can have the same name, but some programmer decided it was okay), but for clarity we will call this second window the Photomerge workspace. If a picture is misplaced, you can use the Select Image Tool (the arrow button—keyboard shortcut "A") in the upper-left-hand corner of the workspace to drag it where it belongs. You will notice it becomes semi-transparent so you can easily align it. As you drop it back into the picture, if you have the "Snap to Image" option checked on the right side of the workspace, the picture should automatically align itself with the surrounding image and blend into it. If it doesn't quite align, try moving it ever so slightly again with the Select Image tool. If it still isn't quite right, you can make a minor rotation of it using the Rotate Image Tool (the circle arrow button—keyboard shortcut "R") in the upper-left corner.

Removing Images

If you included an extra image by accident or just have too many images on the work space to allow you to think, you can remove/dock the images by dragging them off of the bottom white work surface and up to the top white box in the workspace, which Adobe calls the "Light Box" (shown in the following figure). Images stored in this area may later be retrieved if you drag them back down to the bottom white space.

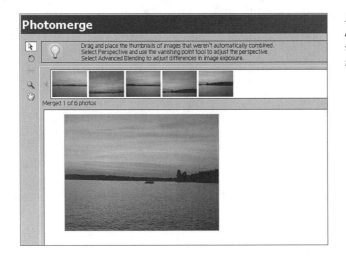

Images stored in the Light Box at the top of the Photomerge workspace are not included in the panorama.

Blending Your Images Together

If you are lucky (or read the entire appendix), your images will blend together perfectly. I seldom have such luck! Fear not, however, because if you read this book carefully, you have the tools to solve the problem. Photoshop will try to blend the pictures together using common points it finds. I find that it is much better at matching them for alignment than it is for matching exposure or saturation settings. If you pre-matched your images before executing Photomerge, you should come closer. Next, try checking the Advanced Blending option in the left panel of the workspace. Select preview using the available button and see how it does. If you look back to the color figure of my panorama in the color insert (or the black-and-white version in the following figure), you will see that the color was partially washed out by me in advance of the merge to get a better blend, and that despite this step, the center image remains much stronger than the outside two.

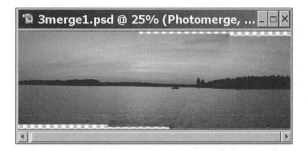

When you run Photomerge, it will match common points (you may need to drag any mismatched/ misplaced photos manually) and try it's best to match the exposure by blending them together, but more work often needs to be done. Here the middle third is signifi-cantly more saturated than the outside thirds.

Using an Adjustment Layer

You might need to select the oversaturated section and apply an adjustment layer by choos-ing a Marquee or Lasso tool from the Toolbox for selection and then from the Menu bar choosing **Layer, New Adjustment Layer, Brightness/Contrast.** You may also try **Enhance, Adjust Brightness/Contrast** and select **Brightness/Contrast.** Use the sliders to adjust only the selected portion to make it blend better. Sometimes setting some feather to your selection will help soften any edges between the adjusted portion and the surrounding parts of the image.

Using the Smudge Tool

After applying some Brightness/Contrast correction, I still often have a bit of an edge between the adjusted area and the surrounding image. I use the Smudge tool from the Toolbox and use both the Normal and Color settings from the drop-down Mode menu on the Option bar (trial and error will usually help you find the right mix of these). Using the Color setting will drag a little color from one place to another to create continuity of color over any edge. Using the Normal setting will soften any edge in the image where contrast stood out. In the sunset image I used, there were two very hard edges where the pictures blended, so I had to go back and forth. This is again a Brylcream example, where little dabs will do ya! Lower the opacity on the smudge tool, probably to the 7 to 25 percent range. Soft adjustments are best. Remember, if it has improved, save an intermediate copy every few adjustments. Also recall that you may want to increase the undo History States (Edit, Preferences, General, History States) for this type of correction as the default is only 20 undos. Because you are making many little corrections, you will quickly exceed that number.

Using the Clone Stamp Tool

In my picture, one of the greatest problems was that the sky didn't quite match at the blend line, perhaps because I tilted the camera (I didn't have my tripod, so I used the boat's windshield). So I used the Clone tool (covered in Chapter 18) to move a little of the sky back and forth over the blend line to create a better line and mask the smudge.

More significant than the sky was the water blending. The center part was much more colorful than the outside parts. I simply copied the more colorful water to the outside using the Clone tool. Again, I turned down the Opacity of the tool, in this case between 30 and 50 percent seemed to work well so that I got a soft copy, but also got some of the water texture.

Restoring Color

In the blending process, I adjusted the color of the three photos to get a better blend. Now I need to restore the color to what my eye saw (or if that isn't good enough to make me happy, why stop at that—but in this case nature had it covered). Using an un-adjusted image as a reference, I applied one or more adjustment layers (as explained in Chapter 20) to restore the saturation and brightness. I cropped and then used the OK button to create the merged panorama. The result is quite remarkable. Remember, I shared only part of the bottom row of my images. Think of what I have when I use all 25 images!

This was one beautiful sunset! See the color insert to see a finished product after applying all the techniques described here.

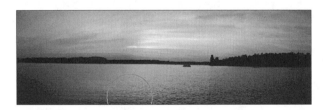

Perspective with Panoramas

Sometimes you will get a perspective distortion when using Photomerge that will make the horizon look as if it is warped. If this occurs, use the Perspective radio button on the left side of the workspace. This will allow you to specify one image in the mix as the center or vanishing point of the merged photo, and all other images will become linked to it. Use the Vanishing Point tool (keyboard shortcut "V"—the option is only available if Perspective is selected on the right) to pick which photo is the focal point. Sometimes this correction will create a bow tie effect, where the focal point image is squished and the surrounding images are stretched in height (this is how the correction was made). To correct this situation, use the Cylindrical Mapping option. Adobe's help section contains an example of this correction.

Fix Problems Before They Exist

One of the best things you can do is take good, consistent pictures to use for panoramas. If you have a tripod available, preferably with a panning head, use it. You want to pan side to side (or straight up—Photomerge works vertically as well as horizontally as demonstrated in this appendix) without deviating from horizontal. Often people will try to keep the horizon or shoreline at a fixed point in the viewfinder, but as you pan, this will distort your picture when you merge it. Instead, make the images in a straight line. Try to keep the exposure and focus settings fixed using manual settings instead of automatic aperture and f-stops. Finally, you should shoot for about 15 to 30 percent overlap between pictures. Less will make it more difficult for the program to find common points, and more may create bad blending.

Other Photoshop Goodies

After you master the Photomerge technique, you should explore the program further. There are many other great features we did not discuss in the book, like animation and three-dimensional imaging and manipulation by rotating. Take your time, and you will find a lot to play with.

Index

W-X-Y-Z

T

U-V